# From Poland to Russia and Back
## 1939-1946

To Sharon & Fred

Sunol Mucy

November 1996

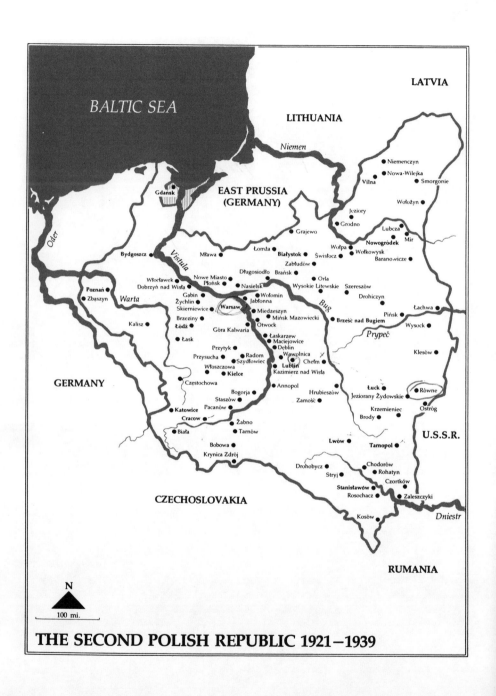

BALTIC SEA

LATVIA

LITHUANIA

*Niemen*

EAST PRUSSIA
(GERMANY)

Niemenczyn ●

Nowa-Wilejka ●

Vilna ●

Smorgonie ●

Wołożyn ●

Gdansk

*Oder*

*Vistula*

Jeziory ●

Grajewo ●

Grodno ●

Lubcza ●

Nowogródek

Mir ●

Bydgoszcz ●

Mława ●

Łomża ●

Białystok ●

Świsłocz ●

Wołpa ●

Wołkowysk ●

Baranowicze ●

Włocławek ●

Nowe Miasto

Długosiodło Brańsk ●

Orla ●

Dobrzyń nad Wisłą ●

Płońsk

Nasielsk ●

Wysokie Litewskie ●

Szereszów ●

Poznań ●

Zbaszyn ●

*Warta*

Gabin

Żychlin ●

Wołomin ●

Jabłonna

Drohiczyn ●

Łachwa ●

*Bug*

Skierniewice ●

Warsaw ●

Miedzeszyn ●

Mińsk Mazowiecki ●

Brzeście nad Bugiem ●

Pińsk ●

Brzeziny ●

Łódź ●

Góra Kalwaria

Otwock ●

*Prypeć*

Wysock ●

Kalisz ●

Łask ●

Łaskarzew ●

Maciejowice ●

Dęblin ●

Klesów ●

Przytyk ●

Przysucha ●

Radom ●

Szydłowiec ●

Wawolnica ●

Chełm ●

GERMANY

Włoszczowa

Kielce ●

Lublin ●

Kazimierz nad Wisłą

Częstochowa

Bogorja ●

Annopol ●

Hrubieszów ●

Łuck ●

Jeziorany Żydowskie ●

Równe ●

Staszów ●

Zamość ●

Krzemieniec ●

Ostróg ●

Katowice ●

Pacanów ●

Cracow ●

Żabno ●

Brody ●

U.S.S.R.

Biała ●

Tarnów ●

Bobowa ●

Lwów ●

Tarnopol ●

Krynica Zdrój

Drohobycz ●

Chodorów ●

Rohatyn ●

Stryj ●

Czortków ●

CZECHOSLOVAKIA

Stanisławów ●

Rosochacz ●

Zaleszczyki ●

Kosów ●

*Dniestr*

RUMANIA

N

100 mi.

# THE SECOND POLISH REPUBLIC 1921–1939

# From Poland to Russia and Back
## 1939-1946

*Surviving the Holocaust
In the Soviet Union*

# Samuel Honig

**Black Moss Press**
**1996**

Published by Black Moss Press
2450 Byng Road, Windsor, Ontario N8W 3E8

Black Moss Press books are distributed in Canada and the U.S. by Firefly
Books, Willowdale, Ontario.

Financial assistance to Black Moss Books
comes from the Ontario Arts Council and the Canada Council.

Edited by Lisa Monforton and Kristina Carroll.

ISBN 0-88753-293-4

The photographs used in this book were sent to our families before the outbreak of the Second World War.

Cover design by Olga Honig.
Type design and layout by Kristina Carroll.

*To my dear wife, Olga, childen, and grandchildren*

As you open this book, you might ponder why so much has been written about the Holocaust. The subject has been covered in such detail, one wonders what else could be said, without repeating what has already been presented.

Yet with each new book, each new study, the story of the Holocaust in Europe during the Second World War has proven to be inexhaustible. It seems writers and film producers can't get enough of the subject of the experience of the Jews in Europe. Without question, in was the most arresting, riveting and tragic event in that war.

Holocaust survivors have come forth all over the globe to tell their stories, and as a result museums and centres have sprung up in every quarter to remember the dead, and to tell the world this was an abomination. And because of that, this desire to keep the story "alive," now fifty years after the Second World War keeps those gruesome realities of the Holocaust still a vivid reality in the minds of people.

My own experience — as a survivor — was different. I did not live in the Nazi war camps. Members of my family did. What few realize is just how many Jewish people survived the Holocaust because they fled to Russia. This story — that personal account — rarely has been written about, or spoken about. The fact is some 250,000 Polish Jews survived because of the Soviet Union. Why this has remained so unknown to most people is because of the long-standing animosity between the Soviets and the U.S. Saying anything positive about the Stalinist regime would have branded anyone a communist. Especially during the fanatical Senator McCarthy era when innocent people's lives were ruined by sheer rumour.

What I have to say in this book is positive. If it weren't for the Soviet Union, I wouldn't have survived. It must also be pointed out that it wasn't a deliberate sympathetic act of the part of the Stalinist government to accommodate these Jewish refugees. These exiled people — including myself — were dispatched to work in back-breaking labour camps.

But we survived. The Russian camps weren't "death camps." We were also treated equally, the same as any other Russian. They didn't kill us. They didn't beat us. They fed us. They kept us alive.

I was born in Krakow, Poland, September 3, 1922. My first memories begin with the birth of my sister Natalie. We called her Niusia. We lived in a small apartment on Barska 34. One day, there was a big commotion in our little apartment. Mother's sisters came. The door to the bedroom was closed and finally, after a couple of hours the midwife, Mrs. Motyszkowa arrived. All the children knew her well and she called us always by our first name. We also knew that Pani Motyszkowa "brought" babies. With all the fuss at home, I was very upset that nobody paid any attention to me. Finally, I fell asleep. When I woke up, the house was still full of relatives. Soon Mrs. Motyszkowa brought us my new baby sister, who had just been born. I was then about five years old. From this time on, I remember more and more of the years gone by.

In order to understand those few years of my life I spent with my family in my beloved Krakow, I must tell you a little about it. A very old one located in the southwestern part of Poland, it is divided by the Vistula River. On the west bank lies most of the city; on the right bank, suburbs and some industrial districts. The whole left bank is surrounded by beautiful parks called Planty. In medieval times the city was fortified and surrounded by a very wide ditch for defense. When this later became obsolete, the ditch was filled with dirt and trees were planted. With care through the years it became a park surrounding the whole city.

It had little industry and had the best schools of any kind in Poland. It was also the most intellectual city in the country. With about 30,000 students attending the university, the mining academy, business school, the art school, and the most famous, the Jagiellonski University of Krakow which was one of the oldest universities in Europe. It was the university of the astronomer Nicolaus Copernicus and many other famous scholars.

We lived on the right bank of the Vistula in a district called Dembniki. Why we lived there, I don't know, perhaps because my mother's sister Frania lived there with Grandma and operated a grocery store. Very few Jews lived in Dembniki. There were three Jewish grocery stores, a pharmacy, kosher butcher, yard goods store and pastry shop. We had our small synagogue and our rabbi, Osher Shayer Halpern, a Hasid. He was always surrounded by the five Rothfeld brothers who were all Hasidim and lived in Dembniki. Our rabbi was very tolerant of the children, and very friendly. He also spoke very good Polish and he didn't mind using it. He would greet the local parish priest or other gentiles, speak to them in Polish and exchange pleasantries.

Demniki had the name of being a rough neighborhood - dangerous for strangers, especially Jews. Sometimes when my school friends came to visit, I had to go to the bridge to escort them to my house. Otherwise, they could be attacked or verbally abused by local youth gangs - some of my Polish friends. Anti-Semitism was a way of life in Poland, although Krakow was more tolerant and civilized than most of the other Polish cities. No killing or serious injuries resulted from those attacks — mostly a kick, a slap or calling you a "dirty Jew." The more you feared them, the more you tried to avoid them - the worse it got. So we the Jews in Dembniki were a different breed. We played with the gentile kids, had friends among them, and acted more like them. When somebody hit us, we hit them back. When somebody called us a "dirty Jew," we called them "dirty Catholics." I, myself, never got a serious beating, never ran away and always fought back, knowing sometimes I would lose and get a kick or two, though I never went home to complain about it.

In the center of Dembniki was a huge market place surrounded on four sides by apartment buildings and four streets leading away from it. One of the streets led to the Vistula River and up the stream to many villages lying on her banks. On this street was located the Brenner's grocery store, right across from the market. Behind the store was an apartment where my grandmother Anna lived, a tall, thin, matronly lady, most of the time in a black dress with a gold chain with a pendant hanging on it. We all loved her dearly. We loved her cooking and baking. My Auntie Frania and my Uncle Shmuel were busy in the store from morning until evening.

They had their apartment on the second floor of the building, but I really don't remember them having spent much time upstairs. They took their meals in Grandmother's apartment where she reigned with her maid Hanka. The store did not resemble the grocery stores of today. You walked about six stairs up to get to the store. On the left side was a counter with shelves. Farther along was a glass cabinet with cigarettes and tobacco. On the right side were all the bags with cereal, flour of all description, and so on. Barrels with sauerkraut, pickles, tomatoes and cabbage. In one corner bundles of dry kindling wood smelling of pine sap. Behind the store was a separate room where they sold only kerosene. The city itself had electricity, but the surrounding villages had none and used kerosene lamps, which were stacked in one corner of the store.

The biggest trade in kerosene was on market day, when the women would come from the villages, bringing their wares - fresh fruit, vegetables, cheese, butter, berries, and so on. They came very early in the morning, sold their wares and did their shopping in the stores, and before noon they returned to their villages and labour, which never ended. It is hard to imagine how hard those poor women worked. In the morning, around 7:00 a.m., the women from the nearby villages came every day, except Sunday, walking most of the time barefoot several miles to the city, carrying two heavy steel containers full of milk. They carried the containers wrapped in a white sheet on their backs and tied in front. Every woman had her customers in the apartments and brought fresh milk every day. Sometimes they had extra butter and farmer's cheese. As children, we knew their names and they knew ours. We greeted them in the street. They became friends of the family. After they sold their milk, they stopped at Brenner's and bought a few things to take back with them.

I remember standing once when I was very young on the high embankment of the Vistula right at the city limits where the dirt road to their villages began, watching the women as they went home. The road was empty and they couldn't see me. Suddenly, they stopped, one after the other spread their legs and urinated on the dry dusty road and continued with their long walk ahead. As a child, I could never forget this. I thought it was very dirty and for a while I resented the milk women. I wanted to tell this to somebody but I was ashamed even to mention it. I lost my appetite for milk for a while. When November came with its heavy, cold rains and dark steel skies, we knew we could expect winter soon. I don't know why, but most of the time the first snow fell at night. In early morning darkness, we were awakened by the bells ringing on the necks of horses pulling sleds headed for the city and loaded with milk as the first heavy snow covered the city. How happy we were running to the windows to see if this was true. I am sure that the peasant women must have been happy too. There was much less to do on the farm, so after milking the cows, their husbands loaded the milk cans on the sleds and drove them to the city. Now all they had to do was to carry one milk can at a time and distribute it to their customers while their drivers were waiting for them.

My Uncle Samuel was a thin, short man, always with an impeccable mustache.He ran the business with Aunt Frania, but somehow, Aunt Frania was the one behind the counter, selling and marking all the sales in a heavy black book. It seems to me that most of the neighbourhood bought on credit. Uncle Samuel had a hot temper and often argued with customers and discussed hot political topics, disagreeing most of the time with everybody. Aunt Frania was tall and heavyset with a beautiful smiling face, her hair always neatly parted, straight, and white.

I liked to spend time in their store, with the smells of the big loaves of bread being cut into four, fresh butter laid out in big blocks on ice, pickled cucumbers, cucumbers in vinegar in big steel tins, and of course, all kinds of chocolates and candies in glass containers. The place was crowded, and all the news came to the store first. The Brenners were the closest family in Krakow and Herman, Moniek and Niusia were my cousins. Niusia was a year or two younger than me, a tall, good looking girl, with very curly hair.

*** 

Every boy has heroes and wishes to be like them. For me, the undisputed hero was my cousin Herman, seven years older than myself. He must have been a very good student in public school because he was accepted to a state gymnasium named after the Polish King, Sobieski. There were seven state gymnasiums in Krakow and they never accepted more than 10 per cent Jewish students. In a Polish state gymnasium, being a Jew, you had to be smart, physically strong and you had to know how to handle yourself with your Christian friends and teachers. You have to understand that most of them were anti-Semitic and prejudiced towards you. As far as I remember Herman, in later years, he was the strongest young man in Dembniki and I dare to say, the strongest Jewish man I ever knew. With all his strength and ability to hit, he never showed it off or used it unless consistently provoked.

The Brenners lived next to the Vistula River and Herman and Moniek spent all their leisure time on the shore playing football, swimming or boating. He and my Uncle Marian owned a two-seat kayak and took long trips on the river. We younger kids used to get a ride with them and sometimes learned how to steer or paddle the boat.

There was a special thing about Herman. He liked all the kids. The Vistula River was their kingdom. In the hot, dry summer, the water in the river would recede and make it sometimes possible to cross without swimming. There were beaches on both sides of the river, but most of the time, the water was deep and with very dangerous whirlpools and currents.

Every summer there were many drownings. About the safest time to go swimming in the river was when Herman was nearby. I witnessed several times how he saved drowning people. It would happen always about the same way - an unsuspecting swimmer or non-swimmer would be pulled suddenly into a whirlpool or current, especially when the water was deep after several rainfalls. You heard a scream for help "I'm drowning!" People became panicky, running to the shore and following the drowning victim. Very seldom anybody had enough courage to jump in and try to save the victim. It was an unbelievable sight when Herman was there. His friends would look in anticipation to see what he was going to do. What was his strategy going to be? To jump in right away? Or to wait until the victim got closer to the shore and then to jump and meet the drowning person? Whatever he decided he always reached the victim soon, if he had to dive into the swirling current, so he did.

Once he had brought the victim to shore, all the people on the bank were ready to help. Herman would just take off with his friends without waiting for thanks from the family of the victim. He would go home for dinner and never mention what had happened.

One time he saved a daughter of our family's friends. Her name was Ceska. He saved her from sure death because she was in the water quite a long time, right on the bottom. He saved her by diving several times.

We lived through a very unpleasant happening with Herman, that worried and frustrated us all. One summer, when he was seventeen or eighteen years old, Herman was swimming and playing with a bunch of his friends from the gymnasium on the shore of the Vistula in the bushes nearby, when he found a bunch of leaflets in the bushes. They were leaflets of the Communist Party. He read one and showed one to one of his so-called friends. The same evening, the police came to the house and arrested him. He was charged with distribution of Communist leaflets and propaganda. We all knew that he had nothing to do with the Communist Party.

You have to understand that in Poland to be a Communist was the worst crime you could imagine — the Party was illegal and hated. Hundreds of Communists and their supporters were kept in jails and concentration camps, especially as political prisoners. It took a few

13

months, the best lawyers and lots of money, before Herman was tried and found not guilty.

After his release, he never spoke about it, just like nothing had happened. He belonged to a local Jewish sports club Macabi, where he played handball and trained with discuss and shot-put. But his best results were on the boxing team. He was a heavyweight and in all the competitions he represented Macabi. He always trained at home and gave his brother Moniek and myself lessons in boxing and self defense which came in very handy in the future.

In one of the fights, he was injured and suffered a broken nose. He went through it with a little local anesthetic, because he would not let the surgeon put him to sleep. After this, his parents persuaded him to temporarily quit his fighting career.

You wonder why I am telling you so much about him. First, I loved him and greatly admired him; and secondly, telling his stories will give you a little insight into what it meant to be a Jew, even an exceptional Jew, in Poland. Herman had a small bunch of close friends from the Macabi Sports Club, good athletes, and they always defended everyone from anti-Semitic outbursts. In the park where youths and Jewish youths used to gather and walk close to the university, quite often a bunch of anti-Semites would attack, abuse and beat some Jewish boys. This never happened when Herman and his friends were in the vicinity. His presence always guaranteed peace for us.

After finishing gymnasium [high school], Herman was inducted into the Polish Army. To pass the medical, every recruit was checked by a doctor assigned to the neighbourhood. Our physics, as they called these doctors, name was Dr. Zamorski, a tall, powerful man. He knew Herman and the family well. One aspect of examination of fitness was a gadget measuring your strength. It was an oval steel gadget called a strength tester and fit in the palm of your hand. By squeezing it, it showed on the dial the strength in your hand. First, Dr. Zamorski had Herman measure the strength in his left hand. It showed almost maximum. Then he put it in his right hand. When Herman squeezed, the needle went all the way and the spring broke, ruining the instrument. Dr. Zamorski was very upset and hollered: "Where am I going to get a replacement for this?" Finally, he laughed and said: "You are already inducted" This incident became known to everybody in the neighbourhood and fear of him became even greater.

And so he was inducted into the army, and being a graduate from a gymnasium, he automatically qualified for officer's school. After a few weeks, he was shipped to Grodno in the northern part of Poland,

14

which now belongs to Lithuania. In the officer's school, after basic training, usually they disqualified Jews for one reason or another. They didn't want them to become Polish officers. With Herman, things went a little differently. They found out that he was a boxer and sportsman. They invited him to join the team of the military sports club W.K.S. Grodno. He stayed in the officer's school and became a Polish Army officer.

After his term in the army, Herman was planning to apply to a medical school in Krakow. His chances were very slim, because after 1935, practically no Jews were accepted to medical school. There was always a quota for Jewish students. The quota was called numerous clausus. As the Jewish population of Poland comprised 10 per cent of the total population, the quota was set at 10 per cent, but after the death of the Polish dictator Marshal Jozef Pisudski, who was fair to the Jewish population, the quota deteriorated more and more and became, as we called it, Numerous Nullus, which meant they didn't accept anybody.

One day shortly before his discharge, a letter came to the Brenners home addressed to Herman. It was an offer for him to stay in the army and being accepted to medical school, under only one condition, and that was to convert to Catholicism. The letter of course, was unsigned. But we all knew it was real.

After his discharge from the army, Herman entered a law school at the university in Krakow. At the outbreak of the war, Herman was inducted in the Polish Army, and according to what I heard, he fought bravely, saving his captain from a sure death. After the fall of Poland, he ran away, not to be taken a prisoner and returned back to Krakow.

Herman had a younger brother Moniek. He was about two or three years younger than Herman, tall, with curly hair. He was the opposite of Herman. He was a poor student, not very neat, always busy with his Polish friends and was into all kind of mischief. He played all kinds of games, like soccer and kept busy all the time.

At one time, his hobby was collecting and playing with buttons. He played games with them like table soccer, and so on. He collected all kinds and sizes. Most of them had to be sanded down to be useful in this game. He was a very good player and would earn full boxes of every kind of buttons. One winter evening, the Brenners had a party at their house and invited family and friends for dinner. When it came time to go home, the people entered the vestibule, put their coats on and none of them had any buttons left.

15

My uncle and aunt were very embarrassed, but they knew right away whose job this was. When they found Moniek, he had all the buttons in his pocket. But for some, it was too late because he had already sanded them down!

He was always hanging around the soccer stadium, trying to get in to see the games, most of the time without tickets. He was caught several times and sometimes he was beaten by the guards. He often forgot the time of day and came home late in the evening while everybody was out looking for him. As he grew up a little, he switched all his efforts to sports. He got very conscious about his looks, and grew handsome and very strong. He finished public school with only passing grades and it became a problem about what to do with him and his further education. With his grades, it was impossible to even apply at a gymnasium. So it was decided to send him to a Jewish business school.

Moniek didn't do very well in school and barely passed his grades. He was very popular with the boys and girls, he was a good organizer, but a really poor scholar. When he passed to the third grade with great difficulties, it became apparent to his parents, after a few months,  that he will never pass the final exam. It would be a waste of time and money to send him anymore. They decided it was time to pull Moniek out of school. My mother was very upset about their decision. She persuaded Aunt Frania not to give up on Moniek. She said: "You spent so much money for two and a half years, why don't you take a chance on another half a year? Try to get him a tutor, and maybe with this help he'll pass the exam. Please take a chance for another half a year and a few more dollars."

Aunt Frania listened to my mother's persuasion, they got him a tutor and a miracle happened! He passed the examination and got his diploma from the business school. As usual, after the final exam, the graduates were introduced to local business people and representatives from local industries. In this particular year, a representative from a famous Italian insurance company - Association Generale Trieste - showed up to look at the graduates. Right off the bat, looking at them, he hired Moniek. I think he hired him for his looks and probably didn't look very much at his records.

I write so much about the Brenners because they were the closest to me and almost every day, I had some contact with them.

My mother, of blessed memory, had another sister, Mania, who lived about 150 kilometers from Krakow in a city in Silesia called Cieszyn. Mania was the youngest sister and was married to my

16

Uncle Henry Steiner. I spent quite a few vacations with them in Cieszyn where I met lots of friends and enjoyed myself very much. It was a small city with a population of about 30,000, very clean and very different from Krakow. First of all, it lay on the border with Czechoslovakia. When you crossed the bridge over the River Olza, taking a short walk, you were in the Czech territory. The name of the city was also Cieszyn, but this was a Czech, Cieszyn. It was very easy for young people to get a permit to cross back and forth across the border, especially when being accompanied by the adults. Practically all people in Cieszyn had a permit. I loved to go there because the Polish currency was much stronger than the Czech krona - about five to one. Everything over there was much cheaper, chocolate, ice cream and exotic fruit like bananas, pineapples, peaches, nectarines and so on. In Poland, these were very expensive. Czechoslovakia, being a highly industrialized country, had much more foreign exchange than agricultural Poland, so they were able to import many more luxury items.

The Steiners were quite prosperous and lived in a fairly new and modern apartment. They had three children, Samek - five years younger than me, Felusia and little Herbert. I made lots of friends there and I enjoyed myself on every vacation I spent there.

*** 

I haven't said so far, very much about my sister Niusia, of blessed memory. I remember her to be a chubby little girl, with chocolate hair and dark eyes. She was always busy visiting her friends and neighbours. She always disappeared on me in somebody's apartment and my most frustrating job was trying to find her. My mother would tell me: "It is time for supper, go and find Niusia." It was a hard task and it took quite some time. I was especially worried when the gypsies came into the vicinity and opened their camps.

At least once a year the gypsies would drive in with several covered wagons, put up their tents and stay put for a few weeks. They would go from apartment building to apartment building and offer to fix pots and pans and do other menial jobs. The word got around that they are stealing and everybody would watch their laundry which was drying outside or anything else left out in the open. Everybody would warn that the gypsies also stole children. That's why I was always so worried about Niusia. People would point out gypsy children with blue eyes or a light complexion, saying they were probably stolen.

I remember Niusia going to her first class in public school. She was very loveable - the teachers loved her, even the school priest was very found of her. She was always cheerful and full of life. Sometimes her grades in school dropped because she couldn't find time for her homework. My task was to tutor her and some of her girlfriends. I took this very seriously and their grades improved in no time. I was rewarded by her friends' parents and I felt very good and proud of myself.

There's not very much more that I remember about her. In 1940, I got a picture of her with my mother which I still have. It is Niusia with mother on the balcony of the Brenner's apartment, wearing the Jewish Star of David on their arms. It was only a very short time that I didn't see her and it was hard to believe how she grew up and got so slim and pretty in such a short time. It hurts me that I don't remember much more. I was a youngster myself, busy with school, sports and friends.

***

My mother, of blessed memory, was called Raizel in Jewish. But as I knew it, her name was Rozalia and people called her Rozia. I have quite a few pictures of her and I remember everything about her. She was born in a village called Zabierzow, not far from Krakow. As a young girl, she and her sisters all moved to Krakow. There were quite a few Jewish families in Zabierzow and the vicinity. Some were farmers and some owned stores and small businesses. The farms were small, and I really don't know how they managed to make a living. Of course, the young people drifted to the city in search of jobs, got married and settled down. I remember very well, as a small boy, we would spend a few weeks a year in Zabierzow, mostly during summer break. We used to go there with all my cousins and relatives, play in the fields and forest. We loved the food, fresh bread, eggs and warm milk. We played with the cows and goats and helped the shepherd tend them. It was so different from the city, so fresh and so pure.

Later as I remember, all the Jews drifted to Krakow and other cities and I don't think that before the war there were any Jews left in Zabierzow.

From what I know, my Father Leon, who lived in Krakow after being discharged from the Austrian Army, met my Mother and fell madly in love with her. When they got married, I don't remember exactly, around 1920, 1921. I was born in 1922.

My Mother was a very special person, and I loved her immensely with full devotion. She was loved by everybody. They said that the whole world's problems could be rested on her shoulders. I never heard her say anything bad about anybody. She didn't gossip about others. She was loved without exception by all the family, close and distant, and all our neighbours.

I was very, very close to her. My father left for work after I left for school, and usually he came home after I went to sleep. So most of the time at home I spent with my mother. I knew her problems and she knew mine. Whenever I misbehaved or got into some trouble in school, my first thought was always what mother would say and how hurt and disappointed she would be. I wasn't afraid to be punished, or when I was small, to be spanked, I always worried about her. The worst was when my mother spoke to me after misbehaving or getting into trouble. I used to call this a sermon and this was the worst punishment.

Mother suffered badly from gallstones. She used to get severe, painful attacks. There wasn't too much I could do. I usually got very frightened. I stayed at her bedside and changed hot water bottles to try to relieve her pain. When the pain didn't get better, I ran to get our family doctor. Doctor Kurtz knew everybody and their ailments. He lived not far from us. In one instance, I ran to Dr. Kurtz because Mother was suffering terrible pains. I burst into his house and found him praying in the morning. I told him what happened and he said "I finish my prayers, have my breakfast and I'll come." Hearing this, I got wild and I'm ashamed to say I practically assaulted him. and his wife had to restrain me. But he promised to come very, very soon.

I would probably have killed anyone who tried to hurt my mother. She was a very beautiful woman. Always very neat and well dressed and I was very proud of her. Unfortunately fate didn't allow me to enjoy her for very long.

***

My Father Leon, was born in the city of Mielec. I was there only as a child, for a very short visit to see my great grandfather who lived to be 105 years old, and I don't remember much about Mielec. The only person I never forgot was my great grandfather. He was a very religious man, a Hasid. He was always dressed in black according to Hasidic customs. He was a very tall person and was the only Hasid that I know of in our family. I would ask my Mother why is grandpa spilling the soup from his spoon and why are his hands trembling? Little did I know that grandpa was over a 100 years old! The other thing I remember when leaving for home, he would call me, put his trembling hands on my head and bless me. I think I was trembling more than grandpa's hands!

Father was the oldest son of Sam and Sarah Honig. He had two brothers and two sisters. The whole family emigrated to the United States before the First World War. He himself, being the oldest, was inducted into the Austrian Army and stayed behind in Europe. The war broke out and he fought with the Austrian Army on several fronts. He rose in rank, and received quite a few medals for bravery. After being discharged from the Army, he settled in Krakow. It was very hard to get a job right after the war and Father worked as a waiter and later as a maitre de in several restaurants. This was not in my time. When I was in my early teens, he opened a bigger restaurant in the Hotel Royale.

I knew that there were good times and hard times. I know there were some problems with partners and one bankruptcy. But Father was a proud person, honest and conscientious and proud of his name. He always paid off all his debts, even if his partners didn't. He was a very hardworking person. I don't remember him taking any vacations for a longer duration. He worked practically seven days a week. He left the house around 10 am and come back around 10 or 11 pm.

My father had a very hard life. When he was discharged from the army with no resources, no family and in hard post-war years, he had to start by himself to build his future. That's why, I didn't have the occasion to be close to my father in those years of my youth. He was always working.

Only on Friday, he came home earlier so we could go the synagogue together. After the meal, he usually would read the newspaper and would fall asleep. On Saturday we went to services and after he would leave in a hurry to be in the restaurant because he had to walk all the way. The restaurant was strictly kosher, and on Saturday they served the mid-day meal, specially with cholent, kishka and kugel. To this day, I don't know how this worked out. No money was exchanged for Saturday meals, and I imagine it was paid later by some arrangement.

In the afternoon, especially in the summer, we would meet Father in the park and spend the rest of Saturday afternoon together.

By American standards, we were very, very religious - I would say Orthodox. Any rabbi could have eaten in our home, it was perfectly kosher, I would say, glatt kosher. As far as I was concerned, I ate only kosher food with all the restrictions and rules. I never travelled on Shabbos, fasted on the holidays, I would never eat traif. I had Christian friends, but when I was invited to their homes, I would not eat any food except fruit.

There were very different religious standards in Poland than I find here in Canada. In our city, there was a large Reform temple. To me, right here now in Canada, when I compare today's houses of worship, it seems our Reform temple was almost Orthodox. Nobody would dare to drive to the Temple on Shabbos or high holidays. The women sat separately on balconies on both sides, the only differences was it had a organ, but it was not used on Shabbos. The sermon was always in Polish. Services in the Temple were frequently attended by Jewish soldiers who were stationed in Krakow and very often were brought to the Temple, especially on holidays, by Polish Christian officers. It was also used by Polish and Jewish dignitaries on official Polish national holidays.

Almost every day, I tried to see my Father, even if only for a few minutes, in his place of work. On the way from school, I would stop in our restaurant to say hello to him. It was always around 1:30 pm when he was very busy, so we would speak for a few minutes. I also had to hurry home for our mid-day meal, which we used to call in Polish, obiad.

I am just trying to write a few words about my family, so later in my writings you will know and understand better what and to whom I am referring.

*** 

I also had an uncle named Marian, a brother of my Mother. He was a handsome man and we were very close to him because in his bachelor years he lived with us for quite a while. My Mother and her three sisters adored their only brother. He worked in a nightclub as a maitre dee. A few years before the war, he moved to Katowice where he owned his own nightclub. I knew where the nightclubs were, but I never went inside any of them. In our time, this was unthinkable and anyway if you were seen in one of them by a professor or teacher, you would be expelled from school.

I want to tell you how strict the rules and regulations were for students attending public schools, especially the gymnasium up to the matura - that means up to the age of 18. For being seen smoking a cigarette, walking anywhere unescorted after 10 pm, attending a restricted movie, you were risking being suspended or expelled. Higher education was a privilege, so you had to obey the rules - that's what we were told.

Once in a while, Uncle Marian would take a short vacation and go to Cieszyn to visit his younger sister Mania. On one of his visits, he was introduced to a Jewish girl named Elsa whose parents owned a tavern. Apparently, they fell in love. Why they didn't get married, I really don't know. At home, children my age weren't told about those things. I suspect that the families didn't approve, or perhaps it was too hard on the courtship to live so far apart.

Not long before the war, Uncle Marian got married to a very petite German Jewish woman named Helen whom he met while living in Katowice. The wedding took place in Krakow and the reception was at the Brenner's apartment. It so happened that my Uncle Jerry from the United States was visiting with us. It was a strictly family reception and was quite moderate.

Uncle Jerry came from the United States to study medicine in Germany and later in Switzerland, so on his vacations, he spent time with us in Poland. Marian, Herman and Uncle Jerry became very friendly, they were about the same age and had lots of fun together, especially in the nightclubs, thanks to Uncle Marian's connections.

The people I've described are the closet family members I had in Europe. Of course, we had second cousins, distant cousins, uncles and so on, but these were the main ones.

# Two

I'll start to write about myself. I'm not quite sure how far back I can remember my childhood, probably not much before I started to go to public school. I remember playing around the house with neighbourhood children. And as always, I also spent a lot of time at the Brenner's, in and around the store where my cousin Moniek used to get me into all kind of mischief.

I remember once how he talked me into throwing a glass pop bottle under the wheels of a garbage truck. He dared me to do it and I did it! Of course, they stopped the truck, jumped out, caught me and gave me a good licking. They brought me to the store where my Aunt Frania bribed them with some cigarettes and they let me go. I got a good sermon from my Mother when I returned home.

We had a maid who used to take me for walks to the park or to the nearby Vistula River. We always stopped at our neighbourhood church and I had to go in with her. She knelt and prayed for a few minutes. I never knelt, but stood and listened to her prayers. Sometimes there were services in the church, so I listened and watched the ceremony. I knew the Catholic prayers by heart and learned from her and my neighbourhood friends all the Christmas carols. But that's as far as it went. I always knew that I am Jewish. Even as a child, I felt very strong about it, thanks of course, to my parents.

When I was about four years old, a Hebrew teacher came to our home twice a week and gave me lessons on Jewish subjects. He taught me the Hebrew alphabet, how to read and pray. We lived in a small apartment at Barska 34 in Dembniki, on the first floor in one unit and the owner of the apartment, a family by the name of Syrek, in the second.

The Syreks were a little different than the other Poles. They were born in Philadelphia in the United States. They had three children, two daughters and a son. The daughters were born in the United States. Only the young son Mietek was born in Poland. He was one year younger than myself and was one of my closest friends. Their father was a great artisan and restored very elaborate, beautiful ornamental furniture. He also made this kind of furniture himself. He had his workshop in the basement of the apartment where he employed a couple of people. The basement was always full of wood,

23

machinery and all kinds of tools. He was brought to Poland by the Polish government to do some restoration in the Wawel Castle on the Vistula River.

Wawel is the most famous castle in Poland and is where all the Polish kings are buried, including Marshal Pilsudski. It is a huge complex with all kinds of medieval buildings and churches and is one of the most visited places in Poland.

What was unusual about the Syreks is that they weren't anti-Semitic, having been born in the United States where they lived in ethnic neighbourhoods with Jewish friends and other denominations. They often received English newspapers and comic books from America, which their older daughter Jadwiga would translate for us as we lay flopped on her bedroom floor.

After school I played with Mietek and the other neighbourhood children. We went to the river to throw flat stones, climb the steep embankments and go back to the meadow behind the apartment to play handball. Our apartment was the last one on the block and had a nice orchard belonging to the Syreks, with a variety of fruit trees and berry bushes. It was fenced off, but we often snuck into it, and other neighbourhood orchards as well, somehow finding the stolen fruit much tastier from that we could have at home. Once we were surprised by an elderly orchard owner close to our apartment. We ran away, but he shot at our behinds with an airgun filled with salt. It burned terribly. Afraid to say anything to our parents, we went to the river to soak our behinds in cold water. What a relief it was!

We didn't have any toys to speak of. We played with everything, buttons, stones, asphalt cubicles, strings. We played "pelant," which was something similar to baseball, but played with sticks. We made things out of cardboard boxes, chocolate papers, blew bubbles from dissolved pieces of soap and straws from the fields close by. We did-n't know what it meant to be bored — our days were all too short. Our big problem was how to get a decent ball to play soccer. We improvised sometimes making a ball from rags, papers, and so on. Later when I was about six or seven years old, I got a regular soccer ball from my Uncle Henek from Cieszyn. He represented many sports equipment factories and in later years, supplied me with skis and skates. I became a king by owning an original soccer ball. Everyone waited patiently until I came to play. We played so much, that the ball needed constant repairs.

The boys I played with were all from the neighbourhood and practically all gentiles. Some of the boys were from very poor families. They were very rough. Most of their parents drank and beat them. They lived mostly in basement apartments. They skipped school and were always behind, but they were good players. I was the only Jewish kid who played with them.

In my free time, I liked to be outdoors as much as possible. It was boring to be inside. After I finished my homework, I ran away the minute I could to be outside, winter or summer. There were no televisions or VCRs. In later years we had a radio with earphones, but we didn't listen to it very much because only one person could listen at a time. The Syreks had a record player and quite a few Polish and English records. It had to be cranked by hand and we could listen only with adult supervision so we wouldn't break it by over-winding it. When the spring was strung, it would play one side without rewinding. If not, you had to bring it alive again in the middle of the record.

In winter, we spent more time in the apartment because it got so cold. If it was bearable, we went tobogganing, with fought with snowballs and built snowmen. We used to slide on a snowy path until it became a narrow strip of ice, and finally became much longer so we could spend a lot of time on it. Our parents didn't like it very much because this was hard on the soles of our shoes. They were gone in no time and to re-sole a shoe was quite expensive.

During the winter I used to get colds and sometimes a fever. My pediatricians were always ladies and I can still remember their names. The first one who took care of me was Dr. Turowa and later Dr. Bornstein. They all made house calls. I didn't know how Mother got in touch with them because we had no telephone. Both perished in the Holocaust.

I was always looking forward to my summer vacations. As a little boy, it was mostly in Cieszyn or in Zabierzow. Mother would rent a house and we'd have lots of fun.

In the village, there was one house in which nobody lived. The villagers claimed that it was inhabited by ghosts. The peasants who passed by would cross themselves. We were all fascinated by this house. Apparently after his wife died, the owner of the house hung himself. That the story they told us. In the evening we watched the house for some lights which supposedly appeared inside at night. Towards the end of the summer my cousin Herman came to spend a few days with us and laughed in disbelief when we told him about the haunted house and all the stories. He looked around and decided he was going to sleep one night in the house. The word spread around, there was lots of opposition and warnings. Yet one evening he carried in a straw mattress and went in to sleep. Everybody was worried, but in the morning he emerged, with a smile. He said he had a good undisturbed sleep and that was the end of the story about the haunted house.

Towards the end of August, before returning home, I spent a lot of time in the marshes and watched the storks exercising and preparing themselves for the long journey south. They would take to the air by the hundreds, organize in V formations, fly a few times in circles then land back in the marshes. Momentarily another group would emerge, doing the same.

The other vacation spot was Cieszyn. Our Aunt Mania would bring little Samek to Krakow, then take me back to Cieszyn with her. When I was a little older, about 10 or 11 years old, I would go to Cieszyn and Samek Steiner would go to Krakow - a practical cousins exchange. I didn't quite travel by myself. I was sent there and back by what you could call the Jewish Express.

In Poland, we had a very organized post office, delivering parcels, letters, selling money orders and even serving as a savings bank. But if you wanted to send something and have it delivered in one day or night, or something perishable, the post office could not help. There were a few trucks going in all directions, but not for smaller parcels or perishables. Here came to the rescue, the fracht (German for "transport") people. The fracht people were a one-man express transport company. They were mostly Orthodox Jews and their job was to pick up parcels and letters from factories, stores, manufacturers very early in the morning or previous afternoon. They took them to the train station in a variety of boxes, bags and parcels and delivered them to various cities and towns along the rail line. Everybody had his customers and his destination. On the way back to Krakow, they would bring some merchandise from the other destinations. It was a back-breaking job. They usually tried to get a separate compartment on the train by bribing the conductor. This way they could avoid being harassed and were able to say their morning prayers in relative privacy.

That's how I travelled to Cieszyn when I was young. My parents would bring me early in the morning to the station and pay a few zlotys to a particular frachtman who was travelling to Cieszyn to keep an eye on me and to make sure I got picked up at the Cieszyn station by my aunt or uncle. It usually went quite smoothly and they gave me a seat by the window because I loved to watch the countryside passing by. My Mother packed all kinds of goodies, I ate, read, watched and kept to myself. To the fruchtmen, I was probably an assimilated goy.

Once on the way back to Krakow, I had a very unpleasant experience. I must have been at least 11 years old because I wore my gymnasium uniform. I didn't look Jewish at all — in fact, I looked more Polish than the Polaks, with light blond hair and blue eyes. My Polish was impeccable, without a trace of the Yiddish accent so common to Jewish homes, where Yiddish was usually spoken.In our home, my parents spoke to us only in Polish.

My aunt took me back to the station and put me in the hands of the frachtman to deliver me back home. We bordered the train without any problem and got ourself a compartment. At the next few station a few more fracht people boarded and the compartment filled up quickly with parcels and people. It was in the morning and everybody said his morning prayers, putting phylacteries and the prayer shawls on. As usual, I sat in my favourite place near the window.

The door of the compartment had a glass window. Suddenly in the window, there appeared a priest who knocked on the door and pointed to me to get out. I didn't know what to do, but after a few more knocks I opened the door, greeted him properly and asked him what he wanted. He said he would like me to go to his compartment next door which was a few doors away in first class. I went, but declined his invitation to sit down. There were other priests with him and I felt quite uncomfortable. He began to berate me: "How can a Polish Catholic boy, a student at the gymnasium, the future of our Motherland, sit together with those dirty, smelly Jews?" I didn't know what to say. I froze. I started to cry. I felt I couldn't speak but finally told him, "I sit with those Jews because *I* am a Jew!" I bolted from the compartment, back to my seat and didn't say a word to anybody. This was the last time I travelled with the fracht people.

One winter when I was sick with too many colds and my resistance was very low, my doctor said I should eat better. He also recommended I should drink a lot of fresh goat milk and eat more fruit. So in the summer, my mother made arrangements to go to a summer resort in the Beskidy mountains called Bystra. She rented a room from a farmer who had goats so I would have fresh warm goat milk, right after milking. Of course, I hated the milk because of its taste and smell. I was bribed by all kinds of goodies so I would drink it. I spent my day with the farmer's children, mostly helping them to tend their cows and goats at pasture nearby. In the afternoon we would climb a wooded mountain nearby and collect blueberries and blackberries. My Mother must have been terribly bored because she had nobody to talk to and there was nobody around that she knew. I probably never appreciated her devotion until I parted with her.

At home, we didn't have refrigerators or ice boxes, so most of the food was bought daily. Sometimes this meant a few trips to the grocery store. Very often my Mother would ask me to go on an errand to get something. Most of the time I would say I'm not going. She would give me a sad look with her beautiful dark eyes and I would do it right away. Why I ever said no in the first place, I don't know.

*** 

The public school I attended was not far from where we lived, about a 10-minute walk. My sister's public school was almost across the street. There were no co-educational schools. I started school right on my birthday, the third of September.

There was very strict discipline in school. We learned al the basic subjects. If somebody didn't get good grades they had to repeat a full year. For sports, all we had was 10 minutes of gymnastics in the morning and 10 minutes later in the day.

In Polish school, part of the curriculum included the subject of religion. So once a week a priest from a local parish came to teach and Jewish kids were excused to an empty classroom where a Jewish teacher gave us lessons in our religion.

After school we walked home slowly, playing on the way. Not very far from where we lived were the city garages with all kinds of vehicles and garbage trucks. I used to pass by there very often on my way to my cousins, the Brenners. Friday was pay day and hundreds of women were waiting for their husbands outside of the gate to make sure they got some of the money they earned before the husbands hit the taverns to drink and spend their pay.

The kids in my classroom gave me a hard time because I was Jewish. They knew that, of course, because I was excused for religious instruction. If they called me names, I called them back. If they pushed me, I pushed back. If they hit me, I hit back. So little by little I was accepted and they stopped bothering me and some of them became really good friends of mine. That's the only language they understood, if you gave in you didn't have a chance.

Once, during a fight with one of the other students, I felt a tap on my back. I turned my head and to my surprise saw the priest standing there. I was frightened, but after hearing my explanation, all I heard was a lecture about how fighting wouldn't solve problems. I was relieved to get away without punishment. The next day at school I was expecting a fight or something bad from the other boy, but he came and shook hands with me. We became pretty good friends after that.

We were accustomed to anti-Semitism. It was a way of life. As long as it wasn't too harmful physically that is, we took it in strides. Then again, we had no choice. Of all the cities in Poland, antiSemitism in Krakow was more tolerable. The majority of the Jews of Krakow lived in Kazimierz. They were mostly Orthodox and many of them were Hasidic. It was an old part of the city with a large market, lots of stores, kosher restaurants, old synagogues, prayer houses and yeshivas. It was practically a Jewish city. Yet in the centre of Kazimierz was a huge Catholic church. On Sunday, the Poles would attend mass. But since it was Sunday, stores were closed and there was rarely any incident. They went to their mass and left. Every year in the Fall a huge religious procession would take place at this church and people would come from all over Krakow, carrying all kinds of holy figures, altars with Jesus with all the saints with the church hierarchy walking through the centre of Kazimierz. Everything was quiet and still as so many people passed by without any incidents. After the services were finished at the church, that was another story. Going back home the crowd couldn't resist the temptation to hit a few Jews, or break some windows in the stores. But the merchants knew about this from experience and kept a very low profile and some of the stores were closed.

Across the street from our apartment was a huge mansion, surrounded by a beautiful garden, all enclosed by a tall fence. This was the home of professor Sawicki who came from a very noble family. He was a geographer and would go away almost every year on expeditions to Africa or Asia. He was a cartographer and published atlases and maps from all over the world. He would be away for a few months, sometimes for half a year. He had a son my age and I would be invited often to play with him. What a treat that was! From his expeditions, professor Sawicki brought monkeys, snakes, sometimes a gazelle or a deer. We were able to play, especially with the monkeys. I think during the winter the animals were taken to the zoo. The next year he would go away again and bring back some more animals.

From childhood I loved music, especially listening to the violin. We had a music teacher in our school who used to supplement his income by giving private lessons in his house. His name was Mr. May. My parents knew that I wanted to play the violin, so they arranged with Mr. May to give me lessons and bought me a violin. I took it very seriously, practising a lot, but I had difficulty learning the notes. It didn't take long before Mr. May called my Mother and told her it was a waste of money. I had no ear or talent for the instrument and that was the end of the future virtuoso. I love to listen to music and I enjoy music, but unfortunately I cannot make music or play an instrument.

All in all, I enjoyed my early childhood years. We had a large part of our family in the United States and there was steady correspondence, almost weekly, with them. Sometimes for my birthday they would send me a few dollars to buy something for myself. Whenever there was occasion and we took some pictures, they were immediately sent to New York. Now, I am recovering quite a few pre-war pictures from my family in the United States.

Mother had a sister named Sally living in the United States in New York. It was a huge celebration when she visited us in 1933. We got a lot of gifts from her. I remember she came on the German liner Bremen to Hamburg. The sisters were thrilled and took her everywhere. There were lots of stories and we kids liked to listen, especially about life in the United States. After that we all wanted to go there.

Sally was amazed we all had maids at home and lots of other help around. She said in the United States only the Rockafellers could afford it. She stayed about three weeks and then returned to the U.S.

I remember in 1935 when the Polish leader Marshal Pilsudski died, I happened to be at the Brenners. When we received the news, my Grandmother began to cry and sob. I tried to console her and asked her why she is crying so hard. She answered, "Samek, from now on there will be very hard times for the Jewish People, now that our Marshal, our grandfather died."

How prophetic her words were. Marshal Pilsudski was a benevolent dictator. We had presidential election and congress, but his words were the law. People said his wife was Jewish, but I don't think this was true. He had a lot of Jewish friends who fought with him in the legions against the Bolsheviks in the 1920s. After his death, anti-Semitism rose immensely, especially after Hitler's propaganda started to filter in from Germany. Grandma died a year or so later and maybe this way she was spared the horrors of the Holocaust. She got sick with a bad ear infection. She didn't complain for quite a while. Our family doctor took care of her but things got worse. She went to a specialist and they decided to operate. The operation was performed in a Jewish hospital by a good surgeon. We were all in the waiting room, but something went wrong and Grandma died. We took this very hard, especially cousin Herman. He was the oldest of us kids. He went to the funeral and we stayed at home. She must have been only in her 60s. After her death, the house at the Brenners seemed to be empty for a long time. We just couldn't get used to the house without Grandma; we missed her terribly.

*** 

There was one more place that I spent some time during the summer with my Mother. It was a village near Tarnow called Zglobice. There lived my Grandfather's brother on my Father's side. This was quite a place. We called him Uncle Psachje. He was married several times and had older children living in Vienna and younger ones at home. He managed a huge farm, forest and a whole village for a Polish count who lived in France on the Riviera. He would come home twice a year to collect his money or to hunt in the winter.

They lived in a huge white house at the top of the hill, actually on the banks of the River Dunajec. There were dozens of rooms, all painted white and when we stayed there we were assigned one. The house was always teaming with activity, lots of maids, workers, drivers. In the morning they would all come to the house and be assigned to their jobs. There were barns for horses, cows, hundreds of sheep in the pasture nearby.

None of this mattered to me. My older cousin, Moniek, brought me a little black lamb and it became my best friend. The lamb followed me all over and slept next to the door. I just loved this cuddly little lamb. There were also lots of cows and calves to keep me busy all day.

On Friday night and Saturday - the Sabbath, everything in the house stopped. All the tumult quieted down. Everybody got dressed and it was a real day off for rest.

There were three cousins there, two girls - Riva and Ida and my cousin Max. They were quite older than I was. Max had a horse, a beautiful white stallion, and he sometimes took me to ride with him. It was terrible when it was time to go home. I didn't want to go home without the little lamb. I cried and fought to stay there.

In early 1939 we received a telegram that Ida, one of the girls from Zglobice, was taken to a hospital in Krakow. We rushed to see her and find out what the problem was. She lay there in great spirits and welcomed us with a very sweet smile. Little by little I found out she had been cut by a rusty nail on the farm and got a very bad blood infection. They tried whatever they could in Tarnow, but she was getting worse so they decided to bring her to Krakow. I believe she really didn't know how sick she was.

Her sister stayed in Krakow and was constantly at her bedside and often she slept at the Brenners. The boys there were close to her age, so she felt very comfortable there. My father saw to it that Ida got the best medical help. He asked the important doctors and professors in Krakow to see her, but Ida didn't improve, her health steadily deteriorated. She had a step-brother in Vienna who sent a famous professor by airplane for a consultation, but he couldn't do anything either. She stayed in the hospital for a few months without any improvement, before one of the doctors suggested we take her home to die. They could do nothing more for her, and he wanted to help us avoid the autopsy which would be performed should she die in hospital, and which violated Jewish laws and customs. Sadly, the family agreed and brought Ida home, expecting her to die soon afterwards. But astonishingly, our own family doctor, Dr. Kurtz, took an interest in Ida's case. Nobody ever told me exactly what he did; they mentioned massive transfusions, and so on.But somehow, he cured her completely. He became a great hero of the family and of the community. Neither Ida nor Dr. Kurtz had long to live; the dark cloud of the Holocaust were approaching and would steal them both from us.

\*\*\*

When I was about to finish my fourth year of public school, the family decided that in September, I should enter private school, the Hebrew gymnasium located not far from our restaurant. This was a momentous occasion, to enter the Hebrew gymnasium, and shaped in many ways my upbringing and outlook on life. This was a place where I made my best friends and spent the best years of my life, my short teenage years.

Our school was the pride of the Jewish community in Krakow and the whole surrounding area. It was the only Jewish gymnasium in southwestern Poland which had full rights and accreditation issued by the Polish government. I think only three more schools were like it in Poland, which had a population of three and a half million Jews. Our gymnasium had the highest standards in Poland. Upon finishing school and passing the matura, a student was entitled to apply to any university in Poland and usually to most foreign universities. To keep this accreditation in anti-Semitic Poland, we had to be better than everybody. Several times a year, the board of education would send, mostly unannounced, several inspectors, sometimes a whole commission of 20 persons or more, to check on the level of our education. They would enter the classrooms and sit, listening to the lectures and asking questions. They also attended the matura final examinations. So the high standards always had to be maintained.

An average classroom in our school consisted of about 50 students. Yet our teachers handled us without problems, achieving great results, incomparable to almost any school on this continent. Whoever finished this school was well prepared to undertake any university studies.

Our school was under the auspices of the Zionist Organization of southern Poland, but financially, it was self-supporting. Being under the Zionist auspices, gave the school the advantage to attract students from diverse religiously observant families, from atheist to orthodox. We were taught four subjects in Hebrew beside our regular curriculum, which was why we stayed in school longer than other gymnasiums. One subject was religion where we learned the basics of the Jewish religion but actual religious observance was up to the parents. Discipline in school was very strict and anyone misbehaving after several warnings was expelled. Anybody who did not get proper marks was forced to repeat the whole year. There was no mercy. Higher educations was simply a privilege and there was no shortage of applicants. The school was very expensive by Polish standards. The atmosphere in the school was like living in a Jewish state. The hours we spent there were like hours of complete freedom. We didn't have to look over our shoulder at who was behind us or hear any anti-Semitic slurs.

We started school at 8 am and stayed there until 1:40 pm, six days per week. Of course, we had time off on Saturdays, and all the Jewish holidays. Frequently, we spent more time after school and in the evenings on extra curricular activities so that most of our life was spent in school.

We weren't always happy, of course. Who would like the discipline, hard studying, exams and very demanding curriculum at our age? I can see only now that those days were probably the happiest time of our lives, with a great school, great friends and our families. I often wish I had thanked my parents more often for all they did for me; at the time, I simply took my father's hard work and my mother's sacrifices for granted.

We each received a copy of the student year book every year. It featured the yearly activities, the accomplishments of the students and professors and the names of every student in every classroom. To my knowledge, only one yearbook from 1937, exists. For this particular yearbook of three classes consisting of about 150 pupils; all but roughly twenty-six perished in the Holocaust.

I remember my Bar Mitzvah very vividly. You can't compare it to the big Bar Mitzvahs affairs in this country. I had already been going to the gymnasium for three years, so to read the Haftorah was not a big deal. After services, all family and close friends came to our house for a reception. I received a few gifts of money and some books. From the United States, my grandfather, whom I had never met, sent me a beautiful prayer shawl and prayer book.

In the last three years of our gymnasium, we had undergone military training, once or sometimes twice a week after school for a few hours we would undergo basic training by officers of the Polish Army. We had to purchase our khaki uniforms to be able to attend. Now, in addition to school uniforms, we had to have military uniforms. We were taught how to use guns, machine guns, bayonets, grenades et cetera. We had day exercises, night exercises and camps and maneuvers for several days in the country.

In July 1939, just before going to the summer camp that I attended every year, we had a huge military training outside Krakow where we got a taste of full army basic training which lasted almost two weeks. We had military maneuvers with other gymnasiums from the Krakow region. We were taught to recognize German planes, how to behave under bombardment, how to protect ourselves from gas, et cetera. We all lost quite a few pounds there. It was good timing because in the near future, the knowledge that we acquired would come in very handy.

The last time I attended the camp was in August 1939. It was beautiful, the weather was great and we had great times. Little did we realize that dark clouds were gathering on the horizon, clouds which would change our lives forever.

## THREE

At the end of our term, we noticed the Polish Army's movement in the area and we stayed close to camp. We were no longer allowed to go on any excursions.

We felt the first sign of unrest when we arrived at the station to board the trains on our way home. There were a lot of soldiers at the station and the train was late. When we finally boarded, it was terribly overcrowded. We arrived late to find our parents worried, but happy to see us. We didn't realize then that we only had a few days left to be together. There was talk about the war for months, but nobody wanted to believe it would really happen.

The situation in Krakow upon our arrival from camp was very tense. People were worried about the war and were listening to Hitler's speeches on the radio as well as the Polish Marshal Smigly-Rydz, who told us that we had nothing to worry about, that we would win the war and that our cause was right and so on. No matter how threatening the situation was, deep down, we didn't believe in war. But on September first, it was happening.

In the morning, we noticed some airplanes in the skies. It looked like a dog fight with lots of acrobatics. There were sirens and people thought it was training exercise or an air raid. Everyone was excited. Suddenly explosions could be heard and I could see the planes dropping bombs very close to our apartment. They were bombing the radio towers which were located very close to us. The people on the street were stunned. Nobody was going for cover. People were still milling about, it was pandemonium. The radio started to play military music and announced that war had broken out. It was really frightening and we had a feeling that something awful was going to happen.

I thought then of 1938, when thousands of Jewish refugees from Germany had come to Poland, thrown out by the Nazis. In November 1938, Hitler and his cohorts arrested 30,000 Jews, claiming they were Polish Jews, though they had lived in Germany for years, even generations. Dragged from their homes without warning, and able to take with them only scanty belongings, they were loaded on trucks and driven to within a few miles of the Polish border. There they had been stranded, unable to return, and unable to cross into Poland because of the border guards, who forbade them entry. Only after strong Jewish and international intervention were they allowed entry. Then they were welcomed by the Polish Jewry, and settled mostly in the southwestern part of Poland, close to the German border.

I had been appalled by that tragedy. My father had brought a couple with a young child to stay temporarily with us until they could find a place to stay. It was crowded in our apartment, and hard for me to study or sleep, but I didn't complain. They stayed with us for the whole winter, never quite believing the situation was anything more than temporary, even when they found a place and moved out. Now I found myself wondering what changes the war would bring to our own lives.

It took the Germans quite a while to destroy the radio towers. In the meantime, they bombed constantly and the bombs fell closer and closer to our apartment. My parents decided that we should move temporarily to the centre of the city to stay with our friends. They lived not far from our gymnasium.

It was unreal. Suddenly, in no time, we had to pack our most precious belongings. Mother and Father packed two suitcases and a few bundles with things they thought we would need right away, of course, with many valuables. My parents helped my sister Niusia to fill her little rucksack. I packed my belongings; it was the first important decision I had to make on my own. We had to leave in a hurry and could hear bombs exploding in the vicinity. I packed my backpack tightly with all my good suits, books, camera, fountain pen - anything that was very dear to me. I tried to put in as much as I could.

People were panicking, they didn't know what to do. Polish radio was sending confused messages we were winning the war, our calvary was counterattacking German tanks. The air force was bombing Germans. What we heard from the German side was frightening.They were attacking Poland from the south from Czechoslovakia from the north from Prussia and on the longest western front from Germany. We heard England and France had declared war on Germany. We were expecting immediate help. Rumours were spreading from every source, every minute. Some people said they had seen English planes coming to help. Some heard France was opening a second front. I didn't want to listen anymore. I was still packing and unpacking my rucksack.

I rummaged through my closet, reluctant to pack everything, when I was sure I would return soon. How long could a modern war last? It seemed silly to me even to pack any of my winter things,

36

though I did tuck a few sweaters into the suitcase. In the outside pockets of the sack I stuck in some more clothing and valuables, my Waterman pen, map of Poland, a few books, my good watch, my favourite flashlight, even after-shave lotion. I packed and packed. I didn't want to leave anything, any of my dear possessions. I looked around my room at the stacks of my books, school books, atlases and encyclopedias, and I realized that I had to leave them all. But, I told myself, I'll be back soon.

In the last few minutes I decided to grab my 1939 report from my gymnasium and a couple of maps of Poland. I can't say why I grabbed those things now, but very little seemed logical at that moment.

Mother was in charge of the packing. She rearranged everything we had packed. Father went to work, promising to return soon with a carriage to move everything. Finally in the late afternoon he came and the carriage was waiting outside. We loaded everything on and away we went.

In our neighbourhood, there was hardly any movement. People stood in front of apartments discussing the events, radio dispatches and all the rumours. They were mostly Christians. It was their country. These were their homes and Hitler never threatened them the way he threatened us Jews. They had no intention to move anywhere and they never did.

\*\*\*

We crossed the bridge over the Vistula and noticed increased traffic everywhere. Army units, some on foot, some on trucks, artillery pulled by horses, were all moving in a western direction. The closer we got to Kazimierz the harder it was to move. People were running in all directions. Cabs, cars, horse-drawn carriages, bicycles, people pulling carts. It was getting late. The bombing stopped and we didn't see any more planes above us. During the day we had seen heavy formation of German airplanes flying very high above but they didn't attack Krakow. They were just flying by. The only two objects they bombed in Krakow were the radio station which was located close to us in Dembniki, and the railroad station. Those heavy bombers were flying very high and were very noisy. They had a specific noise, like on over-loaded machine or a heavy truck trying to carry more than it had to. They seemed to breathe hard. In time we would learn to recognize the noise before the planes were visible.

Finally, towards dusk, we arrived at our friends' home, and unloaded our possessions. The Shicklers were waiting for us with a meal, but we ate the sumptuous dinner in silence. Even the children were quiet. No one knew what to say or what to do. The Krakow radio station had been knocked off the air, of course, so we were listening to Warsaw radio. The Germans had bombed Warsaw but the radio was full of optimistic news. Our Army was regaining initiatives, counterattacking. We were in contact with our allies England and France. In the meantime, German radio was playing marching music and was full of speeches, reporting progress on all fronts in all directions, advancing and capturing all the boarder cities with little resistance. We didn't know whom to believe, but I had a premonition that the Germans were telling the truth.

It was getting late and arrangements were made about where everybody would sleep. It was cramped in their modest apartment with an extra four people plus all our luggage. For me, they put a couple blankets and pillows on the floor. I lay down, and being tired from the day's ordeal I fell asleep immediately. I had terrible nightmares, and woke up in a cold sweat. I realized that I had messed up and wetted all of the quilt. Outside, it was becoming light and everyone was still asleep and I was petrified about how I would hide the quilt, all wet and sticky as were my pajamas. I got up fast, got dressed and rolled up my pajamas and put them in the backpack. I rolled the quilts and pillows in the corner and hoped we wouldn't have to sleep there another night so nobody would notice what I did. For a moment the war wasn't important. Avoiding embarrassment was a priority.

Little by little everybody got up. The radio was on and the news was worse than last evening. They were repeating over and over that men from 16 to 50 years old should immediately leave the city and surrounding towns and move toward the east where they would be inducted and mobilized to join the war effort to fight the enemy. We ventured out of the apartment and encountered a terrible sight. People by the thousands were leaving their homes and moving in all directions with their belongings. I looked toward the main street a block away and saw the same exodus. Cars, horse-drawn wagons were leaving the city. It was pandemonium.

We came to the apartment and the elders were deciding what to do. Father knew a lot of taxi and carriage drivers, but came back in a hurry, unable to get any. In the meantime we realized from listening to the radio and the rumours that there wasn't much time left before the Germans entered the city. Finally we decided to leave on foot, following the stream of people and hoping maybe that out of town we would find some means of transportation. We bid goodbye to our hosts the Shicklers and proceeded on our way eastward. The Shicklers had decided to stay for another day or two to see what they were going to do. There wasn't time to go to Dembniki to see what the Brenners had decided. We didn't expect to go very far. Traffic was awful and to get back to Dembniki would probably take a half a day. We left quite a few things at the Shicklers' apartment because we couldn't carry all that we had packed. It was a terrible decision and time was running out.

We walked with thousands of other people. Everyone was gloomy, looking down and carrying a heavy load. The weather was beautiful. The sky was clear and blue and it was quite warm. We walked toward Vola Duchacka, a small town or village on the outskirts of Krakow. It was very hard, especially on our parents, who had suitcases instead of backpacks, to carry our belongings. We never had enough time to go back to our apartment to repack and re-think about what to take.

It took almost a whole day to get to Vola Duchacka. We stopped over and over, with our loads getting heavier as we went.

My mother had a cousin, Ignace, living in Vola Duchacka. Ignace had been taken prisoner of war in the First World War. He was sent to a camp in Siberia. After the war ended some prisoners returned but he didn't. Apparently he got sick and couldn't return back in time. In the meantime, the Revolution in Russia began and he got stuck there. It must have taken long years and lots of money to get Uncle Ignace out of Russia. I don't remember what year it was, but it must have been around 1935. One day, it was announced that we were going to the train station to welcome Uncle Ignace. We arrived at the station and waited. Nobody knew what he looked like; they hadn't seen him since 1916 and they were all small children then. All we had was an old photograph and I think a small photograph he sent from Russia.

The train arrived and it didn't take us very long to find him. We were all very shocked when we met him. His face was young but his hair was completely white. He wore a big white mustache. He was shabbily dressed and acted very subdued without expressing any emotion. He had hardly any luggage, a small wooden suitcase. We took the carriage outside of the railway station and went straight to the Brenners, who had more room. At the dinner table, everybody was asking questions. We were all anxious to hear his story, but he hardly spoke.

With tears in his eyes he thanked them for their great effort to get him out of Russia. He never told us children anything about his years in the Soviet Union. When you asked him, he froze and didn't say anything. I don't know if he ever told anything to the elders. He stayed with the Brenners for quite a while and helped in the store. A few months later he was introduced to a lady, got married, and with the help of the family, he opened a small grocery store in Vola Duchacka. We visited them, sometimes on Sundays, and he was doing quite well. But as long as I remember him, he was always very serious and I never saw a smile on his face. He probably lost his happiness in the Russian camps.

We were hungry and tired when we arrived in Vola Duchacka, and decided to stay for a few hours and continue on very early in the morning. My parents tried to persuade Uncle Ignace to come with us and avoid capture by the Germans. His answer was plain and decisive. Where could he run but to the east, to the Russian border? And for him, this was impossible. We never heard from him again.

The next day, we got up very early, had breakfast, took some food with us and continued, still on foot despite our efforts to find transportation. The people were still streaming from Krakow as the day before. It was September 3, my 17th birthday. Not much to celebrate. I got a kiss from my Mother and my sister Niusia and congratulations with hope that soon we would be able to celebrate under better circumstances. The morning was hazy with a little fog and we joined the quiet exodus. People were walking, some with pushcarts, some pushing bicycles loaded on both sides. Some had baby buggies and here and there the lucky ones had horse-drawn wagons. You couldn't see any cars. They were probably way ahead of us.

When the fog lifted, the sun became warmer by the minute. We stopped quite often to rest for a few minutes, for the burden of carrying the luggage in the heat and on the unpaved road became intolerable. The traffic was getting heavier and heavier. Some army units materialized out of nowhere. Soon we heard the noise of the planes flying high above us. They were heading to the east or north east.

I don't know how far we got from Krakow, but suddenly the Germans decided to play havoc with our stream of refugees. Out of nowhere a single plane flew over the road and sprayed the road with bullets. We ran into the ditch. The plane kept coming back and back in circles. After he disappeared it was complete havoc. Horses were running all over, some people were wounded. Nobody knew what to do. We got up and continued to walk. But soon we realized we couldn't go on like this. I remember we sat down under a roadside tree and my parents decided to assess the situation. They decided Father and I would continue because of the government's order for men to go eastward. Mother and Niusia would go back to Krakow. If Father and I didn't get mobilized, we would return.

They opened up their suitcases and started to divide what Mother should take back and what Father and I should take. I was scared, but what could I say? I didn't like it but I didn't see any alternatives. To walk like this was getting impossible and very dangerous. The planes would never stop and the weather was great for them to bomb and spray us. The valuables and foreign currency we left for Mother. There wasn't too much money and with us going to the army we didn't need so much. Most of the money my parents had was in the bank but there was no time to withdraw anything before we left.

Mother and Niusia were going back to Ignace There she would stay until she could get some kind of transportation to get back to Krakow. Everything seemed simple and logical. We kissed and embraced and frightened as I was, I didn't realize it was the last time I would see my mother and my sister.

There was no time to waste. Mother and Niusia went one way and my Father and I went the other. I turned and watched them disappear, my chubby little sister holding hands with my Mother.

# FOUR

We started to walk with thousands of others, driven by some instinct to outrun the Germans and not to be trapped. We were dressed in ordinary clothes. The heat was unbearable during the day, so we stopped at some farms where we could to get some rest.

Suddenly we heard our name called. It was a distant relative of my mother's from the village of Zabierzow were she was born. He was by himself, also running with the crowds. His name was Horowitz.. He told us that very soon he was going to leave the main road and try to head into the forest, which he knew very well. Going there with him made lots of sense so we decided to go with him. It was a huge forest, frightening yet tranquil. All you heard was your steps crushing underneath your feet and chirping of the birds.

It was such a relief from the burning sun, so cool and so still. The only reminder of the war were the planes overhead. We didn't see them, only heard their heavy roar which brought us back to reality.

Horowitz certainly knew the forest and all the narrow trails in it. He concentrated on the trail sometimes turning sharply to avoid certain areas. After several hours in the forest, the forest started to thin. Shortly a village emerged. He led us to a farmer's house, and judging by their greeting, I could tell that he knew him well. He didn't know much of what was happening as he didn't have a radio. All he knew was that people were running to the east and towards Warsaw.

We sat down outside, it was late in the afternoon. He brought us dark bread, butter, fresh milk and some baked potatoes. Suddenly Horowitz got up and said that he had made up his mind. He would stay put in this area because he knew it so well and would not be moving any farther. We were shocked. We thought we would stay together and go to the east, maybe the north-east, closer to Warsaw and the Russian border. It was our hour of decision, and for the first time, I referred to my map to see where we should go. I asked the farmer if we could stay overnight. It was getting dark outside and there was no sense in moving on.

He showed us a barn. There was lots of hay and it made a good place to sleep. I was tired and exhausted, yet for a long time I couldn't fall asleep. The picture of Mother leading Niusia by the hand after our separation was constantly in front of me. I started to sob gently until the tears dried up and I fell asleep. This picture will stay with me forever. September 3, my birthday.

In the morning I asked Horowitz to direct us to the main road so that we could proceed. He decided to go with us for a few kilometres. Soon enough we came close to the road. Once again we saw the familiar sight of people streaming with their belongings and all kinds of transportation. We said goodbye to Horowitz and joined the refugees. We never heard from Horowitz again.

The sun was shining and it was getting progressively hot. We were praying for some cooler weather, some cloudiness or rain to help shield us from the German planes and give us some relief to make our journey easier. No one remembered a September like this year 1939. For the whole month, the weather was the same. Hot, early fog and not a cloud in the sky. The German air force had a picnic. There was no resistance in the air and perfect weather. They bombed and strafed anything in sight.

I walked with Father in silence. When was this going to end? Soon there was no time to think. Two planes appeared out of nowhere and swooped so low over the road that you could see the pilots inside. We heard the engine roar and the "ekk" of the machine guns. I ran with Father off the road where luckily there were some thick trees. We leaned against them for shelter and moved around the trees to avoid the bullets, watching the planes to see what direction they were coming from. The two planes were practically playing around with us. It was terrible. People left everything and ran to the forest and ditches nearby. The whole thing lasted several minutes, and when it was over, we were afraid to return to the road. A few horses were killed, some people were killed, others wounded. Belongings were strewn over the road, everything was in chaos. There wasn't much we could do, so having our luggage with us, we proceeded to walk. The sun was low and we hoped that the planes were not going to return. With the few people we spoke to while walking on the road we realized the Germans were not far behind us. Maybe Horowitz was right. Maybe we should have stayed a few days in Zabierzow, see what was going on and maybe return to Krakow.

There was no sign that we would be mobilized. All we could see were remnants of the Polish Army, in small groups, completely disorganized, running to the east or south. It was getting cooler, the sun was setting. Suddenly we heard some horses behind us. As we went to the side of the road to let them pass, Father took a look at them and recognized one of the drivers, called him by name and they stopped. Several of the people jumped down and embraced my Father. They were the carriage drivers who for years had a stand in

43

front of our restaurant. We were welcome to go with them. They rearranged the people and luggage and found a place for us on the first carriage. I sat next to the driver on a very small narrow seat with my Father in the back. The carriages were full of people with bundles hanging off the sides. What a relief it was to sit and rest my aching feet, going faster than before.

It was getting darker and the drivers started to look for a place to rest. It was dark before we found a place close to a brook with enough room for all of us. They unhitched the horses, gave them some oats and led them to the brook to drink. Since we spent quite a few days with them, I learned how much they loved their horses and took care of them as you take care of children. They spoke to them, they petted them. When the going was rough, they never hit the horses. They pleaded with them and the horses made the ultimate effort. With our assistance and pushing, the horses always came through.

The whole group sat down under a tree and started to talk. There were about 20 of us. The drivers were very simple people with no education. They were a rough bunch of guys in the city, but now they were confused and frightened. Among the passengers there was an older gentleman, an engineer, and he seemed to be in charge.

We decided to get up very early in the morning to get a fresh start and gain some ground before the planes started coming from the west. In the early morning it was very foggy and this was the only time the planes couldn't see us. In this period, we tried to cover as much ground and possible. I struck a conversation with the engineer and told him I had a very good map of Poland and maybe we could look up which direction to proceed. He called the map a gift from God. It was getting dark and we decided to look at the map in the morning. We were actually travelling almost straight to the east toward the city of Tarnow. In my opinion, I told him that if we proceeded to travel straight to the east, we would be cut off by the Germans pushing from the south from Czechoslovakia. Everyone was dead tired and wanted to go to sleep. Some slept on the carriage. The drivers lay down on the grass, making more room for the women and children. They had some horse blankets, they gave me a small one, but it smelled terrible from the horse's sweat. I laid down on the grass and used my backpack as a pillow. I tried to fall asleep, it was a beautiful night. The sky was gleaming with a myriad of stars. There was a cool breeze cooling off the earth underneath us. I couldn't fall asleep for a long time. It was the first time sleeping outdoors by just laying on the grass without any shelter or cover. Later that night, as the earth cooled, we got all wet with dew. By morning, we were all completely wet. It was still dark when we got up. Everybody ate what they had. The drivers had pots. They boiled water and we had a little tea. The drivers had a lot of provisions with them and they ate pretty well.

I sat down with the engineer, took out my map and we started to plan on how to continue. He agreed we should move as fast as possible to the northeast to avoid capture and use, if possible, secondary roads, going from village to village, to avoid being bombed by the German planes. We would avoid cities at any cost.

Travelling started to become very difficult. The dirt roads were dusty and full of pot holes, and the drivers started to get very impatient and edgy. It was hard on the horses and the buggies. The horses were used to pulling light loads on city-paved streets. So we proceeded quite slow and very carefully. Most of the time we walked behind the carriages. Quite often we had to forge small creeks and pushed and helped the horses. I learned it was possible to walk while I slept.

The closer we got toward the northeast, the more evidence of the German bombing we saw. We passed villages that were burning and small towns that were bombed out, filled with people around in panic.

When the morning fog lifted on another glorious September clear day, more planes showed up. We decided we would have to move early in the morning and after sundown. We stopped at villages during the day, put the horses under trees and rested a lot. We tried to buy food from the peasants but it wasn't an easy task. They were frightened and didn't want to sell. I was more successful if I went by myself to buy food for two reasons: I was young and I did not look Jewish. I always got something, sometimes for money and sometimes for nothing. When they found out I came all the way from Krakow, they wanted to hear the latest news about the war, what I had seen and what I thought they should do.

Often when we came to a crossroad, we asked the local people for directions. I stopped at homes where I could see light and sometimes I had to wake them up. I became a leader of our caravan. My map didn't show any of the secondary roads, so I had to ask directions all the time. I became somehow proud and maybe even enjoyed doing this. It was something different.

Older people were listening to me, taking my advice and letting me lead them most of the time. I felt responsible for them, so I tried and was very proud when I did something that really worked. Our journey was leading us north of the city of Mielec where my Father was born, towards Tarnobrzeg. The area we were entering was called COP which meant the Central Industrial Area of Poland. There was lots of heavy industry concentrated here. But there was no way we could avoid this area. We tried not to enter any cities and avoided highways leading to them. Now we could see the terrible destruction all around. Towns and cities were burning and we could see fires at night. We passed burnt out skeletons of towns,

When we got closed to the city of Tarnobrzeg, we parked in the outskirts. It was later in the afternoon when we decided with Father to walk to the city and find a relative of ours who lived there. As we came closer, we noticed that the city was bombed. We approached some people and asked if they knew our relatives and where we could locate them. They had a big business producing and exporting all kinds of woven baskets. But we were out of luck. People were frightened. Whoever we asked didn't know them or didn't give us any information. We decided to go back.

Dozens of bombers appeared over Tarnobrzeg, and suddenly all hell broke loose. There was no time to run and no where to hide. Bombs were falling like rain. I dragged my Father to a little field and we lay on the ground, hoping for the best. We could see the bombs falling and could hear them drop, with their shrill all around us. I was sure this was the end. I covered my head with my hands and tried to plug my ears, hoping for a miracle. By the time the bombing stopped, we were all covered with earth. How we got out of there in one piece, I don't know. God must have been looking over us. Everything was burning. Houses collapsed like matches. We practically ran without stopping in the direction in which we left our drivers. We found them and they were alright. They thought we were gone because they could see from their distance what was going on.

It was getting late and we decided to move on farther to the northeast. We walked all night without sleep, realizing we had to go farther ahead. We didn't eat too much because the food was getting scarce and harder to get in the villages. There was also no time to get food.

The villagers didn't know how long this was going to last and did not want to part with what they had. I couldn't blame them. Money was now meaningless. The confusion was terrible. People were going in all directions. Sometimes we met some Polish soldiers. Some were going south, some were going north. You could see they had no communications. We didn't meet any Germans anywhere.

A little farther on, the villages were intact, like nothing happened at all. So far we were doing well.

When we came to a stop, I was the one to get some food and find a place to sleep. We walked all night, with only very short stops and in the morning, when mist covered the earth, making us invisible from the sky. The weather was identical every day. Perfect for the Germans and very hard for us. When the sun came out, the fog disappeared, there were no clouds all day. They disappeared for weeks. The skies belonged to the enemy and had no mercy on us.

We realized that the war was lost, but still hoped that the Germans would stop, take what they need and negotiate. What did they need the whole of Poland for. Maybe something would happen. Whenever the planes appeared in the sky we looked up. Maybe some English or French would appear. But no such luck. When they came closer and started to unload their cargo of bombs, we knew who they were. The heavy bombers, the Junkers and Henkels didn't frighten us anymore. We got used to them. And by not entering the towns and cities, we usually were out of danger.

We were really afraid though of the Stukas. By flying low, they would appear from nowhere and dive within a few metres of the road, drop bombs and strife us with bullets. Anything moving on the road or highway was a target. Once the Germans destroyed the Polish Army and Air Force, the sky was theirs. Sometimes I could see a Stuka attack a stack of hay and strike it until it caught fire. They had a field day. They were getting good experience.

Our next objective was to move toward Chelm, through Krasnystaw. As usual, we started late in the afternoon. The area we were now in was no object for bombing and we were a little safer. However the travel was taking its toll. Nobody was trained to do this. The shoes we wore were for walking in the city, not on roads, fields, grass and stone. They were starting to fall apart and there were sores on our feet. We had to stop more often. Some people tried to walk barefoot. The carriages were overloaded and the horses were tired and worn out. We didn't get enough food and enough rest.

Every day there was more and more grumbling and arguing, but we had one common objective - fear of getting caught. Everything was getting to be a problem. Walking, sleeping, relieving yourself, et cetera. We were all city people, used to relative comforts and in one day became a mass of refugees thrown to the road, running and not knowing where. All kinds of rumours were circulating about Germans killing people,, especially the Jews.

One day, it was kind of quiet. We were resting and waiting for the sun to go down. No planes had been seen for a while so we decided to get going a little earlier. About two hours after sundown, we came to a crossroad of a highway leading to the city of Zamosc. We took out our maps to see what to do. The highway was full of people, vehicles and some army units. The engineer and the drivers decided to take the main highway, going a little to the south and later turning to the east to the city of Hrubieszow.

Soon it would get dark, they argued, and going on a highway would give the horses a rest. It all seemed very logical, but I was against it. I argued that by going on the field roads, we were doing very well and we should continue northeast toward the city of Chelm. I don't know what came over me, but I just didn't want to move on the crowded highway. I told Father that I was not going and suggested that we could manage ourselves. Father wasn't very happy about it, but I became very stubborn and would not go with the caravan any more. We thanked the drivers and said goodbye to them, crossed the road and parted. I don't know what made a 17 year old boy challenge the older people and the engineer but only a few kilomestres after parting with our friends, I heard the familiar roar of the planes — this time they were much, much noisier. We hid behind trees. They approached much lower than usual and began to drop bombs very close to us. We realized that they were bombing the highway, the one that I had refused to go on. The bombing was intense and long. I watched it from afar with tears in my eyes, thinking about my friends who were on the highway.

The sun went down and we stopped in a nearby village. We noticed quite a few peasants with their horse-drawn carts were driving towards the highway. A little later I found out, that after every bombing of the roads and highways, the peasants showed up to collect their booty from the victims and what was left behind by people who ran away.

We got a little food from a farmer and sat outside near the road. We found out from the farmers who gave us food that there was terrible carnage on the highway. We didn't say a word to the farmers or to each other. It was time to go.

My Father and I walked in the darkness hardly talking to each other, probably thinking the same thoughts. It reminded me of the expression "Wandering Jew." All through our history, from the Exodus from Egypt to the destruction of the first and second Temples, we were wandering. But to read about it is one thing, and to be actually wandering is another. Only a short time ago, I never would have imagined I would be walking with a little bundle on my back, my worldly possessions, through strange country, from village to village.

Whenever I fell asleep in a barn, on the floor in a stack of hay outside, which I preferred, I thought everything was a bad dream. Where was my clean bed? Where was my home? Where was my beloved mother, sister and friends? Where is my Krakow? It all happened so suddenly that I just couldn't grasp it all. Now that we were by ourselves there was more time to think, reflect and to worry. Sometimes we tried to cheer each other up. Wars don't last forever. I envied the villagers. Whatever was happening, they were going about their chores. It was their land, their houses, their fields, that's where they were going to stay. Surely they were worried about the Germans. Some had children in the army and did not know what was happening to them. But they knew, they were not going anywhere. This is were they were born and here they were going to stay.

We never stopped anymore for a whole day. The roads were almost empty and when we heard noise in the sky we would hide in a ditch or under some trees. We rested a little bit and then proceeded. This gave us the opportunity to sleep at night and it was easy to get food in the day and directions about where to go. We were getting closer to each other. I loved my father very much, he was a very honourable person who worked very hard all his life. I think his pleasure was to provide for his family, to see that I went to the best school and to buy for my mother everything she liked. No matter how sometimes times were hard, he always provided for us.

Now we were together 24 hours a day. We tried to help each other with whatever we could. We became a good team.

# FIVE

Until the war started on Sept. 1, 1939, everything was done for me. My only duties were to go to school, studying, my personal, youthful life, going out and being dressed well. And my beloved sports. I played everything from soccer to basketball to volleyball. I skied. I skated. I was always busy and everything that I needed I used to get from my father.

To be dressed well was with me a kind of obsession. It started when I went to the gymnasium. Maybe because the gymnasium was co-educational. We had as many girls as boys in the classrooms. To be properly and neatly dressed meant a lot to me, maybe too much. When our maid was pressing my shirts or pants, I sat and watched to make sure she wouldn't leave any wrinkles.

At least once a year, sometimes twice, I would get a new suit. This involved lots of preparation and work, especially for my mother. First, we had to pick out the material, which wasn't easy because I considered it very important and couldn't make up my mind. Then, we had to buy accessories. And finally, we went to the tailor.

The tailor I went to was probably the best in Kracow, and very expensive. But, my father used to get a discount because his shop was very close to our restaurant and he hung around a lot and ate there very often. He was a very famous tailor and he had all the up to-date fashion magazines. Once we decided on the style, he took my measurements, then came the fittings. The last one counted for everything. I went to those fittings by myself so that I made sure everything was to my liking and it fit very well. I must have been a pest to those tailors who were finalizing my garment. It had to fit perfectly. So it was with all my clothing.

In later years, they would call me gigolo because of my immaculate dressing. Before going out, I would comb my hair, put a hair net on and wore it until I left the house. When it was a very important occasion, like a hot date, I would leave home with the hair net on and only take it off when I got to the Dembnicki Bridge. I had a problem with a few hairs, which after parting, stood up to my great annoyance. My mother never criticized my behavior. She probably like me to be neat and clean.

I was very particular about clothing, food and girls. When I was going out with girls, I always tried to be very correct and a perfect gentleman.

Now all of this was gone. I was amazed at how I was adapting to the situation. We stopped occasionally near a stream or river where we washed ourselves and our socks and underwear, because we didn't have much clothing with us. No matter what the situation, we tried to keep clean and shave as often as possible.

The farther east we moved, the more changes were noticeable in the way people lived, compared to the standard of living in the west. It was a different Poland than I knew. It was so poor and different in every respect. The farmers were a mixed lot. Some were Polish, some Ukrainian and some were White Russian. They even spoke their own language. The farms were much smaller, their homes very primitive, sometimes consisting of one big room with a huge oven in the corner taking up half the house. The floor was made of clay. We slept sometimes on those big ovens.

When we came to a village and decided to stop for a few hours or sleep overnight, I always enquired if there were any Jews living there. We would stop at the outskirts of a village and I would usually go to find out where they lived. Father was more tired than me, so I tried to do it myself.

When I found a Jewish house I would enquire what they knew about the situation here. I didn't succeed most of the time. They didn't believe I was Jewish. I didn't look Jewish and worse yet, I didn't speak Yiddish. I spoke to them in Polish and I didn't know if they understood what I was talking about. I tried Hebrew but it didn't impress them either. So I tried to fetch my father and things changed immediately. Father spoke Yiddish well and usually got invited in. Those people were very poor. They lived in peasant homes, terribly overcrowded. Most of the time some more families or friends would be staying with them. They tried to be helpful as much as they could but they didn't have much.

When the night came, they got straw, laid it out on the floor and we were welcome to sleep. But I couldn't fall asleep. There were fleas biting and when somebody at night lit a match for a cigarette, thousands of flies woke up and with their noise they reminded me of the buzz of the airplanes. I usually went outside and found a stack of hay in the field and I buried myself in it.

We found less and less destruction and as we went farther east, we heard fewer planes. Once on the way to a town, I noticed some peasants coming towards their village loaded with bags. So I asked them what they had and what they told me was very surprising. One of them, a young fellow, told me I should go to a bombed-out train

51

nearby with all kinds of food and supplies. I left Father resting by the side of the road while I went to investigate the train. After walking for about 20 minutes, I came upon a scene. There were lots of people from all over pilfering everything possible. I went into one of the cars, and discovered to my delight, it was filled with boxes of all kinds of chocolate from the famous chocolate factory Wedel. I think I ate more chocolate that night than ever before. I loaded all my pockets, and under my shirt. I filled the bag that I had brought with me. When I got closer to Father all smiles, he couldn't believe his eyes. We sat and ate, especially Father, because I had enough chocolate on my way back. Now the question was how to carry all of this with us. It was too heavy and bulky.

We packed what we could and took with us the flat chocolate bars that fitted better in our pockets. I was sorry to leave so many boxes of candies and chocolates.

Our diet was a little enriched with the black bread and potatoes that we ate constantly while on the road. When we approached the bigger villages or shtettles with a bigger Jewish population, we slept and rested quite a bit in synagogues. This was my father's department. He found out these things very fast. We weren't the only ones. In the bigger towns, we met lots of refugees like ourselves filling the synagogues and sleeping there. Some people brought a little food and some invited us for a meal. There was no organized help. Everybody was worried and there was so much uncertainty. We were packed to move on a moment's notice. The rumors were flying constantly. Nobody knew what was happening 10 kilometres from where they were. We slept on the hard benches or on the floor without any bedding. But we felt somehow warmer and safer inside the synagogues, always between people.

Somebody always came to the synagogue with news. They knew how far away the Germans were, what the Allies were doing, everything that they had heard on the road. It was impossible to sort out all the news. One would say the war was over, the next one would say the Germans are very close by. The third one would say that France attacked Germany. One thing we knew for sure — we were running and running and we didn't know where we were going or where the Germans were. All we knew was that we had to go east and east and east, until we came, with luck, closer toward the Russian border.

We continued our journey. The weather continued to be perfect, the same pattern since we'd left Krakow. The country looked beautiful and so peaceful that sometimes it seemed like an excursion in the country. With every day the sky seemed to be more peaceful. We didn't see very many planes and didn't hear any bombing. We did not encounter any destroyed villages or towns. We grew a little bold and walked more during the day, resting when we felt like it, usually during the afternoon heat. We felt more relaxed and safer, but now we started to worry again about Mother and the rest of the family. But there was no way to find out anything. We were getting closer and closer to the city of Chelm. At home when you mention Chelm, a smile came to your face. I didn't know very much about the cities in eastern Poland. But we had all heard about Chelm.

The stories told us that Chelm was predominantly a Jewish town inhabited by simple-minded, goodhearted fools. There were dozens of stories, books full of them, about the stupid adventures of those simple-minded Chelmners. There was a Jewish expression, Chelmnic, and if you wanted to say how stupid somebody was, you called him a guy from Chelm. I soon found out it was a nice town with nice and friendly people. To me it seemed that Chelm was a strictly Jewish city.

The cobblestoned, narrow street led to a synagogue. We slept there overnight and people were friendly. They offered us food in the evening. The great majority of Jews in the shtettle in the east were extremely poor. They lived in terribly neglected, little, old homes, very often with large families. But they were well organized. They had their own Jewish schools. In the bigger places they had a Jewish hospital and a Jewish centre. The youth was also politically organized, like Bundt to the Left and all kinds of Zionist and religious organization. Some had sport activities and they had little teams like volleyball and soccer. It seems that for every few Jews there was an organization or religious school. Soon we arrived towards one of the main Polish rivers the Bug, probably the largest tributary of the Vistula, which we crossed by ferry. Everything was already a routine. We became professional Wandering Jews. There were thousands and thousands like us. Somehow the roads I chose weren't that popular so it wasn't so crowded and it was easier to move. As I looked at the map, I realized we had covered lots of territory and were far away from Krakow. The northeastern part of Poland was far away from us. We didn't have any family or friends in that part of the country. The part of Poland where I came from used to be known as Galicia and belonged to the Austro-Hungarian monarchy. My parents' grandparents were all Kaiser Franz Joseph people. We had family and friends, mostly in Silesia, Vienna and Germany.

One afternoon we came to a large village by the name of Verchy.. It was inhabited mostly by Ukrainians. We stopped on the outskirts. Father was tired, so I decided to look for some food and a place to sleep overnight. In Verhcy, I decided not to ask if Jews live there. I was sure there were some, but without Yiddish I never had much luck. Especially, here so far to the east, some hardly spoke Polish. I noticed a big farm with a nice house and big barns, much different standing out from the other poor farms we were passing most of the time. It had a nice wooden fence, newly painted, beautiful flowers all around and tall sunflowers on the inside of the fence. I really liked the place, so much different and more pleasant than the others. I decided to try my luck. I opened the gate and walked to the house, which was surrounded by huge fruit trees. A tall man approached me and asked in Ukrainian what I wanted. I hardly understood his language and answered in Polish what my problem was. I could see that he understood me quite well. I asked if I could buy some food, mainly bread and milk and if he had a room in the barn for us to sleep. He asked me a few questions and told me to wait outside. He went inside the house and soon came out with his wife carrying bread on a little wooden plate, the butter wrapped in a cabbage leaf and a jug of milk. There was a bench in front of the house and we were told to sit down. It was the first time since we left that we sat down to a meal. There was hardly any conversation at the table. After we finished the meal, he took us to a little building which looked more like a storage room, with a few wooden boxes in the corner. It was clean as a whistle. He told us to wait there and we put our belongings on one of the boxes and sat on the others. A few minutes later we heard someone coming. A girl came in carrying two bales of straw. She greeted us with a shy smile, spread the straw on the floor, making two bed out of it. When she finished I had a good look at her and practically froze with delight. She was tall, with auburn, blond hair with a sweet delicate face, teeth white like pearls. She wore a skirt and a loose blouse. (I found out later they called it a rubaszka.). Barefoot, she was as tall as me. I couldn't take my eyes of her. She walked out and I was stupefied. I didn't know what to say. I wanted to strike up a conversation with her, but I couldn't speak Ukrainian, and probably she didn't speak Polish.

Soon she came back carrying a jug of water and two rolls of dark linen covers, similar to blankets. I started to talk to her to find out if she knew anything about the war, but she was very shy. I think she wasn't very comfortable with the Polish language. I grabbed the two biggest bars of chocolate from my backpack and handed them to her, thanking her for what they were doing for us. First she refused, but I insisted, she took it, looking at me with a very shy smile.

We lay down on our straw bed, the most comfortable bed in many days. It was peaceful, yet I couldn't fall asleep. I went out and looked at the sky which was studded with thousands of stars, watching some fall down through the horizon, and wishing for peace and a return home to Mother. I couldn't stop thinking about this gorgeous girl. She was so different from the girls I knew and reminded me of a painting I saw somewhere - so natural, so wholesome. My father was fast asleep. I lay down and enjoyed the comfort of my straw bed and soon fell asleep. I felt a slight tap on my shoulder, and saw the girl leaning next to me. I looked at her and she was even more beautiful than yesterday. It was dawn outside, very early. She didn't say a word, just indicated that I should follow her. We crossed the yard and approached the big house. She led me inside, and there they were all sitting at the family table having breakfast. They were already dressed to go to their chores. I ate with a great appetite. They spoke about their daily work, then turned toward me to ask more about where I came from and about the war. They were very worried and confused about the future.

They were beautiful people, three generations sitting at the table all tall and handsome When we all finished, one of them, it must have been the father of the girl, called me aside and said if we want to stay another day or so with them we were more than welcome. He also shared some news that he heard in the village, that the Russians had crossed the border and were moving west, apparently to help Poland. The girl came and handed me a bowl of food to take back to my Father.

I told Father about the Russians moving to the west. We felt that they were probably going to fight the Germans. We couldn't explain the news any other way. I remember the anti-Communist speeches of Hitler and the speeches of Stalin and the Russians against fascism and Hitler. What else could it be? They were marching against Hitler. For the last few days, we hadn't seen a sign of any planes. This was very unusual. There was no explanation. It looked like the war was over.

We decided to accept the invitation to stay on the farm an extra day, to decide what to do. Besides, I was happy to stay and get better acquainted with the girl. When I came back to the house with the empty breakfast platter, I found her and her grandmother cleaning up after breakfast. I told her we had decided to stay another day. She seemed happy. I asked her if there was a little river or stream in the vicinity where we could wash some of our clothing and maybe ourselves.

She led us to a brook not far from the farm. The water was cold, but we didn't mind. My father and I soaked ourselves for a long time, enjoying every minute. It was time to do our laundry. We took our clothes and laid them out in the sun, holding it down with little stones. We rested under the tree, watching the blue skies and contemplated what our next move should be.

We figured the war must have ended and we thought we might be out of danger. But it was useless to speculate. All through the war, there were nothing but rumours and contradictions. News reports concentrated on issues about whose fault it was rather than actual progress.

Resting on the grass, in a peaceful setting, we couldn't believe rumours that the Russians were coming to fight the Germans to rescue us and Poland. It was hard to believe and too good to be true.

We went back to our shack and hung out our wash which wasn't quite dry yet. We were invited for dinner and tried to find out if they had heard anything new. The whole family was tense, more than ever before. They were worried about how things would be when the Russians came, since they were the richest farmers in the region.

We didn't know what to expect from the Russians. We couldn't imagine they would be worse than the Germans. We had so many other worries that we didn't have time to fret about this. We needed to keep moving, get food, a place to sleep and to travel in the right direction.

The night was quiet and warm, we stretched out on our straw beds, got up early in the morning and packed our belongings

At the breakfast table, no one spoke. Everybody was rushing to go to work. We thanked the family for their hospitality and offered to pay, which they refused. We had food for the road, and of course, lots of chocolate. As we were ready to leave, the girl came to us and we thanked her for her kindness. I took another piece of chocolate and practically had to force her to take it. I was sorry to leave this place and once again, to wander on the roads.

We felt rested, relaxed and much stronger. The girl stood by the gate and I turned around, waving my hand and threw her a kiss.

# Six

Our next destination was the city of Kowel, a fair sized city, directly east. When we got close it was almost dark. We stopped and asked a few local Jews where we could stay overnight. They directed us to the closest synagogue, where lots of other refugees were also staying. In the evening, we heard shooting in the distance. It was small-calibre fire but we had no idea who was shooting or where it was coming from. We lay on the floor most of the time for protection, waiting for daylight. The local people came to pray and we joined them.

We packed our belongings and set out once more. One of the locals at the synagogue gave us the address of a wealthy businessman named Landau, who he thought could help us. He was an owner of a large hardware store and a factory that produced enamelled pots.

The streets were filled with people. Some stores were open, but not grocery stores or restaurants. The city was practically in a no-man's land. There were no Germans, no Russians. Often we saw small groups of Polish soldiers in uniform, some with rifles and some without. It looked like they left their units and were heading home.

We found Mr. Landau in his store, talking with many people. Apparently, he was the leader of the Jewish community, the *kehilah*. Finally, it was Father's turn to talk to him. Mr. Landau had relatives in Krakow and was anxious to know what happened there.

Mr. Landau had a radio and listened to all the stations outside of Poland. He had tried to listen to English radio, but couldn't quite understand what he heard. In his opinion, Poland lost the war and the Russians were coming, not to help the Poles fight Germany, but to take over eastern Poland after some deal they signed with the Germans. So far, there were no Russians to be seen in Kowel and vicinity. He guessed that the shooting we had heard the night before, might have been between Poles and Ukrainians the remnants of the Polish Army, who were running away from their posts on the Russian border.

Everybody was trying to even up their old scores and complaints by shooting at each other. The Poles, White Russians and Ukrainians never got along because of religious and political reasons.

Everything was so confused, uncertain and dangerous, that upon the advice of Mr. Landau, we stayed overnight in Kowel. He let us sleep in his store and provided food for everyone who stayed there. We didn't know what to do. Father and I concluded our next destination would be Lvov, where we would figure out what to do next.

We wanted to make sure there were no Germans there and find out about the possibility of getting there by train, since it was so far..

Lvov was the biggest city in southeastern Poland. It had a large and powerful Jewish community. Most of the refugees, sooner or later, were hoping to get there. Everybody wanted to get to Lvov to get their bearings.

It was hard to believe Poland was defeated and was being partitioned again after only a few years as an independent state. I was born in independent Poland, unlike my parents, who were born under the Austro-Hungarian monarchy. I didn't know any other country. Polish was my language. I studied Polish history and literature. I served in the para-military service as part of my high school education. I believed the Polish Army was powerful, patriotic, invincible and capable of defending itself and the country.

In school we celebrated the Polish national holidays. We were proud of Polish successes in sports or any other international acknowledgements, as were all other Poles. We were Zionists and dreamt about our land of Israel, but it was a faraway dream and hope. Meanwhile, Poland was home to three and half million Jews.

We had a decent sleep in Mr. Landau's store, got up in the morning and had a bite to eat. Out on the streets, thousands of people were milling around. From what we heard, it became clear the Russians were in Lvov and moving west. It appeared they made a deal with the Germans to divide Poland. Nobody had any idea how far they would go and what kind of an arrangement it was.

We realized it was time to go to Lvov. We packed our belongings and said goodbye and thanked Mr. Landau.

As we neared the railway station, we saw thousands of people — locals and refugees — waiting for trains.

We slept outside the station one night. Before noon, the next day, we finally got on the train. We were packed like sardines. The train stopped at many little stations. We arrived late in the evening, and were welcomed by the first September rain.

We disembarked in pouring rain. We didn't know where to go or what to do. It was also the first time that we saw a lot of Russian soldiers. We sat on the floor like the others and slept overnight at the station.

58

***

Lvov was the third-largest city in Poland, but was bursting at the seams with refugees. Russian armies and Russian civilians converged on the city. The streets were crowded and it was hard to pass by. Little by little, as we moved forward. we could see people being reunited with relatives and friends, who arrived in Lvov from different directions. Some lucky people, who left before us on September 1, got there by train, some by bus and cars.

Father met some people he knew who told us that many people from Krakow frequented a coffeehoue in the centre of the city. It was called the Cafe de la Paix. We got there around noon. Hundreds of people were on the street and around the cafe. We met quite a few people that Father knew, who for years were guests in our restaurant. I stayed with our belongings while Father went up to the cafe on the first floor of a building.

In no time he found our Uncle Henek from Cieszyn, who had arrived alone several days before us on the train. On the first day of the war, he had been taken by the Germans to a forced labor camp. Somehow, he escaped to the nearest railroad station and was lucky enough to get transportation to Lvov. We found out his cousins, the Steiners, were here and also Uncle Marian, his wife and some very dear friends of Father's. Father's best friend, Schickler, had been here with his wife and son.

Now, we didn't have to worry about the bombs and the war. Our goal was to settle, at least temporarily, in Lvov. The biggest problem was to find a place to live. With the thousands of refugees from the western part of Poland, who had been cut off from their homes by the new Russian/German border, this was going to be a chore. Lvov was the new southern centre for the new Russian administration, government and army. Whole families came to the city's well stocked stores on shopping sprees. They had never seen such an abundance of quality merchandise. They started to buy out the city. It was funny. The Russians came with bags of rubles and exchanged them for Polish zlotys. For a while, both currencies could be used. The Polish currency was always strong nationally and internationally. Poland may have disappeared, but people were happy their money was still worth something. But the business only came from one direction.

The Russians went crazy, purchasing everything. They didn't ask the price. If they came to a jewelry store for one watch they bought

59

ten. If they came to a camera shop, they bought three cameras. Within a few weeks, the stores were completely empty. Whatever was left or saved was only now available on the black market.

The Russians came with orders to spread the word about the abundance of everything in the Soviet Union. So when you asked a Russian: "Do you have a lot of watches?" They would answer: "Yes, we have a huge factory in Moscow, producing watches by the millions."

You wondered why they were buying everything they could get their hands on. Some of the watches the Russians wore, were the size of small alarm clocks.

One day, a smart alec asked a Russian if they had factories producing bananas and oranges. "Oh yes, we have quite a few!". This is how we learned what Russian propaganda meant.

That afternoon we met in a wine cellar. Uncle Henek, his cousin Salek, my Uncle Marian, the Schicklers and some other friends. They had been in Lvov a few days before us and were more or less settled.

Finding a job for my father was no problem. All the restaurants were doing a fantastic business, full of Russian civilians, soldiers, especially officers, loaded with all kinds of money. The only worry the restaurants had was that the food would run out because the Russians' money never did.

In the wine cellar, everyone was telling stories of how they got to Lvov. We speculated about how long it would be before our families could meet us here, or when we could meet them in Krakow. We had very little information about what was going on. Our main sources were the Russian newspapers and radio, which were filled with propaganda. The German stations spewed their propaganda and glorified their conquests all over Europe.

The BBC was the only thing we could trust but it was jammed. The new border between Russia and Germany was still fluid and many people smuggled themselves to the Russian side. This was the best proof things were not good. Why would so many people still run away? Only time would tell.

After dinner, we talked and decided to keep in touch as much as possible. We spent the night with the Schicklers, who had rented a couple of rooms . The next day, Father went with Mr. Schickler to look for a job. He returned shortly announcing he had been hired at a small restaurant with a beer and liquor outlet. He was to start the next day. The owner, a local Jew who resided in Lvov for a long time, had good connections and promised to find us lodging, too.

60

Father worked as a waiter and helped with other problems that arose. The owner soon recognized Father's abilities and was grateful for Father's business expertise. So, he tried very hard to find accommodations for us. It was a formidable task. In a couple of days he took us to a building in Zolkieski Street. He knew an orthodox Jew who had a stand at the local market. He talked him into taking us in. The place was located in an old apartment complex with a huge, common courtyard.

Upon entering the apartment, there was a huge room with two large windows facing the street. In the corner was a kitchen with a big wooden table and few chairs. There was little furniture and it looked rather empty. In the corner were two beds covered by a curtain-type of divider.

There were two old spinsters who lived there with their father. As soon as he entered, the negotiations started. The conversation was in Yiddish, so I didn't understand much, but it was very animated. He showed us a fair-sized room with two narrow beds. There was a dresser in the corner and a couple of chairs. I don't remember how much money he asked for it, but it was a very steep price. The deal was made by Father and his new boss who had a little leverage with these people. The setting didn't appeal to me but it was a place to sleep, rest and put our belongings. The daughters of the landlord were polite to me. They cleaned up the room, changed the beds. We were now settled in Lvov.

They had a stand at the market with some used and new clothing. Renting the rooms to us added to their income. Five days a week, from early morning until dark, they stayed at the market in a little canvas booth. Rain, snow, frost and heat didn't deter them.

There were hundreds of stalls similar to theirs at this huge market. It was a messy, smelly and dirty place where you could buy food, clothing, furniture, household goods, anything you could think of. Much of it was used. People were haggling, swearing and arguing. It was a noisy place. It took lots of guts to exist and do business in a place like this.

So it seemed our problems were settled. We had a place to live and Father had a job. Our lives were becoming normal. Father made a living and I was to continue my education. Father went to work in the morning and later I left the apartment to go to the Cafe de la Paix to get more information and to see who else had arrived from Krakow.

Around noon, the place was teeming with people. I found my cousin Moniek Brenner, who brought some news from home. He spent a few days under the German occupation of Krakow and told us my Mother and sister had returned safely home to our apartment. Things were getting rough, but in the few days he was there, he did not find out much, yet he decided to come to Lvov. He felt it would be safer to live under the Russians than the Germans.

I also met quite a few students from our gymnasium, some who had already reported to a new school in Lvov. I decided to do the same. Some of them encountered difficulties in enrolling because they didn't bring their report cards with them as proof of attending a gymnasium in Krakow. I had no problem because I had my 1939 report card which I took with me. I don't know why I packed my report card. I must have felt it was my most important document. It was the biggest achievement in my life so far. In fact, I carried my report card from 1939 with me throughout the war, and when I returned to Poland after the war, it helped me to enroll in the university in Krakow. I even have it in my possession today.

The gymnasium in Lvov was impressive and named after the famous Polish poet, Adam Mickiewicz. It was much different than our school in Krakow. The biggest stress in the curriculum was to study communism, Stalin's constitution, the works of Marx and Engels, especially Marx's Das Kapital. There was a shortage of books. The Polish teachers were frightened. It was a poor atmosphere altogether. The refugee students, like me, felt like strangers.

After school, I always managed to stop downtown at Akademicka street where the famous Cafe de la Paix was and visited Uncle who was always there. I met new friends, former teachers and girlfriends.

One day I met Lola, just walking on Akademicka Street. We were school friends and attended the same class for several years. We knew each other well. She was a stunning girl about my height with a beautiful figure and a friendly face, full of tiny freckles. She was always smiling and had a sweet personality.

I liked her very much, but at home I didn't have the opportunity to get very close to her, except during some school activities. She came from a wealthy family that owned international enterprises. On vacation, she spent a lot of time abroad.

Although we attended a co-educational gymnasium I don't know of anybody having sexual relations. Having a girlfriend meant kissing, a little hugging, being together, going swimming and having fun. The sexual needs of the boys, if they had the guts, were provided by prostitutes, and sometimes by the maids who worked in their homes. The relationships with the girls at school were platonic.

Now in Lvov, I had the opportunity to get closer and spend more time with Lola. We met in the parks, went to swimming pools, the movies to watch Russian films (even though we didn't understand three quarters of it!). I took her home in the evening, but never went upstairs to here family's apartment. Everyone's accommodations were very compact.

The times were quite pleasant. The school we attended wasn't taken seriously like back in Krakow. We skipped a lot of classes, especially political ones. I don't know why, but I didn't try at all to learn Russian. Instead, I got some books to help me learn English. We had little family supervision and felt like we were on our own..

We knew winter was fast approaching. We had to buy some warmer clothing and in some instances I had clothing made to order. Father was earning enough money to afford life's necessities

It was interesting to see how the Russians solved the monetary problem. Until their arrival, the Polish zloty was the only currency in circulation, but everyone was apprehensive about what was going to happen to the zloty. Nobody knew how long both currencies would be valuable. At one point, the Russians made the old Polish money more valuable than the ruble. Everybody was relieved and normal trading continued unimpeded. But we soon found out, it was a Russian ploy. One day, there was a proclamation the zloty was not going to be recognized as a currency and the ruble was going to be the only legal currency in the Soviet Union.

There was no promise about exchanging zlotys. We were part of the Soviet Union, so rubles were our currency. By artificially boosting the value of the zloty before the proclamation, people lost a lot of money and in some instances all their savings. This was one way the Russians got rid of capitalists and speculators. We were lucky to have more rubles than zlotys, which we simply threw out.

These were crazy, terrible times. Nobody could understand what was going to happen, what our status was. We had been uprooted from our homes and families. I longed for my mother, sister and the rest of the family.

Life was hard in Lvov, but it must have been worse in Krakow. At least we weren't subjected to physical abuse. Despite our problems, it was better living under the Russians.

We had little news from home but one day in October, a couple that lived in Dembniki arrived in Lvov. They had left Krakow a few days ago and were smuggled to the Russian side.

People were trying by the hundreds to do this but it was getting harder every day. That November, my cousin Herman Brenner, attempted the same but was not successful and had to return to Krakow. We found out from the people about our families. They were already forced to wear the arm bands with the Star of David and suffered of all kinds of discrimination. But they were managing Occasionally we would receive news from Mother through an underground mail system. It was expensive, and unreliable, but it was the best we had.

We met with our family in Lvov in the wine cellar, exchanging our hopes and fears for the future. Despite Lvov's Jewish population of about 80,000, we felt unwelcome — refugees, who had lost everything we had.

I returned to my room one day to find two men unpacking their belongings. The owner had rented out half of our bedroom and added another bed. It was ridiculously crowded, but we had nowhere else to go. We tried to find another room, but the situation was getting worse and more and more refugees were coming to the city. Our new roommates were twin brothers from Germany, expelled first from Germany and then, a year later, from Poland.

Little by little, the area was becoming more and more Russian. The stores were empty of goods and shortages were constant. The black market was thriving. From the beginning, people welcomed the Russians as saviors from the German barbarians and Hitler and his henchmen. The local Jewry welcomed them as saviors against anti-Semitism and the Orthodox Jews called them the "Leftist Messiahs."

The Russians began a campaign, offering all unemployed locals jobs in the Soviet Union, especially in the Donbas Region in the Ukraine. People registered by the thousands. They were promised housing, good wages and great benefits. There was great euphoria. The poor, unemployed people were finally able to get steady jobs and opportunities to live better.

It didn't take long before letters and news started to drift in from Donbas Region that the situation was rough indeed. The region of Donbas, on the River Don basin was rich in coal and full of coal mines, and work in the coal mine was a far cry from what people had expected when they left. Little by little they sold their belongings or traded them for food and necessities. When this ran out they started drifting back to Lvov and their homes.

One day after school I went to Uncle Henek's apartment. The landlady and another woman answered the door. Their faces were white and they were trembling. I knew there was something wrong. My uncle was no where to be seen. When I asked what happened, they both started to talk at once. I hardly understood what they were saying, they were so agitated.

I soon found out. A few civilians had entered the apartment and took Uncle Henek away. They gave him a few minutes to get some belongings together and without a word to the landlady, they were gone. She saw him getting in a car with the men and they drove away. This is all I learned from her. Everything had happened so quickly.

I was baffled, but ran to tell Uncle Henek's cousin, Salek. He was working in a huge restaurant. When I finally got there, I couldn't catch my breath. He led me to his office, and brought a glass of cold water. Finally, I could talk enough to tell him what happened. We decided to call the family counsel for the evening and meanwhile, Salek would try to get information or talk to a lawyer he knew.

We met in the small wine cellar, my father, Salek, Uncle Marian, our friend Schickler and others. Salek asked some lawyers to come, but they didn't want to get involved with the Russian law. We didn't know of any Russian lawyers practicing in Lvov. The counsel decided everybody in his own way would try to find out what happened. The best way would be to ask some Russian military acquaintances at their workplaces.

We couldn't find out anything. The police didn't want to talk to us. Uncle Henek's disappearance was not our business, they said.

The only lead was through our friend Schickler. He got an address and a name of a Russian prosecutor. I went with him to the prosecutor's office, located in a huge building, occupied by the military. I waited outside for him. It took a couple of hours before he emerged. I was afraid he had been detained as well.

As we left the building he told me about the meeting with the prosecutor. The prosecutor was a man in his mid-50s, wearing the uniform of a high-ranking officer. Salek told him the story and then was told to wait. Finally, the prosecutor called him to his office and said: "If you don't want to go where your friend is going I'll give you one piece of advice. Stop looking for him. It is not your business. Get out of here in a hurry!"

We later found out many people disappeared this way. We couldn't imagine what Henek had done to deserve being arrested so abruptly. He was the first casualty of the war from our family. We decided not to notify his wife, in enough difficulty already living under Nazi rule. It wasn't until after the war that we learned what had happened to Uncle Henek.

Apparently, he had written a letter to my aunt in the United States, describing the situation in Lvov, and detailing the recent events since the Russians had come in. It was a detailed letter, and sadly it was intercepted by the Russians who were censoring mail. They picked up Henek, and he was tried without representation for being counter-revolutionary and spreading false and derogatory information about the USSR. He was sentenced to ten years, but was released two years later, deathly ill, suffering from malnutrition and other diseases. Such sick prisoners, called Dochodiaga ("people at the end of the road of life") were often released. Many died on their way home. Some, like Uncle Henek, survived.

He found out about a Czech army hospital in Buzulox. It was a miracle. He stayed in the hospital for quite a while. One of the doctors knew him from Czech Cieszyn and registered him as a Czech. Uncle Henek lived through the war and returned to Cieszyn, where I later met him.

Nothing was the same after he was taken. We were bewildered and frightened, and became increasingly suspicious of the USSR government.

Real news was scarce. Newspapers and the local radio were full of positive news about what was happening in the Soviet Union, glorifying Stalin and his constitution and the good life in the USSR. Unfortunately, we didn't see any of the "prosperity" in Lvov.

I spent most of my time at Father's restaurant, sitting in the corner for hours, struggling over my homework. The Russian language was difficult to master, the Cyrillic alphabet completely different to my own Polish script. The Russian soldiers frequented the restaurant, ordering several beers at once, fearful the beer would run out. They were friendly, and invited me to join them, but I was always apprehensive, thinking of Uncle Henek.

\*\*\*

The time spent in Lvov was like living in limbo. The weather became dreary and as autumn approached, rain intensified, interfering with daily life. The parks were empty and I was getting lonely. Trams were the only transportation and they were always overcrowded with people hanging off the sides or holding onto the railing. Even the steps were full. The store shelves were empty, and buying necessities was a chore.

But we were never hungry thanks to Father's job at the restaurant. We had enough money to buy whatever we needed, but there was not much available.

Lately, news from home was coming at longer intervals. The borders were getting tighter, and the trickle of people running away from Germany to Russia was tapering off because patrols on both sides of the boarder increased to stem the flight of refugees.

A German delegation arrived to register refugees who were willing to return to their homes now under German occupation. Tens of thousands of people lined up daily at the villa on the outskirts of town to register. We all went there a few times, but the crowds were so large it was impossible to get into the villa.

In the two months since we received the letter from mother asking us to return, we knew the situation had worsened.Besides, if we didn't register, we'd have to accept Soviet citizenship. We tried, apprehensive still of the USSR government, but the registration process was erratic and overcrowded. Half the time, the office was not even open. They distributed registration papers, but you could never get into the office. Some people left addresses for future registration, but this was a charade. The only thing accomplished was that the Germans and the Russian NKWD (later to become the KGB) received thousands of names and addresses of the refugees.

Some people, usually whole families who had escaped together, applied for Russian citizenship. Among us, only Mr. Shickler applied with his wife and son.

Our morale was low. Winter setting in and there was no good news on the horizon. School didn't interest me much and I had no friends in the gymnasium. The curriculum became more political.

Many Polish professors disappeared making everyone afraid to talk to each other at school. I kept to myself, going through the motions, just getting passing grades. I started to think it was pointless to study. Besides, we knew no refugees would be accepted at the universities.

## SEVEN

By the end of December, I was feeling ill and thought I was coming down with a cold. I had indigestion and I lost my appetite. It was freezing, and there simply weren't any decent winter clothes to buy.

One morning while shaving, I noticed in the mirror my eyes were yellow. I didn't give it much thought. But the next day, I noticed it was getting worse. My skin was yellowing, too. I knew that I had yellow jaundice.

Father decided to wait a few day, hoping it would get better, but instead it got worse. I was getting more yellow and I couldn't eat. Father became worried and started to look for a doctor. We knew Dr. Wohlfeiler, a gastro-intestinal specialist from Krakow, was in Lvov. He was related to the Brenners, who arranged an appointment for me.

The doctor took one look at me and told me I did indeed have hepatitis. I was ordered home to bed, and Father had to search desperately through pharmacies before finding at least some of the medication I needed.

That winter, the four walls of our sparse apartment, with the dismal view of the courtyard, became my cramped prison. There was nothing to look at, nothing to do. Even my diet was reduced pretty much to dry toast and a few other bland foods.

The toilet was outside, which we shared with a few apartments. I had to walk on the open-air courtyard catwalk to get to the toilet. There was no light in the washroom, just a little window. At night I used a bidet for urinating. We used a huge sink in the kitchen to wash ourselves with only cold water. If we wanted warm water we set up a little kerosene heater.

Father worked hard at the restaurant and took care of me, without ever complaining, Only now do I fully appreciate the sacrifices he made for me.

Father and I agreed we would not let Mother know that I was ill. She would only worry and, things were getting bad enough at home.

Winter's deep freeze was setting in with lots of snow and unbelievably low temperatures. I lay in bed alone with barely anything to read. The days were short and only one small electric bulb threw light. There was no radio and nobody to talk to.

I lost contact with all my friends and acquaintances. We never visited anybody and they had no idea where I was. It wasn't uncommon for people to move from Lvov to other small cities, where it wasn't so crowded and accommodations were easier to find. Some moved deeper into the Soviet Union, others were arrested and simply disappeared.

After everybody left for work, I would read an old newspaper or textbooks, including a Berlitz book to help me learn English. It became my hobby and helped me overcome the loneliness.

Every morning I would look in the mirror to see if the yellow in my face had disappeared, but to my dismay it was getting worse. I felt weak because I had lost weight on the strict diet.

After a couple of weeks with no improvement in my health, Father notified Dr. Wohlfeiler. He examined me and made the prognosis that my liver was enlarged and the symptoms were worse. He lifted my spirits by telling me I would eventually get better. He also ordered me to eat as many sweets as possible and order some new medicines.

The sugar was easy, with Father's connections in the restaurant. The medicine was impossible. I did my best to eat as much sugar as I could, hoping it would strengthen me and make me well.

I remained optimistic I would get well again. I never cried or complained in front of Father, though I cried often when alone, wanting home, and my mother.

The days grew more bitter. My window was completely covered by ice, thick grey flower-like patterns of frost. The room became depressing, cold and unfriendly. I covered myself with the feather quilt, tried to close my eyes and forced myself to daydream of the happy days at home.

All the homes in Lvov and the majority of cities in Poland used coal for heating. During the summer and fall, people would purchase and accumulate coal for the winter. Our landlord had little coal reserves and in a few weeks it had run out. Coal was expensive, and during the harsh winter, was simply impossible to get.

My dear father with his connections to the Russians and the people he worked for, once in a while, would get a bag of coal. The problem was transporting the coal to the apartment. The only way was to carry it. So when Father got just a little bit, he brought it on his back in a little burlap bag. When he got lucky and got a little more he used a child's sled to bring it home. In the snow and cold he pulled the sled for miles.

Our bedfellows, the German twin brothers, tried to help , but they usually were only lucky enough to get a few pieces of wood. It helped to make a fire so Father could defrost and prepare food for me.

It took several weeks, but finally we were able to get some of the medication I needed through the underground post office from the German site. Our money bag became much lighter, but still I failed to improve. I checked my eyes and skin every morning. Days, weeks and months passed and I saw no improvement. I was getting weaker. I was tired of going outside to the bathroom in the bitter cold. Depression and loneliness were my constant companions.

For the first time I started to worry I wouldn't get better. Going to the hospital was out of the question. They were overcrowded and a refugee's chances of getting in the hospital were slim. There was a shortage of medication at the hospitals, too, and the doctor said I would be better convalescing at home.

The letters from home were scarce and we had little opportunity to write back. I never wrote about my illness,a nd had little else to say.  My letters were short. With the little correspondence we received, we now knew life under the Germans was getting worse by the day, but we had no detailed information.

The days were getting longer. In late February,  my thoughts turned to spring, but I lay here wasting away. I finally asked the doctor point-blank what was going to happen. Did I have a chance for recovery? He assured me I did, but I was not convinced. He tried to explain why I was not improving. He said the ducts leading to the duodenum  from my gall bladder were blocked for reasons that he wasn't quite sure. He needed a medical instrument called a *sonda*, that he was unable to get. Father was determined to use up the slender resources of our money-bag to try to get hold of the instrument through the letter smugglers.

Meanwhile, I was getting weaker, sleeping most of the time, huddled in dirty clothing and bedding that could not be washed because the coal was far too short to heat up water for laundry.

One night I dreamt I was trying to return to Krakow and to my mother. In my dream I travelled the many miles, and finally neared my home, growing more excited by the minute at the sight of familiar streets and landmarks. But as I neared our street, I noticed two men in trench coats behind me and realized they were following me. I was unable to shake them off. When I reached the apartment, I ran up the stairs and knocked at the door. My mother answered, but

70

when she looked past me and saw the men, she didn't say a word, only shut the door, then returned with a chunk of bread and whispered, "Go back." She closed the door again.

I awoke drenched in sweat, and have never forgotten the dream.

After several more weeks without improvement, Dr. Wohlfeiler arrived at the apartment, opened his black case, and with a smile took out the instrument we were waiting for. Father had received it that morning and rushed it to him. When I saw the instrument I was a little shocked. He showed me a piece of very thin rubber hose with a small metal head at one end. Was this simple instrument the key to my cure? Dr. Wohlfeiler said we would have to work hard. I didn't understand what he meant.

He took a glass of warm water from the kitchen and took out a big syringe. He explained I had to swallow the rubber hose until it reached into my duodenum. I couldn't imagine how I could swallow such a long rubber hose. But with coaxing, choking and encouragement, it went down. The doctor insisted and for the first time he hollered at me to follow instructions. He turned me in the bed while I swallowed. Finally, he was satisfied the instrument was in the right position. He attached the syringe to the end of the rubber hose and started to draw out the intestinal juices. When the syringe was full, he emptied it into the glass. The liquid was slightly yellowish, but very light. He turned me over on my side and told me to swallow some more. He must have done this hundreds of times before.

Next, he took a glass of water and dissolved epsom salts in it, filled the syringe attached to the rubber hose and by squeezing the syringe put it inside me. He asked me to tell him how I felt. Suddenly, I felt a strong cramp. I saw a little smile on his face. He repeated the procedure once more and in a few minutes started to draw the juices into the empty glass. Several, thick dark green drops of liquid appeared in the glass. He extracted more juices with the same results. He started to pull the tube out of me. I was exhausted.

He sat on the edge of the bed and looked in my eyes with a little smile and he said the sweetest words, which I had dreamt of hearing for such a long time.

"We made it! You will live and recover very soon," he said.

I knew he was serious. I burst into tears. They were tears of joy. He explained to me that without this instrument he wouldn't have been able to help me.

He repeated this procedure seven times in short intervals. He gave me more medication and relaxed my strict diet. Slowly, I started to feel physically better, but emotionally I recovered quickly. I felt optimistic again. Father became more relaxed and cheerful. He felt he had won another war.

The days got longer, the sun shone and most of the time my window was clear of ice. I started to walk around the room, looking outside to see the sky. Everything I did gave me pleasure and satisfaction. The snow melted. I could see women in the yard opening windows, putting their down quilts on the window sills to air them out after a long and bitter winter. Soon, the children were outside playing. Still, I stayed in bed quite a bit, but I was getting stronger every day.

Spring was coming fast. The doctor came to see me less and less. It must have been April when my doctor came to examine me again. He was satisfied with the progress I was making and ordered me to see him at his office in two weeks. I was overjoyed at this announcement. Finally, I would get outside to see the world.

He allowed me, when the sun was shining, to go outside for a few minutes. Father was elated, and began trying to bring me some more tasty foods to eat from the restaurant.

Now we sometimes ate a meal together in the kitchen. We started to assess our situation and all the rumors we'd heard. The news we were getting from the German side was getting worse. The Germans celebrated victory after victory. It seemed to be safer on the Russian side. They had signed a treaty with Germany and got involved in a bloody, prolonged war in Finland. We thought they would defeat and occupy Finland in a few days, but it took a year. We started to doubt their military power.

A few people were still trying to get Soviet citizenship, but it was difficult. No one was able to return to Poland. Those caught trying were arrested by the Soviets and immediately deported.

I thought of my dream about Mother and returning to Krakow. I believed it was a sign not to return.

## EIGHT

The day arrived to go see Dr. Wohlfeiler. It was sunny but cold. I dressed warmly and walked a short distance to get the tram, which brought me to the vicinity of his office. He examined me and was satisfied with my progress. He warned me to take it easy and dress warmly. I was to see him again in a few weeks.

I walked happily to the tram and back to my apartment. I started to read more, and when the weather permitted, I took short walks to the main street. I felt much better, ate more and felt stronger each day.

We met in the restaurant with the rest of the family. They were all well, but unfortunately there was no good news to hear.

The Germans were invincible and we didn't trusts the Russians. We couldn't figure them out or what their intentions were. At least there was work available, and money to be earned. Father paid off all the debts connected to my sickness and our little money bag started to fill up again with the rubles.

As the weather got warmer, I ventured outside more. I started to gain weight and my strength was coming back. Sometimes I would take the streetcar, in the afternoon, to the restaurant where Father worked. I would sit at the table reading, and watch the Russian soldiers. They were full of joy and good humor. I envied them.Officers brought their families and children to the restaurant and they enjoyed the rich life of Lvov.

I waited for father until he finished work and we had a meal together and went home together.

My skin was still yellow and I was not ready to see my friends. I longed to see and talk to Lola, but I couldn't make myself do it in my condition. I still looked sickly and yellowish.

I decided to visit the gymnasium. I reported my sickness and was given some school material to catch up. I had little emotion or ambition for it. I was beginning to think of university or medical school, but without Soviet citizenship, I was unlikely to be accepted. What future did I have?

One warm day, I decided to stop at the Cafe de La Paix. The crowds were still milling about there, and on the street below. I met a couple of my school friends. They were amazed to see me and wondered where I had been. They thought that I had been arrested and deported deep into Russia.

They had little news that they could share with me since the last time I saw them. The uncertainty and confusion was greater. I met my friend Zygmund in a park. He was more fortunate because he was with his family, but he also sounded pessimistic.

***

As refugees we were treated at every level of daily life like second-class citizens. Not only by the authorities, but also, unfortunately, by our fellow Jews. I never expected to be stigmatized by our own community.

To the Russian authorities, we were intruders. In their closed society they looked upon us with suspicion because we didn't want to accept Soviet citizenship.

Right now, I was interested in seeing Lola. I decided I would make myself look presentable. Late one afternoon I found enough courage to go to her apartment. A woman, not her mother, opened the door. I asked for Lola and she invited me inside. Lola appeared and in the happiness of seeing each other after so long, we embraced in front of her parents.

I was invited into a room, cramped with beds and a little furniture. Her mother served us tea in the kitchen. Lola was worried about me and disappointed, even angry, that I hadn't let her know I was ill for the past several months.

We went for a walk to the park and talked for hours, kissing and caressing each other.

We tried to make jokes about our situation in Lvov, about the local people and the Russians. There was a lot to laugh about, especially the Russians' propaganda about the wealth of their country. The Russian women could be seen in the evening strolling in fancy negligees and night gowns which they thought were evening dresses. They often bought merchandise they'd never seen before.

When I took Lola home, the world seemed a happier place to me. I finally had someone to talk to. We saw each other quite often.

Spring was full of beauty after such a harsh winter. It was refreshing to walk in the parks, woods and streets and enjoy the fresh air, instead of sitting half frozen in a cramped apartment. We visited museums and old churches. We sat at cafes or ice cream parlours and occasionally met mutual friends from home. We speculated on the outcome of this crazy war. How long would it last? When would the United States get involved?

Between school and shopping and dating, I was very busy. I spent very little time in our room. The weather was warm and the days became longer. I felt good physically, almost normal. Only my eyes were still a little yellow. My doctor was satisfied with my recovery.

\*\*\*

At the beginning of June, a rumour spread like a wind storm. The Russians had decided to deport the refugees to the east, deeper into Russia. From time to time we still heard how people were being arrested or simply disappeared. We also heard they deported Polish intelligentsia, big landlords and even some priests, but we never heard about the deportation of Jewish refugees on any measurable scale. It was hard to believe, but little by little we realized this was not a rumour, but reality.

At night, the Russians came with trucks and picked up refugees with their belongings, taking them to the outskirts of Lvov, a few kilometres from the main railroad station, where they were loaded on trains.

People became panicky hearing these stories. There was no place to escape. Some people wouldn't sleep at home. They tried to change their addresses and spent all night in parks, anywhere but where they lived, and returned home to sleep in the daytime. The days remained peaceful while the dirty work of deportation was carried out at night.

We tried to keep in touch daily with the rest of our family in Lvov, hoping this would blow over. We thought we would avoid deportation because we all worked.

To our surprise, the first to be taken away was my cousin Moniek Brenner. He was working as a stock manager in a huge bakery run by the Russians that supplied bread for the army. He started to work there in a menial job, but they recognized his education and ability and he was promoted rapidly. If he was taken away from such a position, we realized we had no chance.

A few days later, Salek Steiner disappeared. Now there was only Uncle Marian and his wife. The Shicklers had their citizenship, so they didn't have to worry.

Father decided we couldn't stay in our apartment any longer, and he made arrangements with the restaurant's owner. We moved in secrecy to the basement there.

It was a deep basement full of beer bottles, chairs and all kinds of junk. It was cold, damp and dark. We put some old tables together to make a bed to sleep. The owner brought us a couple of pillows and some blankets.  It was a scary, dingy place.

I sat in the corner of the restaurant until late at night, dreading the thought of going downstairs.. In the morning, I got up, washed and went for a walk to shake off the chill and the smell of the basement. I had my breakfast and walked towards downtown to check on Uncle Marian to see if he was still there. I didn't go to school anymore. Everything became gloomy and useless. I checked on Lola. So far, they were safe, but her parents didn't allow her to go out on dates.

We did not know how long this situation would last. There was no one to complain to, no one to defend us. We were at the mercy of the Russians. Outspoken criticism or resistance meant instant arrest. In their system, we were somehow the enemy.

For a few days it was quiet, and we thought maybe they had filled some sort of deportation quota. We were always looking for a glimmer of hope.

But this was not only happening in Lvov. We soon realized this was going on in all the territory occupied by Russian, which amounted to about one third of Poland. Some people came from smaller cities and towns to Lvov, hoping they could avoid the deportation.

On one bright sunny morning, Father went to work and I went to check with Uncle Marian. I entered the restaurant but couldn't find him. I asked about him and was told he hadn't shown up for work. I had a bad feeling.

I ran like a madman to his apartment, not bothering to wait for the trolley. I just ran. I soon found out what I suspected. Marian and his wife had been taken away late at night. I was stunned. I didn't ask any questions. I knew what had happened. I ran back to the restaurant to share the news with Father. When I came back huffing and puffing, Father knew what had happened.

We knew we were the next to be deported. We decided we should take our belongs and get immediately to the railroad depot, where the NKWD was putting the transports together. Maybe we would find Uncle Marian and join him on the same transport.

I had never seen Father make a decision so quickly. Somehow it seemed strange and senseless to become prisoners of our own volition.

We brought everything we had. Father told the owner we had to leave. He packed all the food he could find — bread, salami, pastrami, rolls and pastries. The owner couldn't understand what we were doing. The *droszki* stand was around the corner and Father knew many of the drivers who came into the restaurant, stopping in every few hours for a glass of vodka. The driver was stunned when Father told him where we were going, but he agreed to take us.

It was a long ride in an unfamiliar part of the city. The tall apartment buildings gave way to smaller ones, and finally small homes with big yards. We could see people working in their gardens.It seemed so peaceful and cheerful, and here we were driving to give ourselves up to be deported somewhere.

In the distance, we could see several freight cars. But as we came closer, we could see the whole area was enclosed by a wire fence with soldiers walking in all directions..I noticed some freight cars with their doors open wide and people standing inside the doors looking out. Our driver didn't want to go too close to the gate. Understandably, he didn't want to get involved with the NKWD. I looked at the people standing in the doors of the freight cars, trying to see if Uncle Marian was there.

Something came over me and I jumped out from the *droszki*, ran a short distance to the fence and tried to look into the occupied cars. I took a deep breath and hollered, "Marian, Marian, Marian!" The guards on the other side of the fence looked at me.I kept yelling, "Marian!" Suddenly, there was a commotion in the car opposite to me and Uncle Marian appeared, waving his hands..

I ran back to the *droszki* and Father and I approached the officer at the gate. I tried to explain what we were doing there, but he didn't understand. The officer called one of the Ukrainian soldiers, who spoke a little Polish. I told them they were looking for us, but we had been away and they had taken part of our family away last night. I pointed to the car where Marian and my aunt were and told him we wanted to stay together.

The soldier didn't want to accept us because we were not on the list. We insisted they had to take us. I only yelled "family, family, family!"

An officer showed up and they had a little conference. They came back, asked our names and dutifully added us to the list, marking all the details we gave them. We took our bundles and were escorted with by the officers to the car where Uncle Marian stood.

We threw our belongings on the train car and with the help of the soldiers, climbed in. We embraced Aunt Hela and Uncle Marian and went into a corner where they had their belongings. Hela was a petite woman, always perfectly dressed, groomed and elegant. She looked out of place in these, filthy cramped quarters. There was not much room and we had to struggle to find a place on the floor next to them.

Jewish people from all walks of life — laborers, intellectuals and Hassidim — were crammed into the car. It was silent as people sat speechless and stunned. A few were sobbing quietly. The euphoria of getting together with Marian passed and we became depressed and anxious. Where were they taking us? There was nobody to ask.

An elderly lawyer named Mr. Garber sat among us. He spoke Russian perfectly, because he studied law in Warsaw before the First World War. At that time, the city belonged to the czarist Russia. He became our spokesman and tried to ask the soldiers where we were going, but they didn't answer. I am sure they didn't know either.

The train's toilet facilities consisted of a square hole in the floor. There were lots of women, young and old among us.. People tried to wait until dark to relieve themselves. During the day, someone would hold up a bedsheet providing privacy.

It got dark and we laid on the floor, fully dressed trying to get some sleep. We were so excited and distraught we didn't think about eating. During the night, we could hear trucks arriving with more people, talking and marching towards the other empty freight cars. I woke up several times and tried to look through the narrow opening of the door, but it was impossible to see anything. The windows were too high and I had nothing to climb up on.

Around 7 a.m., they opened the door, but didn't allow anyone outside. Everything looked like the day before.

The NKWD operated at night. They didn't like to be seen doing their dirty work during the day. Later in the morning they brought us bread and pails of water.

People were quiet and sad. Everyone was worried and contemplated what the future held. What crime did we commit to be treated this way? Most of the people in our car were middle-aged. I didn't see any teenagers and there were only a few elderly people.

The religious people took out their phylacteries and tallaisim (prayer shawls) and said their morning prayer. We sat on the floor for hours, only with our thoughts.

By noon, it was very hot and they opened the doors. We tried to take turns standing by the open doors for some fresh air and to see the world outside. All I could see were the cars next to ours, full of people standing like us in the doors. The soldiers with their guns walked back and forth. We asked how long we were going to stay in this station. They didn't answer. When they did they always said: "*Ne znaju!,* I don't know!"

I thought about Lola, the Schicklers and a few friends from home. I wondered if they were still free in Lvov. I realized I was being taken farther away from my mother, sister and family. I confided my worries to Uncle Marian. He tried to sound optimistic, but I could see he was also worried. I felt like crying, but I was too ashamed to be seen.

While I was sick I had become a cigarette smoker. Father and Uncle Marian had some cigarettes, but were trying to conserve them. I satisfied myself with a few puffs. In the late afternoon, they brought some bread again, some sausage and hot water. Only a few people ate the *traif*, or non-kosher sausage.

The cool evening breeze brought a little relief to the overheated cars. But still, there weren't any signs of departure. I was anxious for the train to move. I wanted to see where we were going. The uncertainty of where and when we were going was troubling us, especially because we had nothing to do but think and worry. Finally, I fell asleep.

Suddenly, in the middle of the night I heard and felt a jolt. The car moved a little, probably the locomotive getting hooked to the transport. I felt the train moving slowly. Our journey began.

I was glad we would finally find out what was in store for us. People got up, though it was still dark. They spoke to each other, trying to guess the direction in which we were going, how far and where the Russians were taking us.

The USSR was such a huge country, it was hard to guess and useless to speculate. The women and some men started to cry and sob quietly. Some prayed and wailed. I don't know why, but I felt calm. I realized there was nothing I could do.

It didn't take us long to realize we were going to the east. To some of us it was a certain relief because we thought they might hand us to the Germans, and call it repatriation.

The rest of the night the train sped along passing little stations without stopping. We all tried to peek through the crevices and the lucky ones, who had sturdy valises, stood on the top of them and watched through the windows, relating what they saw.

It was late in the morning when the train stopped. But there was no indication of where we were because we had stopped far from the station. We saw lots of buildings and homes. If we were going to the east, it must have been the city of Tarnopol, in eastern Poland.

We stood there for a while, listening to the noises outside of our boxcar. We could hear the soldiers walking next to the cars, speaking Russian. I don't remember how many people were in the car, maybe 50. Finally they slid open the door, and to our relief, the light and fresh summer air filled the car, clearing the stench and smells. Now everybody wanted to stay next to the door and there was a little pushing and shoving. But I must say, in general, people were civilized under the circumstances.

It was confirmed we were in Tarnopol. Mr. Garber found out we would stay here for a while to get food and provisions. We could see Polish people near the tracks. Some tried to come closer to see us but were chased away by the soldiers. Soon, they started to bring pails of water, bread, sausages, margarine, even a little marmalade.

Through Mr. Garber, we found out we would get some boiled water from the locomotive boiler. Within a few hours, the soldiers had done their jobs and we were on our way, but to where? The guards were all saying the same phrase "Ne Znaju!" "I don't know."

The train made more short stops, but the doors didn't open. Early in the evening, we stopped again and the doors were opened. We got our dinner, including cabbage soup. We were close to the station and lots of local people could see us. Something unusual happened. People moved close to the train and threw us some candy, chocolate, bread and rolls.

Word of this incident must have spread, because at some other stops, people threw food to us, too. The guards were amazed and didn't know what to do. They tried to chase the people away, but they kept coming and finally the soldiers closed the door. We weren't hungry, but we were inspired by this unselfish deed.

We stopped in the city of Stanislawow. This was the last stop of the 1939 Polish territory.

Life on the train became routine. People became friends and helped each other. When somebody became ill with a fever or stomach problems, everybody chipped in with medication that they brought with them.

The Matzners, a Jewish Austrian couple had a violin. He would play and his wife Stella sang. We begged him to play more often. He played Viennese music mostly , but sometimes mixed in Jewish and Gypsy songs. At some stops, when he played, the guards would stand near our car to listen.

Sometimes in the middle of the day, in the middle of nowhere, the train would stop. The guards would open the door and allow us to get some fresh air, exercise and relieve ourselves outside.

We were now in the flat steppes of the Ukraine. From the steppes and the easterly direction, we knew we were moving straight through the Ukraine. The train always stopped on the outskirts of the cities. The guards had a long way to bring us food and water. If we stopped close to a station, our cars remained closed and they would load the provisions on the car next to the engine and distribute the food at a later stop.

Inside the cars the mood became more somber. People didn't talk too much. There was absolutely no way to find out anything from the soldiers and the guards. Our spokesman, Mr. Garber, tried to talk with them, hinting and hoping for some clues, but to no avail.

We had been travelling for two weeks and as far as we could tell, we were still in Ukraine. We stopped at every little town, sometimes for hours. But as long as the train was kept moving, we felt we were getting closer to our destination. We were powerless to do anything about it. It is hard to understand how we felt. I tried to be optimistic and always believed things would get better and with time, we would survive.

The night stops were the worst. We often thought we had arrived at our destination. The silence was frightening. The few Hassidic Jews in our car prayed twice a day. We were worried about the consequences and how the guards would react. So they would pray quietly.

We discovered we were heading north or northeast. When we were sure about the direction, our mood became gloomy. Heading north meant moving toward cold weather. The clothing we had wouldn't accommodate the bitter Russian winters.

We passed small, unfamiliar stations, and the stops became farther apart. The rumbling of the wheels relaxed me at night. It was almost like music. When we did stop, we became frightened and worried. Was this our destination or was it only a stop? We were left to speculate. Some of us clung to the windows, trying to see where we were, but most of the time the stops were in the middle of nowhere, on the outskirts of towns and cities.

Boredom and apathy were taking over. We sat for hours at a time just brooding or daydreaming. Only during some day stops, would they open the door and let us out.

I tried to stay neat and clean. I changed my underwear often. When we got a bucket of water to wash, which was seldom, after washing myself, I would dip my underwear in the water and hang it to dry on a nail which stuck out of the wood close to the window.

We passed the large city of Voronez. The weather was still beautiful, sunny with comfortable temperatures. When the train stopped, we could see more and more forests. Most of the trees were leafy birches. But further north the birches gave way to pines and spruces.

Weeks were passing by and the food we brought with us was running out. We had to depend on food given to us by our captors. We were becoming hungry. This constant hunger, of varying degrees, was to become my companion in the years to come. We were given a metal pot with a wire handle which the Russians called a *kotelok*, and some wooden spoons. These, too, became our constant companion. We used it for receiving food, for hot water and for drinking water and washing.

We sometimes frowned at the food we received, but our escorts just smiled. They knew, sooner or later, we would eat everything that was given to us.

This became true in a matter of weeks. By now, a majority of people were dependent on the food we got from the guards. It varied from station to station. We got a chunk of bread, sometimes black, sometimes white, sometimes stale or mouldy. I was always a fussy eater and it took real hunger before I could eat this food. I still didn't have all my strength back after my lengthy illness. Father was worried and coaxed me to eat everything we got. I eventually got used to the food and looked forward to it. The food consisted mainly of bread, some thin cabbage soup, sometimes cereal, a piece of greasy sausage and sometimes a piece of sugar.

The boxcar got filthier by the day. People were taking off their clothing and checking for lice. The women were picking lice from each other's heads. Things were happening that I abhorred and never saw in my life. People were getting nervous, edgy and from time to time there were arguments. They were hungry and some were getting sick. Then came the pushing for food when it was distributed. Mr. Garber, our spokesman with the Russians, was trying to organize some kind of order and vented our complaints to the soldiers.

Our Russian escorts were never brutal or mean to us. Sometimes you could even detect a little compassion or sorrow. They treated the women more kindly than the men.

We passed the station of Tambow. The countryside was less populated and the forest grew more dense. There were only single rail lines now.

I began to regret our decision to give ourselves up for deportation. Maybe we should have tried to hide ourselves for a longer period of time. I didn't share my thoughts with Father, realizing nothing could be done.

We had no blankets and the nights were getting cold and damp. People were coughing and sneezing. Some had fevers and there was little aspirin to go around.

After about five weeks of travelling by train, we  stopped one sunny morning Our door didn't open for hours, but that was not unusual. We suspected the guards were getting supplies, so we sat patiently waiting for food. Finally, the door slid open to the beautiful, warm sun, which brightened our mood. I looked outside, there was nothing unusual upon first sight. We were allowed to leave the boxcar. There was no station to be seen, just a few old buildings without any names on them. It felt so good to stretch in the fresh warm air. I couldn't inhale enough of it. I walked toward the locomotive under the watchful eyes of our guards. They knew no one would try to escape. Where would we run in this giant country, full of police, army, strange languages and people? It never crossed my mind or anyone else's.. As I came close to the locomotive, I noticed something unusual — the track ended a few metres from the engine.

I went back towards our car to tell Father and Uncle Marian. We decided to keep the information to ourselves and see what was going to happen. There was no use disturbing the rest of the people. Meanwhile, we got some bread, margarine and pails of hot water from the locomotive. After we finished this so-called breakfast, the cars were left open. We noticed in the car next to us, people were leaving with their belongings and marching toward the other side of the track.

I leaned against the car, taking in the warmth of the sun. The guards kept watching us. Some were walking, some sitting on the ground. They seemed to be in a better mood. I noticed a soldier walking slowly past the cars, stopping and looking inside each car and giving instructions. Slowly he came to our car. He was short and dressed in a better uniform than the others. He may have been an officer. He suddenly stopped in front of me, and to my surprise, started to talk to me. I had no problem understanding him. He spoke slowly in a combination of Ukrainian and Polish.

"I see that you are worried," he said.

"Of course I am," I answered. "I don't know where I am. I don't know where I'm being taken to, and for what purpose."

Then, he asked me a very unusual question. Had I left behind a girlfriend  that I intended to marry in Lvov. I was shocked. Why would he ask me this?

I told him I had.

"Maybe you have a picture?" he asked.

I did and he asked to see it. I hesitated, but I thought, what can happen? He noticed my reluctance and said not to worry. He wouldn't hurt me in any way.

I took out my billfold and removed the picture of Lola, handing it to him. He looked at it for a long time, lifted his head and I noticed tears in his eyes. He asked me her name. I told him it was Lola. What a beautiful name he said in a sad voice. I was sure he was sincere.

But he frightened me with his behaviour. Why did he have tears in his eyes? Was it because he knew our fate or was it because he was sad about my separation from my girlfriend? He took me by the hand and led me to the end of the car. He probably didn't want anybody to hear what he was about to tell me. We stood between two boxcars, almost in the middle of the track. He asked me my first name. I told him it was Samuel.

"That's a biblical name," he said. "But there's no first name like that here in Russia. Your name here will be Sasha."

For the next four years I was known as Sasha.

"Sasha," he said, "Look, I am returning to Lvov. If you give me the address of your girlfriend Lola, I'll look her up and give her the address of where she can write to you."

I froze. How can I give him her address. Maybe they would take Lola and her family. Am I going to betray her and regret this all my life? I stood there, leaning against the car, closed my eyes, frightened, not knowing what to do.

He must have understood my position and my thoughts. "Sasha," he said. "I swear to you I am not going to betray your girlfriend. I want to do a good deed, because I see so much misery and injustice around me."

He tried to, in a mixture of languages, to make me believe his intentions. He just wanted to help. He took out a pad of paper and a pencil.

"Write her address, sign your name, I'll give her your address and deliver it if I find her still in Lvov."

I looked at his face and his sincere expression and I did what he asked. I handed back his little pad of paper and I burst into tears. He put his hand on my shoulders and with his misty eyes , he said: "Don't worry. I am sorry. I cannot tell you any more."

He started to walk toward our car, turned around and walked briskly toward the command car. I was in a daze. Did I do the right thing, trusting him? I decided not to tell anyone about this.

Our car was almost at the end of the transport. The day was getting warmer and the morning haze was gone. The door of our car was wide open. A few people sat on the floor, dangling their feet. I didn't feel like talking to anybody and walked as far away from the car as the guards would allow and sat down on the grass.. I buried my head in my hands and sat there for a while with the sun on my back, fighting with my thoughts and worries..

I daydreamed and saw Lola opening the door to an unknown officer and him handing her the little piece of paper. I wanted to forget everything for a moment. I opened my eyes and one look at the transport brought me back to reality.

Meanwhile, people were leaving the cars with their belongings. The guards were marching them toward the locomotive, turning left away from us. We started to pack our things. There wasn't much. My backpack, one valise and a bag.

By late afternoon, it was our turn to leave.

Two soldiers jumped inside the car to check if anyone was hiding or had left anything behind. We were marching towards the locomotive. It was a sorrowful picture. We walked in silence — young and old men unshaven, women in wrinkled clothing with untidy hair, with sadness in everybody's eyes, carrying their meager belongings..

We turned left and saw trucks loaded with people from previous cars. We stood on a wooden platform. Two trucks were just departing, leaving a cloud of dust behind. When the dust settled, we could see a city in the distance. We could distinguish clusters of buildings, some of them several stories high. Is this the place we are going to stay, live and work? What is the city's name? Where is it located? We tried to ask the soldiers but they were tightlipped and would not say a word. They seemed to be less relaxed. Their only words were "uvidisz" — "You will soon find out.".

We waited. Open stake trucks with two drivers each approached the platform, turned around, raised a dust cloud and backed up to the platform. They jumped out, opened the gate and we hopped in. The drivers were of Asian origin, which made us think that only God knew where we were. Maybe we were in Asia.

They spoke a strange language and uttered a few words between themselves while we got in the truck. They were quite polite and did not use any force. They were doing their job. Sometimes they smiled at us.

When the trucks were full, we were on our way down some dirt road. The dust was so thick we couldn't see much in front of us. We approached the outskirts of a city on a hill. The air cleared and the road was paved. It was a good sized city. We saw people walking on the streets. A mixture of Asian and European faces greeted us. It became apparent we were not going to enter the city centre. Our truck was still climbing as we took a road to the outskirts of the city and began to descend. We made a sharp turn. Suddenly, an unusual sight appeared before our eyes. It was a strange horizon, resembling clouds. The trucks descended further. Houses became rare. The clouds became closer and finally I realized it was not a cloud, it was a body of water

I could see the banks of a huge river, like I'd never seen before. We could see boats and barges plying the water. We noticed on the horizon, the opposite banks of this huge body of water. What river was this? The only name that entered my mind was the Volga. It looked like a port, full of all kinds of boats, ships and barges. We drove straight towards the banks. Empty trucks were passing us and we realized this city was not our destination.

Two big barges were anchored to the bank. Our truck stopped, and we were ordered out. I approached one of the drivers and asked him if this was the Volga. He didn't speak but nodded his head affirmatively. We got our luggage and marched towards the river.

We were led to a barge. We walked on a wooden plank, leading to the barge from the shoreline. There were more than 200 people in each barge. Father and I tried to stay together with Uncle Marian. We searched for a few feet of open space to sit down and rest.

The sun was going down. We were hungry, depressed and worried. About an hour later a tugboat approached our barges and maneuvered to position itself in front of the first one. It hooked our barges with chains and now we knew we were going upstream.

A truck approached from the shore and started to unload food, mostly bread and other boxes. After a long time we were given some unfamiliar salty fish. I tried to eat it, but it tasted terrible. It was just as well; those that did manage to eat it suffered all night from horrible thirst.

The sun sank behind the steep shore and only part of the river was flooded by bright sunshine. It was beautiful, almost exotic, and had a calming effect on me. My head was full of thoughts.

Only nine months had passed since we'd left Krakow. So many things happened in such a short time. Every day was different and a story in itself. The normalcy of a safe and stable life was gone and forgotten. I think this was the beginning of our fight for survival.

The journey was awful, more cramped even than the boxcars, and fully exposed to the elements...and to the swarms of mosquitoes who tortured us through the nights despite the protective clothing we wore.

The third day on the barge, the fog became so thick that the barge had to pull into shore and anchored at a village or settlement. We stayed there until dawn. In the morning we received our usual breakfast and were on our way again.

The river was shrouded with a mist. It looked like a delicate white blanket covering most of the river. The sun started to shine through the mist. The eastern side of the river was already covered with sunshine. It was a beautiful and serene sight.

When we left the Volga and moved into a smaller river, the mosquitoes were even worse. They buzzed around us all day. It was quiet and there was no breeze. As the sun went down, we came to a stop. We received our hot water, bread and little pieces of sugar with some drinking water. The only thing we found out from the guards was that the river was called the Vetluga. They also told us we would arrive at our destination shortly.

We heard no news about the war. Was it over? Little by little, I didn't care anymore. Our daily task was making sure we got food and to kept ourselves as clean as possible. More and more people were scratching themselves because they were full of lice. I would wash myself the best I could every morning with the little piece of toilet soap that I had brought with me and rationed carefully.

One morning, we started as soon as the first light filtered through the forest. Around noon, I could see areas on the shore where trees had been cut down. I also saw a few barracks or some kind of buildings, but no sign of life. We approached some kind of wooden docking facility, resting on wooden poles.. The tug started to manoeuvre our barge, bringing us as close as possible to the dock.

Apparently, we had arrived at our mystery destination.

## NINE

Guards appeared on the docks as our barge was being docked. We also noticed some people high above us. We were ordered to get out of the barge and take all of our belongings.

We went up the primitive steps with its planks broken and rotten. For weeks we did not get any exercise or walk very much. People had trouble going up the stairs, especially the women and older people.

I reached the top of the steps and found myself amid a beautiful green clearing, surrounded by young trees. Men, mostly in NKWD uniforms, ordered us to sit on the grass and rest. Our escorts stayed down at the barges until everybody was at the top.

It was a beautiful day, reminding me of the smell of the woods at home on my vacations. I looked down on the winding river below. The scenery was lovely. I lay on the grass, stretched myself out and enjoyed the luxury of space around me.

More and more NKWD people appeared. Apparently, they were waiting for something or someone to come. Some of the deportees took off their dirty shirts, soaking up the warm sun.

I sat with Father, Uncle Marian, his wife and our interpreter Mr. Garber and a few other people we met on the train. Mr. Garber had given up his effort to try to find out anything from the guards and the NKWD officers.

Within a couple of hours, we heard engine noises and we saw some trucks approaching. They were strange looking vehicles. The cab was narrow with a cylinder attached to either side. The drivers stopped, opened the gates and began the process of loading people and their belonging into the trucks. As soon as two trucks were full, they closed the gates, revved their engines, which were extraordinarily noisy, and away they went. We weren't in a hurry to move because it was so pleasant laying on the grass. I could have waited forever.

While they were loading the trucks I counted more than 450 deportees.

We left on the last two trucks. As the sun set we got on the last truck. It was quite roomy because there were only about 20 to 25 people left.

We travelled along a bumpy, dirt road through a forest of young trees. Our truck turned to the left and the one ahead of us proceeded straight. We became uneasy. The road got narrower, more like a grassy patch than a road. Trees on both sides were tall and and darkness was setting in. It was a slow ride as the driver swerved to avoid the big holes in the road and the engine spewed smelly fumes.

We came to a clearing with a lonely wooden barrack with an old well next to it, standing on the right side of the road. The truck stopped in front, the guard and the driver got out and went inside. They returned and ordered us to get out of the truck and take our belongings with us. We were petrified. It was almost completely dark. As we entered the barrack, it was obvious no one had lived here for a long time. Part of the barrack was divided into cubicles with two bunk beds in each. I called them beds, but they were only three slats across and up and down. The other part of the barrack was empty.

We threw our belongings on the floorand went with Mr. Garber to confront our guards.

At first Mr. Garber was polite, and then he demanded an explanation. We stood behind Mr. Garber, raising our voices in support of him. I noticed the guards seemed intimidated and started to back away from us. They eventually explained we would only stay here overnight. There was a shortage of accommodations in the camp where the rest of our transport had been taken.

It was hot and humid in the barracks. I couldn't keep myself covered from the mosquitoes for long. I must have fallen asleep uncovered because I woke with a terrible pain and itch from a bite in my ear. I got up, opened the door and went outside. The sky was bright with the light of the moon and stars. The air was still. I walked over to the well. It was full, about even with the surface. I bent down, took some water in my palms and started pouring it on my face and into my ear. I spent most of the night outside, and once in a while I heard the noises of some small animals rustling about. I ran back to the barracks, closed the squeaky door and listened. As soon as the noise abated, I went back outside and splashed water into my ear. I grew tired, went back to the barracks and fell asleep.

I woke up as it was getting light outside, and left the barracks to relieve myself. We had run out of all paper — napkins or newspaper — whatever we had was gone. Our only choice became leaves which became the norm for a long time.

When it was completely light outside, our prayers were answered. We could hear the sound of a truck coming.

Our guard and the driver got out and greeted us good morning. They were apparently in good humour. They opened the gate and we were politely invited to get in.

We were told we would arrive soon and join the others.. After a half an hour drive through thick forest, we came to a huge opening and saw a village in the distance. We entered a main road with buildings on both sides, the same type of barracks, built from timber, as the one we spent the night in. We were happy to see people milling about the buildings and walking from one building to another. They were all from our transport.

The truck stopped at the end of the road, in front of a bigger and longer building than the others. We could smell food cooking. We were ordered to get out from the truck and leave our belongings.

We entered the building and inside there were two rows of long wooden tables, filled with people eating on either side. We lined up in front of a wooden counter, took a wooden plate and spoon and received our first meal. It consisted of oat cereal with a puddle of oil floating in the centre, a chunk of dark bread and a dark liquid, which was supposed to be coffee. It didn't matter, we were so hungry.

Our driver and the guard ate the same food we were served. We finished our meal and were ordered back onto the truck, which took us a few hundred metres further, to the end of the settlement. We stopped in front of a large, log building and were led inside. It was a long building with windows on both sides.. At one the end was a podium, a kind of stage, and pushed to the sides were rows of benches. There were lots of people from our transport there, settled on the floor of the building. We were assigned a place and told to put down our belongings.

Besides our guard, we were met by a man in civilian clothing who gave directions to the driver and our guard. He tried to explain something to us but we couldn't understand. As usual, we delegated Mr. Garber find out what he was trying to tell us. He was able to decipher that we were in a place called Niuziary. We were in the cultural centre building, but only temporarily, because the barracks were not ready yet. This evening, there would be a meeting and everything would be explained to us.

I noticed some people had straw to lay on. We would probably get some later, I thought. The people who had come here last night didn't know much more about our situation.

The weather was pleasant. I went outside to get my bearings about where we were. We were on the shore of a body of water. It looked like a lake On the other side, as far as I could see, there was nothing but forest.

People were washing themselves and doing laundry in the lake. I also could see a little island in the centre of the lake. The water was yellowish, but when I took it in my hands it seemed quite clean. I was happy to be near water. At least there was a place to wash and maybe even to swim.

It felt good to take a stroll and not be watched by anybody. Noticeably, there were no children. Apparently, the transport had been selected this way. The Russians knew all along where they were sending us and knew it would not be suitable for children.

I didn't see any guards or NKWD. It seemed nobody cared about where I was walking or what I was doing. Everybody was busy, unpacking and trying to settle into the barracks. Women were cleaning and washing, airing the clothing. There were probably 50 people in our building, which they called The Club.

An NKWD officer came in and spoke with Mr. Garber. We were to make as much room as possible for the meeting to be held in our barracks at 6:00 p.m. Everybody was to be there. We had to put all the benches back to the centre and move our belongings close to the walls to accommodate everyone. The anticipation ran high. Finally, we were going to find out about our situation and maybe our future.

The Spielman family, who had a ten or twelve-year-old daughter was assigned to our barracks. I was surprised because all through our journey I hadn't noticed them. They settled next to us in The Club. The girl was shy and frightened and her parents tried reassure and comfort her.

They were also from Krakow. Mrs. Spielman was a practical nurse and her husband was a businessman. We became very good friends and I tried to help them with their daughter,Ruthie. I called her Ruti and liked her a lot. She somehow reminded me of my sister Niusia who I missed so much. I told Ruti stories about my sister and often took her for walks by the lake. She was a very lonely and she often cried. She was the only child in the camp and had nobody to play with. She had a hard time adjusting to the food. People were kind enough to give her morsels of food they had brought from home — a piece of sugar or chocolate. Ruti became kind of a mascot to everyone in the settlement.

The afternoon before the meeting people gathered together around The Club early, sitting on the floor and benches, taking up every inch of space. We kept the door and window open because it became very hot. Father and I stood against the wall with our belongings around us.. Everyone waited with great anticipation. There wasn't enough room for everybody. Some stood next to the windows. It felt like we were the accused standing in court, awaiting our sentence.

Three uniformed persons entered through the side door and went straight to the stage. The man in the centre went to the podium and the two guards with their rifles sat down on chairs on either side. The room was silent. He was a good-looking man, very tall, and wore a NKWD uniform with an officer's insignia on his epaulet. He greeted us in Russian and started to speak. We listened intently as if we understood the Russian language. Once in awhile, he would stop to let Mr. Garber catch up with his notes. He spoke for about a half an hour. I understood very little only catching a few familiar words. But his last sentence many of us understood. He pronounced it very slowly to make us understand. These were his words:

"You are here to stay to work for our country, to live here and die here."

The silence of the room was broken. People became agitated. Women and many of the men started to cry. It took some time for them to quiet down and give Mr. Garber a chance to tell us more about the speech.

The guards stood by, but the officer left the club. The outline of the speech  brought no explanation, just the grim facts..We were in Maryjska, ASSR, a republic that I'd never heard of. Our status was that of special re-settlers. We were living in a special camp called Niuziary. We were not allowed to move or travel anywhere unless we got  special permission. Our main job was going to be lumberjacking — to supply the great Soviet Union with lumber. We were also expected to do all the jobs around and inside the settlement.This was to be our  home. The better and harder we worked and behaved, the better life would be. The following day we would be organized in groups and shown our duties .

We were going to live in The Club temporarily while they assembled new barracks for us. People had more questions but they were not answered.  Everybody left The Club with heavy hearts.

When the barracks had cleared, we went back to our corners and sat on the floor. Father, Uncle Marian, his wife Hela, who had tears in her eyes,  were all completely shocked. I was the only optimist among us. I wouldn't accept or believe this situation would go on forever. I tried to lift their spirits, but I couldn't find the right words.

***

The next day, all the men were to be ready in the morning  for work. We had an early breakfast in the dining room and waited outside for the authorities. Our guards  marched towards us with a group of men in civilian clothes. We realized there were actual Russian inhabitants, other than us,living in Niuziary.

We were divided in groups of about 10 and assigned to one civilian. He was introduced to us and we were led away. On the shore of the lake, stood a little warehouse full of axes, steel spikes and large saws.

The man in charge gave our group two saws, four axes and some spikes. We were marched out of the settlement towards the forest. About a half an hour later, we turned down a narrow path and became surrounded by a thick forest with tall trees. The man in charge led us to a small clearing and we were told to sit down. His name was Kowalenko. He was about 35 and wore a fine mustache. He rolled himself some kind of a cigarette in a piece of newspaper with a strange looking tobacco that came in a little pouch. He lit it and a terrible smell filled the air. He offered some to us, but there were no takers. Many of us were craving a smoke but not this kind. He had a few puffs and started to explain what our work was going to be and what was expected from us. He spoke slowly, using more Ukrainian, and it was possible to understand most of his speech. He told us we were to become lumberjacks. We were going to be divided in smaller brigades once we learned our trade. The more wood we cut, the more food we would be able to buy.

We were dumbfounded. I couldn't imagine becoming a lumberjack, and most of our group didn't look like they could do the job. The men in our group were younger and included Uncle Marian. Father was in another group. We later found out, Father was considered old. He was only about 42, but with his mustache and his unshaven face after our long journey, he looked much older than his age.

Kowalenko spoke only about work — our duties in terms of quotas or how many cubic metres we were to cut. It was, to us, mumbo jumbo and I didn't believe we could ever accomplish what he expected.

I had never worked in my life. The thought of becoming a lumberjack seemed outrageous to me. Kowalenko didn't answer any of our questions . He was friendly, polite and smiled, but he spoke only about cutting trees. When we told him we had never done this kind of work, he simply responded: If you want to eat and live, you're going to work, if you don't you'll starve.

It was a beautiful and warm day, so peaceful and quiet at the edge of the forest. I laid down trying to listen to what he was talking about, but most of the time I closed my eyes and tried to forget where I was. The past 10 months of my life were so unbelievable.

But when I opened my eyes I knew where I was. Kowalenko finished his talk, took out some tobacco and rolled another cigarette in a piece of newspaper. He had pieces of newspaper neatly cut in a certain form and kept them in his tobacco pouch. He told us not to worry. Sooner or later, we would learn this work like everyone else had.

Kowalenko finished his cigarette, selected a man from our group and handed him an axe. He took the other one and we all moved to the trees at the edge of the opening. I remember this tree very well. It was a tall, straight pine tree with very few branches at the very top.

We got a demonstration about how to fell trees.. With axe in hand, he pointed to a spot on the tree where he was going to start cutting. He started to chop the tree on an angle. He called upon the man he had selected tried to teach him to do the same. The man, like the rest of us, probably had never done anything like this. The axe was flat and sharp on a very long handle. He held his hand and showed him how to hit and chop. The tree had to be chopped from both sides in a vee shape, until a groove was formed. This was going to be the side the tree would fall. It took a long time until the vee groove was formed. Our guy was hitting and chopping all over, very seldom hitting the right spot. Then Kowalenko would take his hand, steering the axe to hit the right spot. Finally, the groove was formed. Kowalenko let the man rest and said "*harosho!*" That's good! He used this word often to encourage us. Now he looked around for another student. He pointed his finger at me and called me to come. He picked up a saw and I followed him.

The saw was very large with long, sharp teeth, about one and half metres long, with wooden handles on both sides. He told me grab one side, bend down and indicated a line where we were going to cut. It was exactly opposite the vee cut done before with the axe. Now we bent down and started to saw, slowly, until the blade was well wedged in and then he increased the tempo.

The saw was very sharp and the large teeth were biting into the tree quickly. About three centimeters from the vee cut in the tree, we stopped. Kowalenko got hold of the steel spikes, took one and inserted it in the incision. After hitting it several times with the axe, we heard a crack and this beautiful, proud tree started slowly to fall to the ground. Finally, it hit with a loud thump. This was my initiation as a lumberjack.

With the tree on the ground, he showed us how to chop off the branches very close to the stump. Then he took a measuring tape and measured to cut the tree in three pieces. For cutting the three pieces he chose another man. I had enough for the day. Kowalenko told us that the norm for two people is eight trees like this a day. If they were thinner, the quota was more, if they are thicker maybe less than eight. He also said most of the people, if they worked hard should exceed the norm. I thought he was crazy, but later I found out he wasn't. He showed us how to put the branches together in one place. He cut several trees that day, always picking a different man to do it, so that everybody learned something.

Late that afternoon, one man swung the axe too close and cut his leg, which started to bleed. It wasn't a dangerous cut, but we didn't have anything to stop the bleeding. I tore a sleeve off the guy's shirt and tied it around the cut and from another sleeve made a tourniquet above his thigh. The bleeding stopped and Kowalenko decided we should go back. He watched how I applied first-aid and asking if I was a doctor. I answered I was a student doctor and he smiled. There was a nurse back at the camp who would take care of the man. We helped him walk back to our camp. He ordered the men straight to their barracks, but told me to accompany the wounded man to the clinic.

He turned right and we entered a little street. I noticed several homes were situated before the entrance to the camp. They were built from wooden logs, similar to the barracks but had many windows. The first was the Komandant's office with a small addition on the side. We walked in with Kowalenko and met our camp nurse, Zina.

She was a pretty girl, about my age, maybe younger. Kowalenko told her the problem and introduced me to her. He smiled, saying I was a student doctor. He went inside the Kommandat's office, probably to make a report and I stayed with Zina to take care of the patient. Zina opened a first-aid kit. It contained cotton, gauze, alcohol and iodine and a few boxes with some other medications. We washed Alex's cut and I helped her to bandage it. I told her it could use a few stitches and asked if she could do it. She smiled, turning her head. She was really cute. I liked her and did most of the work, as she watched me with curiosity. Our conversation was limited because of the language barrier. But through smiles, we understood each other. We stayed inside waiting for Kowalenko.

Zina asked me if I would sometimes come to the infirmary after work. I told I would be happy to.

Kowalenko walked me back to the main road and told me to notify the others that tomorrow, after breakfast, we would go back to the woods for more training.

I realized there were quite a few people living in private homes separate from the camp. These were people who had also been deported from different parts of Russia and were here to teach us how to work.

We were not allowed to go to the part of the camp where they lived, only to the Kommadant's office when some problem arose. They never spoke to us accept about work, weather and food. Apparently, they had been told not to have any personal contact with us.

I returned to the barracks exhausted, ate my dinner and slept in our corner, dreaming about my next visit to Zina.

I went to see her on several occasions. She was friendly and I knew she cared for me. I would help her sort out the measly supply of medication she had. She always prepared tea and sometimes treated me to a piece of white bread with jam. My Russian was improving by the day and I could understand her more and more.

My friendship with Zina came to an unexpected end. One evening, while I was having tea with Zina, one of the NKWD guards, the short man, who we later called Poldek, burst into the infirmary. He started to holler at me, half of which I could not understand. He ordered me to get out and warned me never to come back again.I said goodbye and I left. I understood later, that my visit there and socializing was against regulations. But the main reason was Poldek's jealousy. This was the end of my friendship, or romance, with my first Russian girl. I met her later, but only on business and it was always during the day.

Our lessons in lumberjacking continued in earnest. We realized we had better take this seriously, and the sooner the better. Kowalenko never threatened us. He tried to persuade us that this was for our own good. Every day we learned more and more. I worked with Uncle Marian as a team and we were getting quite good at our new trade.

We went to work in our own clothing but in a few days, my pants, were falling apart, having been torn by the branches and stumps. In the evenings, with the help of some of the women, I tried to sew them. But the next day they would be ruined again. I had a pair of shoes, one of the three pair I brought. They fell apart in only a few days, to the point where I kept the soles together by tying strings around them.

We asked Kowalenko if we could get suitable clothing. He said that as soon as we learned to work and fulfill our quota, we would get everything we needed. Kowalenko had a pair of pants made from a sturdy material and a dark heavy, cotton shirt. He wore heavy leather boots but I had noticed Russian workers usually wore some kind of sandal made from the bark of trees. They looked very odd. But after seeing what was happening to my shoes after such a short time in the forest, I started to think about those sandals more seriously.

Little by little we became familiar with Niuziary and the people who came in our transport. Almost everybody went to work in the morning and only a few older people were left behind. The women were taught how to cut lumber into small pieces. The lumber was brought to them. They put the logs on two special stands and cut them all day. They called it *ciurki*. The lumber had been dried, mostly from dead trees abandoned in the forest. These *ciurkis* were piled outside to dry even further.

I eventually found out why the transport trucks we had arrived in, had steel cylinders on either side of the cab. That's where the *ciurkis* ended up. They provided the fuel for the trucks. The cylinders were filled up and a little kerosene was sprinkled on the wood, lit and closed. This wood gas ran those trucks for miles and they were capable of carrying heavy logs, too. I admired this innovation.

There were stables in Niuziary with a few horses that looked sickly and undernourished. There were a few volunteers who knew a little about horses and formed a brigade to drag logs from the bush to the nearest road by horsepower. There was also a brigade that built new roads and removed tree roots and stumps. The older people were assigned to all kinds of easy jobs around the kitchen, steam bath and general cleaning. I was getting better at cutting down the trees. Kowalenko was right. The sooner we learned our trade, the better it would be for us. There was no way out. Finally, we were allowed to choose partners who we liked to work with. My partner became Uncle Marian.

Father, with the elderly people, was assigned to a brigade of about 10 people, who did all kinds of jobs inside and on the perimeter of the camp. Sometimes they cut wood for the dining room, did a little road work and sometimes helped to load the trucks with timber. Aunt Hela was assigned to cut the *ciurki*.

Our initiation as full-fledged lumberjacks involved getting new pants, dark shirts called *rubashkas* and a cap. We looked like typical Russians.

Around six a.m. each day, we went to the dining room, got our hot cereal, almost always oats, very seldom some corn syrup, a little sunflower oil and a ration of dark bread. It was quite substantial. We ate with wooden spoons from wooden plates and drank from wooden cups. After we finished our meal, our Russian brigadier took us to the tool shed where we were given two axes, one saw and two steel spikes.

Then we were led to the bush. We walked for almost an hour until we got to our destination. We were led to a thick forest and our leader showed us where to start. We were assigned a woodlot about 100 square meters for me and Uncle Marian. This was our *delanka,* or our section. The border of our section was marked with white paint. We were advised to start cutting in the centre and move outward to the perimeter. It wasn't easy and it was dangerous. Kowalenko or others would share some advice and help if there was a problem.

Some trees were easy to cut, especially those straight ones with a few branches on the top. But you had to cut them into pieces and clean off all the branches. The branches were put separately in one big stack. I had no choice but to learn how to wear the bark sandals which were called *laptie.* Sometimes, I put my socks over the sandals. I learned from the ladies how to darn my socks and I became quite good at it. To walk in this strange footwear and to properly bind them was quite an art which took some time to master.

In a few months I became an expert lumberjack. I could put down a tree in almost any place or in any direction. We tried to achieve our quota daily, and often exceeded it. It often depended on the type and size of the trees we were cutting. The second most important factor was how sharp and properly adjusted the teeth of our saws were. After work, we deposited our tools in the little shed to be sharpened for the next day.

I learned from the "King of the tool shop," an elderly Russian named Rubtsow, how to sharpen the tools, which made the work much easier. I became quite friendly with Rubtsow, but he would never talk about anything else but work, Niuziary, the lake and the weather.

I found out that some newspapers were delivered to the camp, but nobody would talk about it. Once in a while, I would come across a piece of old Russian newspaper, and would struggle to read it, learning with the help of Mr. Garber. I didn't get much information from them, and what I did learn was depressing.

98

The Russian newspapers served a dual purpose. I didn't see many Russians reading the newspapers, but instead used them for cigarette paper. Everybody had run out of real cigarettes. When we arrived at the camp, they had some fine cut tobacco in the warehouse and we were given some. But there was no cigarette paper. We tried all kinds of paper, including the Russian newspapers, but it didn't work at all.

The only tobacco in the camp by the Russians was called *mahorka*, with the exception of the Komandant, who sometimes smoked real cigarettes. *Mahorka*, which consisted mostly of stems and roots of tobacco plant chopped into tiny pieces. The Russians rolled it in a piece of newspapers, making a little funnel and smoked it like a little paper pipe. They called it *trubiczki*. They invited me to take a few puffs, but they were strong and made me cough. It didn't taste like a cigarette. They laughed, and told me I'd get used to it. I didn't believe I ever would, but in a short time we were happy to get it.

Of course, the newspaper was also a luxury to be used as toilet paper. But most of the time we didn't have any and got used to leaves.

Sunday was a day of rest, but it became cleaning day. We had more problems keeping clean, because our group still lived in the social hall. We were anxiously waiting for our barracks to be built, but it took a long time.

After a few weeks, something unprecedented happened. Once a week, a letter carrier would come and bring mail to Niuziary. It was quite an event. He would bring the mail to the Komandant, often a bunch of newspapers and some packages. After work, all the locals would go to the office to pick up the mail. None of us expected any mail. We didn't know our address. Suddenly, Poldek, the short guard, came to our hall and called my name, hollering for me to come to the door.

My new Russian name was Sasha Gonig. From Samuel, they decided on Sasha and they didn't pronounce an "h" so I became Gonig instead of Honig. I was frightened to follow Poldek to the Kommandat's office. I stood in front of him and he handed me a letter. He was curious about how someone had found out my address in such a short time. He asked me to open the letter and find an explanation. The letter was from Lola in Lvov. Apparently, the NKWD hadn't caught up with them. I knew right away how I got the letter. The decent NKWD guard delivered my note to her. This was the man in Czuboksary who felt sorry for me and whom I had trusted with Lola's address.

I read the letter in front of him. She didn't write much, only a few words. She was still safe with her family. She missed me very much and was happy that I was well. I told the Komandant that there was no clue in the letter as to how my girlfriend got my address. I practically translated the letter word by word. He shook his head and let me go. Now I was a celebrity. I was the only one to get a letter, and had the address of where we were. Nobody could understand how I got it. I never disclosed my secret, except to Father and Uncle Marian.

I didn't receive any more letters from Lola. After a couple of months, we were allowed to write and receive mail. It brought a great relief to communicate with the outside world. I wrote to Lola, but never heard from her again. I was sure she was deported and I hoped to hear from her. But I never did until my return to Poland in 1946. I found out she died from typhoid fever in central Asia. I accidently met her parents in Krakow. They didn't recognize me and I had no courage to ask them what happened to Lola. I was very sad. We expected all the refugees in Russia would return alive. We found out later this wasn't the case.

We wrote a letter to Mother and the rest of the family, hoping they would receive it. Father wrote to his best friend Shickler in Lvov and I wrote, against everybody's advice, to the aunt and uncle in Washington. Everyone said I would get into trouble, but I always believed if the Russians knew you had a family abroad and the family knows you are in Russia, then your chances of survival might be better. I wrote only a few words, that we were safe and well and we hoped the war would soon be over.

The only answer we received was from the Shicklers in Lvov. It was a short letter in which he told us he was sending us some food and clothing. We were overjoyed to hear from him because we knew he somehow would let our family at home know where we were. Everything we received was worth more than gold. It helped us to supplement our insufficient diet, and the clothing allowed us to barter for food and other necessities.

Shickler wrote that everything was fine and that his son was going to school. They seemed to be living a fairly normal life. They still worked and lived at their old address. We never found out what happened to them after the war. They disappeared without a trace. Most likely they were caught by the Germans and shared the fate of 99 per cent of the Lvov Jews.

The days at Camp Niuziary were warm now. The forest was full of blackberries, raspberries, blueberries and little red ones I'd never seen before. With a piece of black bread, they sweetened our meals.

The majority of people in Niuziary were Jewish from rural Poland. They kept to themselves and most of them created their own brigades. Some of them were farmers and the work came easier to them than to us city people. They usually got jobs with the horse brigade and as lumberjacks. They were doing better than us when it came to tree-cutting quotas. I wanted to catch up with them, and in a few months we had nearly caught up to them.

Except for cuts and scratches we got on the job,we stayed fairly healthy. But suddenly people started to get sick, especially in our barracks.

There were 60 people living close together on the floor. The symptoms were diarrhea, accompanied by a high fever, that ran higher during the night. The diarrhea stopped, but the fevers persisted. A few older people and little Ruthie became sick. I thought it might be a cold or the flu. Zina distributed aspirins, but the sickness persisted and more and more people became victims. Zina visited the barracks more often, but couldn't diagnose the illness. She promised to try to get some doctors to come, but nobody showed up. Little Ruthie lay sad and motionless with a high fever, sleeping most of the time.

I started to think about the sickness and what could cause it. I became very curious.I noticed none of the Russians got sick, only us. The Russians suspected we just didn't want to work and this was some kind of conspiracy.

I suspected the drinking water, which came from the lake, was the culprit. In the morning and evening we received boiled water from the kitchen. Outside the kitchen there was a tap to get water at any time. The local people sometimes drank water straight from the lake. There was no other water supply because Niuzary was surrounded by swamps. If you dug a few feet into the ground a yellow, murky water sprung out. The lake was the only source.

I didn't believe that they boiled the water to a proper boiling point. Sometimes the water wasn't that hot. Maybe they were immune or maybe they boiled it again in their homes. Ruthie's health was getting worse. Her mother sponged her with cold water to keep her temperature down and gave her aspirin, but it didn't help.

\*\*\*

In the middle of the lake was a small island. Some days after performing my chores, I paddled a little boat, which was anchored near the kitchen, to this little island about 200 metres from the shore. It was a wooden boat which was seldom used by anyone else. I never understood why there were no fish in this lake. I never saw one, nor did I ever see anyone fishing. Yet the name Niuziary meant Pike Lake. It would have been nice to catch some pike. Maybe the water was so polluted they'd all been killed off.

I loved to spend a few hours on the island. It had beautiful trees — birches and big willow trees. It was so peaceful and quiet. I would sit on the shore and soak my feet in the water, close my eyes and relax.

Thousands of water lilies floated around the island. I liked to go there whenever I had a chance. On the way back I would pull out a few water lilies and brought them back for Ruthie. She wasn't getting any better and I was worried. She always gave me a smile, especially when I sat next to her and told her a story. I told her about the beautiful island I visited, how I got the flowers. I promised her I would take her there when she got better.

The next Sunday, I started working to create a filter system for our drinking water. I brought home a good sized empty bottle and by putting a string soaked in kerosene around the bottom and lighting the string, I was able to cut the bottom off. It created a good sized funnel. This became my first funnel filter.

I used paper, sand and lots of charcoal which we had in abundance as my filter medium. From that day on, we used only filtered water, day and night. Mrs. Spielman and others who didn't go to work, maintained the filtering system. It filtered drop by drop. Ruthie was given only this water. Our family, fortunately, never got sick. Within a week, Ruthie started to improve. Her temperature went down, she started to eat and in a short time she was well.

Word of my innovation spread and more and more people created all kinds of filters. I earned a reputation in the camp and people started to come to me with all kinds of medical problems.

When the epidemic started, Zina was worried and had notified medical authorities about the problem. About a month later, about 10 people came to Niuziary. We didn't know who they were. They came in two black cars, women and men. They went straight to the Kommandat's office, arriving while we were at work. We found this out from people who were working inside of the camp.

I entered our barracks and started to clean up when the short guard, Poldek, came in and told me to go to the Kommandat's office. I couldn't imagine what they wanted. It usually meant trouble to be called to the office.

I walked in and all the people from the health commission were there, including Zina. They were polite and offered me a cigarette. There were four women and six men. I was introduced and they started to question me.

A woman, a medical doctor, wanted to know what kind of medical training I had. Zina informed her about my water filters and how it had helped stop the spread of an epidemic and other medical problems I had helped with. She wanted to know where and when I obtained my knowledge. I didn't know what to tell her. My knowledge was limited to courses in first-aid from student paramilitary training at school and at home. I had read many popular medical books as my dream had always been to become a doctor. I read about Pasteur, Semelwiess, and Weigeland. Anything that had to do with medicine I wanted to know. I even neglected certain subjects in school that I didn't think were important to my future study of medicine. I had excelled in subjects such as zoology, chemistry and anatomy. I wanted to help people .

In our daily life in Poland I had seen a lot of sickness — young people dying from tuberculosis, people who couldn't afford a doctor, and people who never saw a doctor. When I read about Louis Pasteur and the others I dreamt about being like one of them.

The doctors I knew in Krakow were not rich. I respected them because they worked hard for small financial rewards. The Jewish doctors helped in the Jewish hospitals without any fees.

They wanted to know who taught me about water filters. Was it my idea? Where did I hear about it? Finally, they told me I did the right thing and promised to help me continue with my future medical studies in the Soviet Union. They asked if I had any suggestions that they could help implement for the settlement. I was afraid to make too many suggestions. I asked if they would ensure our water was properly boiled. I also asked for more bandages and medication. I thanked them and expressed my appreciation for their promise to send me to school in the Soviet Union.

Nothing became of such promises. Later, when I had spent more time in the Soviet Union, I learned to understand the system. I was convinced the medical inspection team was sincere to help me, but the system wouldn't allow it.

Still, I became more respected in the camp and became more adventurous in my medical endeavors in many circumstances during my years in the Soviet Union. With the hundreds of inexperienced lumber jacks and other connected jobs who worked with saws, spikes

103

and axes, imagine how many cuts, sprains and broken bones that need to be treated almost daily? Zina couldn't handle it alone. There were cuts that needed stitches, but she would not even try.

Mrs. Spielman and I did all the stitches, using a regular needle, the smallest we could find. We sterilized and did the best we could. The patients screamed with pain, but they endured. The only result from the inspection was that Zina got more supplies and even some pain killers and a bottle of ether.

All in all, people remained healthy, and in some cases became physically stronger, in their new lifestyle. Our diet consisted mainly of dark bread, cereal, very little fat, which usually only consisted of a little sunflower oil, cabbage and pumpkins. People who had suffered from all kinds of digestive disorders were miraculously cured. The obese lost weight.

There were few rainy days  we hated them because we still had to go to work. Once we arrived at our section of the forest, we tried to burn a little fire to keep dry. When it rained hard, we hid under the trees, powerful pines that were so thick that no matter how hard it rained, their branches kept us completely dry.

The worst problem was coming back to our barrack, there was no place and no way to dry our clothes. We asked the Komandant and Poldek and their answer was always: "Don't worry, pretty soon we will get barracks for you." One day, almost at the entrance of the camp, a few trucks arrived, and dropped off what looked like old timber. We soon realized they partially disassembled old barracks at another location that were reassembled at our camp. Within a few days they had the first barrack constructed. About 30 of us were told to get ready to move in on Sunday.

Our barrack was quite long with little rooms on both sides with a small stove at the entrance. Following a narrow corridor there was another little room with another little stove.

The beds were two-storey bunks. Father and I got one little room. Uncle Marian and his wife got anther. We were lucky to have a small window to ourselves. Our room was very tiny, consisting of the bunk bed and a little wooden bench. There was hardly any room to move around. We brought the rest of our belongings in and  were allowed to get some hay  for our bunks, from the storage next to the horse barn. We slept very soundly that first night in our new room.

A couple of nights later, I felt I was being bitten by something. I couldn't see what it was. I lit the kerosene lamp and to my despair, I saw many bedbugs in my bunk and on my body. It was a constant and losing battle with them.  Bedbugs were supposed to hate kerosene, so we spread some on the walls next to the bunks, but it didn't help. The bed bugs even dropped down on us from the ceiling.

The bedbugs, mosquitoes, fleas, horseflies, lice made our lives miserable. The mosquitoes were by far the worst. The barracks were full of them. We had no screens or nets to protect us. In the evening, when you wanted to walk outside you had to take a tree branch with leaves to fan away the mosquito clouds. Most people became immune to the bites. But some people, especially with a light complexion, suffered terribly. Uncle Marian was one of them. He was a deep sleeper and would wake up in the morning with his face so swollen he could hardly open his eyes. Some people even tried to commit suicide because of the torturous mosquitoes. We had to cut down from a tree one man who attempted to hang himself.

Not until the first frost did we get any relief from them. Bed bugs were fought by covering ourselves in newspaper. And, the lice we kept at bay by keeping clean even though soap was in short supply. Sometimes a month went by without having any. We substituted with sand, lime, soda ash, whatever we could lay our hands on.

In our barrack there was a widow, Mrs. Schwartz, who had two teenagers, a boy and girl. Cyla, the daughter, was about my age. Mrs. Schwartz wasn't required to go to work, because she was considered a widow with two working children. Instead, she took care of the barracks and cooked the little food we were able to scrounge.

Another couple, Dr. Kaminski and his wife lived in our barracks. They were descendants of Polish nobility and didn't mix well with the Jews, although they were very polite. Dr. Kaminski was a psychiatrist, who had trained at the University of Krakow, a distinguished looking man, tall and handsome, with white hair. In the evening, they visited other barracks where other Poles lived. His wife kept her little room very tidy which always had wild flowers in a vase. He never administered medical care in the work camp because he was afraid to get involved. However, we did take his advice on many occasions.

A brother and sister named Poznanski lived in our barrack. They were from the city of Chorzow, Silesia, where they owned a candy factory. Mr. Poznanski became very sick. We were sure he had pneumonia. He had a high, persistent fever of about 41C to 42C. I asked Dr. Kaminski what we should do. He said the only way bring the fever down was to sponge bathe him with cold water around the clock.

We started immediately. Miraculously, the fever broke and he fully recuperated.

# TEN

It was late summer and the forest was full of berries, which added to our daily diet. And after the rains, the forest was full of mushrooms. They grew to the size of children's umbrellas. When I went to pick mushrooms, in a few minutes I would fill my bag so I could hardly carry it back to the camp. We boiled the mushrooms, and when we could get a little fat, we fried them.

Mrs. Schwartz would string them up to dry. We knew it would be hard to get food in the winter so we tried to stock up.

The Club, where we spent our time before moving to the barracks, was now ready for meetings and entertainment. The Matzners, the Austrian couple in our barracks, entertained us occasionally. They had been thrown out of Hitler's Germany in 1938, because they were Jews of Polish origin, though their family had lived in Germany for generations.

The Matzners were performing musicians. Leo was a violinist and Stella was a singer. He was much older than his wife, bald, with white sideburns.. He had a sweet, friendly smile and spoke in the oddest language — a mixture of Yiddish, German, Russian and Polish.

Nearly every day after work, Leo and Stella entertained the people in their barracks and I would always try to see them. He played mostly popular Austrian and Hungarian melodies and Stella would sing quietly. The Komandant soon found out find out about them and he often invited them to play for him and the guards.

The Matzners were delegated to organize a concert in The Club, newly named the Culture Club. There was also a Russian who played a small Russian accordion, called a *garmoszka*.

There wasn't enough room for everyone in the building. People sat on the floor and window sills and some stood outside the open windows, waiting anxiously for the event. The Komandant and his entourage sat in the front row.

The concert was a great success. The Matzners played familiar melodies. A few Russians joined in with their harmonicas and everybody sang together. The Matzners even mixed in some Jewish melodies.. The music lifted everyone's spirits and somehow it made us feel more human. The Matzners became famous in Niuziary and were rewarded with light jobs..

106

Knowing how to play an instrument, especially accordion, harmonica and violin, in Russia, was the best profession. The Russians loved it, appreciated it and rewarded the musicians richly. The second best professions for deportees included, good tailors, shoemakers and barbers.

Our work in the forest provided well for us. Uncle Marian and I achieved our quota of five cubic metres of lumber per person. If the weather was favorable, we often exceeded our norm and got extra pay.

I found out we were about 15 kilometres away from a good-sized Russian village, called Juryna. We were curious about who lived there and what we could buy or trade for food. We asked the Russians and our guards if we could go there. They said it could be possible in the near future, providing we consistently met our lumber quota. The Poles were the first to apply for permission to go to Juryna because they were good lumberjacks and exceeded their norm almost every day.

They left on a Sunday and the rest of us were curious about what they would find there. The following morning, I asked Dr. Kaminski how his friends' journey turned out. He was not normally talkative and didn't share too much information, yet, he told me they had brought back some potatoes. That was good enough for me. Potatoes sounded like a treasure.

Uncle Marian had a friend named Polek Treister. He was a good worker who always exceeded his lumber-cutting quota. I knew Polek well. He was at Niuziary with his sister. We decided Polek and I should apply for permission to go to Juryna for a "shopping" trip. Permission was normally given to pairs, because it was too dangerous to go by yourself.

We were granted permission and began our journey early one Sunday morning, along a narrow, dirt road, which wound through underbrush and forest.

Besides the danger of getting lost, there were also bears and snakes to worry about. But during the summer, food was plentiful in the forest and the bears seldom attacked people. We were told they could if they felt threatened. The Russians informed us that it was no use trying to outrun a bear. Their advice was to lay on the ground and play dead. The bear would only sniff the person and leave. We often saw bears in the distance, but they would just mind their own business. Only on one occasion did I have a rather scary and unexpected encounter with one.

We were sent, about 10 of us, one morning to clear a parcel of land of dry and diseased wood. The job site was about a few kilometres from our camp. We finished the job quite late and were waiting for the foreman to check our work and bring us back to the camp. Meanwhile, we lit a fire and roasted a few potatoes and toasted some bread. I was sitting by the fire roasting a good sized potato, when the foreman showed up. It was getting dark. He quickly looked at our work and was satisfied.

My potato wasn't done yet, so I asked the foreman if I could finish cooking it. He agreed and told me to catch up with the rest of the group shortly. I stayed behind for a few minutes, finished cooking my potato and put out the fire. I ate my potato while trying to catch up with everyone. The narrow track was about a metre wide, cut out recently through a thick underbrush, leading to the dirt road. Suddenly, I heard a noise in the underbrush a few metres in front of me. I was sure someone was lost or had gone to relieve himself. I took a few more steps, then noticed that the noise was getting closer. I looked up only to be face to face with a huge bear, standing on his hind feet, about a foot from me. I froze. I couldn't cry for help. I couldn't move. This confrontation may have lasted seconds, or moments, I don't know. The bear turned his head both ways, crossed the path and disappeared into the trees. I stood for a moment like a pillar of salt. Finally, I started to run and holler. My friends heard me and came back towards me. They knew something had happened but it took a few minutes before I could babble my experience. I have a feeling that the bear was equally frightened of me.

So there were Polek and I with our burlap bags, converted into knapsacks, on our way to Juryna. We took some rubles and few things to barter, a couple of shirts, some handkerchiefs, some kerchiefs and other womens' accessories, including stocking. We also brought combs and a few pencils and pens, and a couple pairs of slippers. We had no idea what we'd be able to trade.

The whole area was full of water and swamps. We were warned to stay close to the road. You could easily drown or be sucked into those swamps, which happened to one of our camp residents. We were able to save him by pulling him out using a rope and some logs. This incident also convinced everyone that escaping from the camp would be next to impossible.

It took us about three hours to get to the outskirts of the village. The weather was warm and sunny and the way through the forest was cool and quiet. The village seemed long, with one dirt road and log homes on both sides. At the entrance, the first home on the left, was the police station, the NKWD post. We stopped there to show our permits. He nodded and let us go with the advice that we should leave a few hours before sundown.

We proceeded toward the homes in the village. It was strangely quiet, with nobody on the road, except for a few children playing outside.They were barefoot, wearing dirty shirts and pants and had protruding bellies.

We started to knock on doors asking for food to sell or trade. Those people were very poor. Their diet consisted mostly of bread and potatoes and probably what the forest yielded. In most of the homes, there were only women. The men had likely been sent away to work. I was sure these people had not come to this area voluntarily. No one would want to live in this depressed area.

The residents didn't talk much and we didn't ask them for anything but food. We were able to get some potatoes, a little bread and a bottle of milk. Some of the households had a couple of goats or a cow. We spent a few rubles and traded a few trinket.

Although quiet, the village people seemed friendly and maybe felt sorry for us, even though they didn't have much themselves. As we sat outside eating, a woman came out and gave me a piece of baked squash. I had never eaten this before. It was a sweet treat. I vowed the next time I came back I would buy one.

We began our walk home, loaded with 16 kg each. Our homemade backpacks weren't very helpful after all. The strings cut into our flesh and made us lift the bottom of the sack to make it easier on our shoulders. We had to stop often for a rest. For our next trip we planned to cover the ropes with some material.

We returned exhausted to the camp after dark, pleased with our mission. We were to repeat these trips several times during our stay at the camp. But the more people that got permission to go, the harder it was to trade. The village people became wise and the prices skyrocketed.

I became friendly with a young woman in the village who had two children. I never saw her husband and when I asked about him she told me he was working somewhere far away.

On one of our trips we had a terrifying experience. I don't remember why, but we arrived in Juryna a little later than usual. Trading had become difficult and we were delayed on our return trip. It started to rain and we realized we weren't going to make it back before dark. About three-quarters of the way to the camp, we decid-

109

ed to take a shortcut through the forest. We thought we'd save lots of time. We knew the general direction. How wrong we were. It became a nightmare and an experience I'll never forget.

When we entered the forest it started to rain heavily, and darkness surrounded us. The ground was full of water and we realized we were in a swampy area. We tried to backtrack to the road, but by doing so we lost our way in the forest amid all kinds of frightening noises.

We saw lights, but they were only fireflies. Dry trees rubbing on each other made eerie sounds. Every little breeze filled the forest with new noises. We thought of bears, wolves, all kinds of animals lurking among the trees. We tried to talk to each other, we hollered and made other noises to keep the creatures at bay. The echos of our voices frightened us even more.

It took about six hours to go a short distance. We were about to give up and wait till morning, but we noticed some lights in the distance. First, we made sure it wasn't our imagination. It might be bugs. We kept going in this direction and little by little the lights got closer.

We finally made it to the camp, and everyone was awake, looking for us. That's why we noticed the lights. We learned a lesson — never take shortcuts again through the forest.

***

I kept very close relations with the widow in our barracks, Mrs. Schwartz, and her two children, a daughter Cyla and a son Henry. They were from a small city in Poland. Henry was a couple of years younger than me and Cyla was about my age, the only female teenager in the camp. I became friendly with her. Since my sickness in Lvov and the deportation, I had only dated one girl, Lola.

During the long deportation, especially the weeks on the trains, I dreamt and daydreamed about girls. But I hadn't met anyone compatible and besides there was no privacy on the train. In Niuziary, life was a little more normal. My short crush on Zina, our nurse, was rudely interrupted, besides we both understood it was impossible.

Cyla was a pleasant looking and shy girl, with dark hair and a nice figure.

Because there were three people in the Schwartz family, their cubicle was a little bigger than ours. There was even enough room for a few primitive chairs and a little table. Their room was at the

110

back of our barrack, near the second cast iron stove. In the winter, their room was warmer and Mrs. Schwartz would make soups from whatever she could scrounge. While everyone was at work she would boil potatoes for us, make some soup or fry mushrooms.

In the evenings, I usually stayed in their room, playing cards and dominoes with Henry. We always talked about our homes that were so far and the frustration with the lack of news. When I did get some newspapers, I would read them slowly, trying to find some news. Hitler was still going strong and it didn't help our morale. I hated the Russian newspapers, Pravda and Investia. They glorified the leaders of the USSR, especially Stalin. and their achievements in every field. People who worked above their norms became labor heroes and received medals for exceeding quotas.

The long, hard work hours and trying to find food kept us busy. Yet, I found time in the evenings to spend with Cyla. We stayed up alone, long after everybody went to sleep, trying to take short walks, but the mosquitoes usually prevented it, unless it was a windy night. Most of the time we spent siting on a bench outside the barrack talking, kissing and fondling each other. But our privacy was often interrupted by someone going to the outhouse. The only time we had some privacy was on Sundays when we could leave the camp for a walk in the woods.

If I had been living in Krakow, Cyla would not have been my choice for a girlfriend. I preferred popular girls, who were blonde with light complexions. We became friends, trying to help each other with our loneliness.. We tried to cheer each other up and forget our grim reality.

Father and Uncle Marian were concerned about my relationship with Cyla. They didn't have anything against her, but felt we were becoming too serious, especially at such a time.Uncle Marian lectured me on day about it, and I took his advice to heart.

A group of orthodox Jews , who had been deported as a group, lived close to our barrack. They prayed secretly in the morning and evening and always on Fridays and Saturday nights.They did not want to offend or get in trouble with the authorities. I got to know some of them and admired their commitment to Judaism under our circumstances.They worked on Saturdays, the Sabbath like everyone else. They didn't complain. They believed this was what God intended and with God's help things would get better. It was uplifting to talk to them. and sometimes on Friday nights, I would sneak into their barrack and pray with them. They had only a few prayer books so I said my prayers as best I could from memory. I stayed with them after prayers were finished and they would ask me what I had read in the newspapers.

Autumn was approaching and the days were getting cooler. The birch and maple leaves turned beautiful colors. Evenings were quite cold and only a few mosquitoes were in the air. The berries were gone and soon winter would be here. This worried us .

I went to pray with the Hasidim one Friday night and found out that in two weeks  it was going to be Rosh Hashanah, the Jewish New Year.

I returned to my barrack and told everybody about the approaching holiday. Little by little, word spread throughout the camp. We didn't know what to do. It was still unthinkable to go to work on Rosh Hashanah and Yom Kippur. At home in Poland, people who never attended synagogue would come to pray on those holidays.

What could we do about the holiday in a work camp in  Russia. We were afraid to ask or express our opinions.

As the holiday approached, we became more uneasy. We started to talk about it among ourselves.

When the eve of Rosh Hashanah arrived you could feel something unusual was going to happen. The barrack of the Hassidim was full. People asked them  for advice, butt they gave none. We  knew they would not go to work on those days.

On the morning of  Rosh Hashanah, we went, as usual, for our early morning breakfast and  returned to the barracks. Something unbelievable happened. Without any organizing or talking about it, nobody moved to go to work. People who had prayer books,  or siddurs gathered around one book to pray. The same scene occurred in every barrack except the one inhabited by the Poles. They all got up and went to work as. did Dr. Kaminski from our barrack.

To this day I have never forgotten the courage and devotion to Jewishness by our people. Not only the Orthodox, but everybody whether they were observant or not. They believed this was the new year and we were entitled to a day off.

Poldek and the other guards and some Russians and leaders of the work brigades, came running from barrack to barrack to see what was happening. Everywhere they got the same answer — today is our new year and our holiday and our God doesn't allow us to work.

They didn't understand our actions. This was, for them, beyond belief.  They shouted and threatened us with dire consequences. To them, this was rebellion and in the Soviet Union it was probably punishable by death.

The work camp leaders were deportees themselves and probably deep down in their hearts they admired our courage. Although, to them, religion was far too risky to rebel about. They probably wondered what we hoped to accomplish by our actions?

About 10 o'clock, Poldek came running back to our barrack. . He ordered me to follow him to the commandant's office, who wanted to see me. I could see the worried looks on the faces of Father and Uncle Marian and most of my friends. I was frightened, too. I followed Poldek .

When we got to the commandant's office, I was relieved I wasn't the only one there. About 10 men and a few teenagers were waiting outside the commandant's office. The door opened and we were all invited in. The commandant's name was Ivanov, who was in his late 30s, tall and good looking, with a pleasant smile. We were offered a real cigarette and invited to sit down and he began his speech.

He started mildly, saying it had come to his attention we refused to go to work because of some religious holiday. He tried to appeal to the young people in the group by suggesting we young people had been influenced by our elders. There is no religion in the Soviet Union, he said, and beside everyone celebrates the new year January 1.

No one in the group said a word. He realized his speech didn't have much impact on us so he then tried to bribe us. He then promised us we would get the best jobs in the camp, maybe even a foreman's position, if we returned to work.

He waited for our answer but nobody spoke. He then asked us individually. All our answers were about the same. We said we had celebrated this holiday all our lives as did our parents grandparents. I told him we didn't mean to be disobedient and that we would work longer and harder to make up the two days we were going to take off work.

He became angry and threatened to punish us. He called us enemies of the Soviet Union and told us we'd be sorry for our actions. He said we were being treated well and that we were ungrateful.

The meeting ended with us pleading that he respect and understand our behavior.

Everyone was relieved to see me return to our barrack and I told them what had happened at the meeting. We hoped somehow we would not suffer any consequences.

Things returned to normal after Rosh Hashanah and we worked very hard to make up our quota. It looked like we might have gotten away with it, but next we'd have to face Yom Kippur, the Day of Atonement and fasting.

***

I began working temporarily with a bigger brigade of men. There were about 10 of us. We were assigned to a large parcel of forest that they wanted cleared in a hurry. It was a little further away from Niuziary. There were many dried and diseased trees, almost as if the forest had been attacked by some infection. Our foreman was a Tartar, named Iskakov Mizbah.

Ishkakov was strict and demanding. He had oriental features but he was rather fierce looking and serious. His eyes sparkled like fire and he never smiled.

The day before Yom Kippur, we went to work as usual, planning to pray the holy prayers of Kol Nidre when we got back. The next day we planned to take a chance and disobey the authorities. But we came home to some unexpected news. The camp was teeming with NKWD soldiers who wanted to make sure we wouldn't repeat the Rosh Hashanah incident.

We prayed Kol Nidre in our barracks. I didn't go to the Orthodox barracks, because I was worried about putting them in danger of influencing our behavior.

At the entrance of every barrack, we were greeted by half a dozen NKWD soldiers.. Everyone got ready and went to work. We had no intention of being heroes.

Our group left with Ishkakov to the forest, carrying our tools. It was a long walk and everybody was quiet. Most of us hadn't eaten or drank anything since the night before. When we arrived at our work area, we sat down, as usual for a little rest and a smoke before starting our work. This was standard procedure.

Only Iskakov rolled his *majorka* in the newspaper and lit up. He seemed to be acting a little strangely. Suddenly, he got up and started to talk. I remember the few short sentences of his speech.

"I know that today is your very important holiday. I know you are not allowed to eat or drink or smoke. I respect this. Go deeper in the forest and say your prayers and rest. If I need you, I'll call you."

He then turned to me, calling me by my name.

"Sasha, he said, "You are the youngest and you will stay with me. We have to work very, very hard to cover for all the others. God will forgive you for this."

114

He finished his cigarette, took his jacket off and we started to work. Ishkakov was a man who worked like a demon. He cut so fast that the axe in his hand was a blur. He made me work as I never worked before. I prayed to God that he should give me strength to keep up with him. I didn't want to break my fast. Since I was 13, after my Bar Mitzvah, I had never missed a fast on Yom Kippur.

We finally took a break. I laid down and realized I had no more strength left to work with Ishkakov. He realized it too. When we got up he told me we would take it easy now. Then he did an extraordinary thing, which I can only call cheating. When it was nearly time to finish our work for the day, a Russian foreman would always come to measure the amount of timber we had cut. He would stamp every log we cut. He measured the logs and entered the cubic metres in his log book. This was how they kept track of how much we produced.

I got up on my wobbly legs. I hadn't eaten or drank anything all day. Ishkakov took some dry wood and branches and started a small fire. He took a saw and called me to help. I understood very well what we did that afternoon. He picked up some logs and we cut off slices from previously cut logs and stamped before. He knew exactly which logs to cut to be least recognizable. We threw the slices we cut up in small pieces and threw them in the fire.

Late in the afternoon, he called everybody back from the forest. Strangely, the man who stamped the logs didn't show up. Maybe Ishkakov had made a deal with the foreman.

We extinguished the fire and began to walk back to the camp. Everyone thanked Ishkakov for his kindness, and all he said was: "We worked and we did our share and this is between us, your God and me."

The following day Ishkakov became his usual self, the strict demanding disciplinarian. No one knew what his beliefs and religion were. I suspected he was a Muslim, but I didn't dare ask him. A couple of months later, I had the chance to find out a little more about our mysterious leader.

One morning he asked me to accompay him outside of the camp to work. He didn't give me any details and only told me to wait in front of my barracks, the next morning. I waited for him, for several hours until he finally appeared. He explained we were to go with a truck to pick up some supplies for the camp, but the truck hadn't shown up.It was already late in the afternoon when the truck finally arrived.Two hours later, in the darkness we pulled up to a warehouse in the middle of a large village.

The warehouse was closed and we would have to wait until it opened the next morning. It was Friday and I wondered where we would spend the night. The driver went down a street and stopped to drop us off in front of a house. Ishkakov knocked on the door and was welcomed in an unusual foreign language. We entered a vestibule and I was asked to take my shoes off. We entered a large room, lit by a couple of kerosene lamps and an unusual sight greeted me.

In the centre of the room was a large table full of all kinds of strange foods and a big samovar. At the head of the table, sat an older man with a long beard. Next to him, sat an older woman, a middle-aged man, other women and a few youngsters. All of men wore a type of brightly colored head-covering, similar the type I had seen in oriental pictures at home. The woman wore white scarves on their heads. They greeted Ishkakov warmly.

We were invited to the table for the feast. The food was strange, and included meat, which I hadn't had for a long time, some sweet white bread with tea. Their conversation was in a strange language, which I assumed was Tartar.

We ate and after dinner, the host brought a couple of straw mattresses on which we went to sleep immediately. I couldn't figure out if this was Ishkakov's family or just some friends.

Early the next morning, our hung-over driver showed up and took us to the warehouse, where we loaded our supplies in a hurry. When I returned to Niuziary, Father and Uncle Marian were worried about what had happened to us and were relieved to see me return safely.

## ELEVEN

Niuziary was located in Maryjska, USSR and the inhabitants of this region were called Maryjcy. I hadn't seen many of them around. They live in temporary barracks, similar to ours. They were of some Asian origin, with slanted eyes, wide cheekbones and darker, yellow skin. They spoke their own language. The capital of their republic was Yoskarola. I found out later that we were about 200 km from their capital. While we were living isolated in our camp, I didn't know anything about them.

We learned in a few months that the Niuziary camp was called a special settlement and we were dubbed special deportees. The words we heard from our commandant in his speech to us the first day were ominous to us.. We were going to live here, work here and die here. There were millions of people deported from their homes, cities and republics, mostly to Siberia and other north and eastern republics. They lived their lives without permission to leave or travel to their original homes.. Sometimes, whole generations were born in exile. Our situation seemed hopeless.. When the war ended, we discovered we had it easy compared to other people who had been sent to much more harsh camps.

Single people sent to the brutal Gulag camps, some located further north, in the Arctic circle or in far eastern Siberia were forced to live with criminals and political prisoners. Compared to them, we lived in a country club. If Father and I had not voluntarily decided to join Uncle Marian, we would have surely been sent to the Gulags. This is when I truly began to believe in fate. Although the food supply wasn't adequate at least we were not physically abused. To a certain extent it was bearable. There was no fences or watchtowers hovering over us, but everyone was wise enough not to attempt escape. And the Russians knew this.

Meanwhile, the weather was changing and fall was upon us. The skies were cloudy most days. It was rainy and the temperatures were falling slowly. The birches and the other trees were losing their leaves. The forest was damp and seemed sad and unfriendly. We returned from work soaking wet and chilled. We tried to dry our clothing by the two wood stoves in our barrack. The smell of drying clothes and our bark sandals and foot wraps was overpowering.

One day, by chance I stumbled upon a small treasure. I was walking around our eating room and noticed some yellowish paper in the garbage. I took a closer look at what appeared to be a type of wax paper, enforced with threads throughout. I was struck by an idea. I took all those papers, even the small pieces, folded them neatly and took them to the barrack.

The next morning, it was raining again. I put the rags around my feet and in between I put a sheet of the paper I had found. I also put pieces under my jacket, over my shirt and around my shoulders. A small miracle occurred. I returned from work with dry feet. My shirt and shoulders were dry also. I shared my paper with Uncle Marian and it proved to be a great innovation.

It was getting colder and washing in the lake was getting impossible. The air was frigid and the clouds were dark and threatening. We knew and felt that the winter would soon be upon us. Everybody feared the oncoming winter. Nobody knew how hard or how cold the winter could be here.

My Russian was improving, especially my reading. I would get a few used Russian newspapers once in awhile, with short articles buried in the paper about the state of the war. The news was getting worse, with a string of German victories in Europe. Where was the mighty USA, England and the rest of the world?

Sometimes I would get bitter asking these questions. We all hoped Germany would be defeated, the war would end and we'd be free and eventually be reunited with our families. Sometimes hope has no logic and certainly with our knowledge about the war it was a dream, a Utopia.

My social life, like anybody else's was limited. Anyway there was not much time for it. I spent the evenings with Cyla when possible, but I was always careful and listened to the advice of Uncle Marian, not to get involved too seriously. But the Russians had told us we were staying here forever. To my knowledge there were no marriages or pregnancies at the camp.

The days were getting shorter and we were returning from work a little earlier. Once a month on Sundays, the Matzners organized a concert. Sometimes, we listened to the Russians playing their accordions. I enjoyed their lively melodies, which invited your feet to dance. Their music seemed to be two extremes, sad melodies or happy ones. It all depended on the mood of the player.

I learned to love their music.

It was now late October. In the evening, a cold wind blew from the north. When we woke up in the morning the whole world was white. The wind subsided and the snowflakes were falling majestically to the ground. The snow was dry. It wasn't like at home, rain mixed with snow, and then wet snow. Here, the first snow that fell stayed on the ground until spring.

We were issued some old quilted jackets and pants and old fur hat, but no shoes. They claimed the bark shoes we wore were warmer and better than anything in the cold weather. They gave us a few pieces of cloth to better cover our feet.

At the beginning of November, winter was in full swing, a winter we only heard of in books at home. The temperatures started to drop from the beginning to - 20 C and later to - 40C and lower. We were obliged to work up to - 40C. We were getting up in the dark and returning in the dark.The worst part was the march to our job site. The snow was deep and the wind was bitter in the open spaces. We tried to cover our faces to avoid frostbite.

When you urinated outside, it turned almost immediately to ice. When you had to move your bowels and take off your pants it was a disaster. We tried to hold on. The only consolation was the mosquitoes were gone. The rest of our lot in winter was much harder, physically and mentally. The woods were a relief. It was still and peaceful, and we were able to warm ourselves and cook our meals once we lit the fires. We also had to quit much earlier to be able to return to camp before darkness and had to fill our quota in a shorter time.

Our barracks were always cold, despite the ovens going all the time. The windows were frozen and the outside walls were covered by frost.We slept in all the clothes we had, and were still freezing. We were only able to keep clean with a great amount of determination. I was lucky Mrs. Schwartz who stayed in the barracks all day, helped me keep my things dry and clean.

Once in a while we were allowed to go to the steam bath. It was only a small one, and for about 400 people it took a long time to get your turn. It felt wonderful to get undressed and wash your whole body.

By December the winter started in all its fury. The snow fell day and night. Our barracks were covered by snow, half way up our doors. Sometimes the wind would blow away the snow from one side and pile it up metres high on the other. It was so fine and dry, just like powder. It was almost impossible to get to work. The roads were impassable.

The Russians had their special way of dealing with this problem. They had plenty of experience.When the snow was so high that everything became paralyzed, we became the snow ploughs of Niuziary and the area.

The job was called *toptat*. To translate, this meant to press the snow with our feet. We were told to get dressed warmly and be ready to get to work. When the Russian foreman showed up, we were ordered to get in rows, about 15 in one row and 15 behind us. Lined up this way, we were told to put our hands in each other's underarm, to be as close to each other as possible. And we started to march in a chosen direction. The snow was very high, and light as a feather. We were marching in two rows, one in front of the other, pressing down the snow and creating a passable road. We changed from first row to second row, every half hour, because the front line had a harder job than the one behind. This road-cleaning was done for several days, by the whole population of the camp. After a few days, the roads were open and we returned back to our wood-cutting.

Men working in the horse brigades started to take the logs from the forest. It showed that people could do anything. As long as you had such cheap labor, who needed snow ploughs?

One extremely cold and snowy day, we heard the noise of a tractor approaching the camp, and saw a powerful tractor pulling a huge wooden cistern filled with water on a kind of sled. As the sled was moving, being pulled by the tractor, a groove about 10 cm wide was created on the road. The water from the cistern was pouring steadily into the groove. The water froze almost immediately, creating a perfect frozen track.

The tractor came to the outskirts of the camp, turned around and stopped for a rest. Our task now was to fill up the cistern with water. A hole was prepared in the lake and we filled drums with water, using wooden pails. As the drums were filled with water, they were transported on a sled and emptied into the cistern. Everything was done by hand, no pumps or any other equipment. When the cistern was full, the tractor turned around and went to another village on the shores of the Vietluga River. In the next couple of days we understood the fantastic means of transportation, I am sure the most unique in the world.

The logs from the forest were brought in by the horse brigade, very close to the tracks created by the tractor. The next day, the tractor approached the village, pulling large sleds with wooden platforms and stacks on both sides. They looked like railroad cars on sleds, moving in the ice grooves created. It was an ingenious transportation system for bringing the lumber towards the river.

120

It seemed to us the job priority during the winter was to deliver the lumber to the point from which in spring it would be transported out of our region. When the tractor came, we were called to load the lumber on those sleds, as high as the stacks allowed. It had to be done neatly and the weight evenly distributed. It was a hard and dangerous job.

When all the sleds were filled, the tractor was hooked up and to our amazement the whole train moved effortlessly forward. The ice in the groove was hard as a rock.

Winter was getting harder and harder to take. The food supply was not adequate for a long winter and some people started to show signs of scurvy. Their teeth started to wobble and they got boils and sores. Zina tried to do her best to help them. She snuck some garlic and onions from the kitchen, thought to be a treatment. They were a little frostbitten but she distributed them to those people suffering. Most of the people who followed this aromatic diet improved in no time. Zina did the best she could to treat the ailments in the camp. She was compassionate and did the best she could with what little supplies she had. Many people got colds and fevers, but with aspirin and few days' rest, they recuperated. To my surprise, there were no fatalities.

On New year's Eve 1941, we got a day off, a little better food and a concert with the Matzners. There were even a few bottles of vodka, and if you wanted to gulp from the bottle you were welcome. The guards, the commandant and the Russians drank a lot and were in a great mood. The next day, the place was dead. Everybody slept late.

I was 18 years old, and no matter how hard I worked and how hard life was in Niuziary, I felt the biological urge for some female companionship. There were no girls my age at the camp, except Cyla and Zina. I couldn't have anything to do with Zina because Poldek, the NKWD guard, was crazy about her. There were some older women I felt I could have gotten involved with, but I didn't think it was the right thing to do.

The most convenient relationship was with Cyla but under the close scrutiny of her family and my Uncle Marian, we only sat around the stove until late at night, kissing and necking.

When I finally fell asleep in my cubicle, I dreamed of summer, swimming and washing daily in the lake, of the berries in the forest and of going to Juryna to buy some food. I dreamed about not being cold and dressed lightly, being in the fresh air. When I was hungry I always dreamt about food, the great food that my mother prepared.

I dreamt about my mother, my sister, friends and family. I longed so much for my mother and the uncertainty of our situation, made my longing worse.

As winter passed slowly, the days grew longer and the temperature warmed up a bit. On sunny days you could feel the warmth of the sun rays ever so slightly. During the winter, the color of the setting sun was deep red and the more deep it was the colder the night would be. Now, the sun seemed more friendly and the redness of the sunset disappeared.

In early April, it got much warmer, the winds changed and they came now from the south. First came a wet snow, but soon it turned to rain. Our ice railroad was gone and roads became impassable because of the water.

We had at that time a very bad medical emergency. Mr. Green, a man in his 40s, an engineer from Silesia, apparently sustained a small cut to his leg. We weren't sure what to do about it. His leg swelled in one spot, like a boil, and he began to run a fever. He was nearly unconscious most of the time. We looked at his leg, and it seemed to be full of pus. Mrs. Spielman said we should drain the leg, but how to do it? I decided to ask Dr. Kaminski, but as usual he didn't want to get involved in anything connected with health care, though as usual, he agreed to give me verbal advice. We decided we had to lance the leg. We got hold of a straight razor, which we sterilized by boiling it. We tied the patient down, and tried to put his to sleep with a makeshift rag soaked in ether; I don't know if it worked or not. We were both very nervous, but the lancing only took a few seconds. His temperature went down immediately and he began to recuperate. It was a great success.

Complete isolation set in as the camp became an island surrounded by water. We couldn't get to our jobs in the forest, but soon there was lots of emergency work to be done. The water was creeping up to the barracks, especially the kitchen and buildings sitting in lower areas. We had to build an earth wall around them, to prevent them from flooding. It was hard work because the ground was still frozen. We had to dig draining ditches and break the ice in the lake. Our feet were always wet. We caught bad colds and sore throats. Even in the kitchen, the food was disappearing. The soups were thin and cereal portions became smaller.

Late in April, the roads dried enough for the trucks to bring more supplies. The tobacco shortage was over and the newspapers came in bundles but they were one or two months old. Now, we had enough paper to roll our cigarettes and sometimes, we enjoyed the luxury of toilet paper. The backlog of the papers came in handy, but the news about the war didn't improve.

We received a couple of letters and some food packages from the Schicklers in Lvov. Some food had spoiled because it took two months or more to get it to us. It had defrosted several times. but whatever we could salvage, especially, some fat, came in handy. The letters we got were short and only spoke in generalities. They were afraid of censorship.

***

One day, Ishkakov announced we were going to a job outside the camp. We were to be away for three days. The next day a truck came and picked us up. There was 12 of us to work in one brigade. It was a long ride through thick forested territory over very bumpy, narrow roads.

It was quite a long ride before we came out of the forest to a huge clearing. And the sight we saw was quite unexpected. In front of us, stood on a rail track, a train consisting of platform cars, with stakes on the sides. The clearing was full of stacked lumber. The difference was that whole, uncut trees were being prepared for loading. Our job was to load those trees onto the cars. We loaded lumber in the camp on the sleds in the winter and on trucks in the summer, but never whole trees. It was difficult and very intricate work. They were much heavier and the bottom part of the tree was awkward to move.We had to keep switching men to keep them on the same level.And we had to pile them quite high. The natives were way ahead of us in quota. They had probably done this for years. It was after lunch before we had loaded the first car, when from the far end of the train I noticed a group of men walking from one car to another. When they came closer, it became obvious from the way they were dressed that they were a bunch of big shots. We call them *nachalniks*. They came to our car and watched us work. We were about to roll a heavy, large tree on top of the pile but we decided to change the log for a thicker one, so it wouldn't break.

One of the big shots yelled to me not to change it. According to him, this log was sufficient. So, we started to roll it on. Sure enough when the tree was almost on the car, it broke in two pieces like a match. The tree fell off and luckily, everyone jumped to the side and nobody was hurt.

123

I became very angry and I swore in Russian, using Hitler as the object of discontent. It was the most popular Russian swearing. It sounded like "Fuck Hitler's mother."

The *nachalnik* became angry and called Iskakov over to ask who I was. Then, he walked over to me and said: "In our country, we don't swear and don't say dirty words about the head of the government that we are having friendly relations with. In this case Chancellor Hitler. I warn you, these people go to jail."

They didn't send me to jail because I think they realized that I was already in one.

We stayed in this outpost for four days, until all the lumber was loaded on the railroad cars and shipped away. The worse part here were the nights in the barracks. The smell was overwhelming. It was damp, wet and cold. We never took our clothes off. Everybody, including the Maryjcy slept in their clothes. This didn't prevent them from their nocturnal activities. They were noisy all night, talking, whispering and they didn't hide their sexual activities from anybody.

When the time came for the trucks to pick us up, we were happy to go back to our camp. It was something like going home to see family and friends. Iskakov promised we would get to go to the steam bath, as soon as we got home and he came through on his promise.

The roads dried up and days became much longer and we were back to our normal routine. Most of the timber was shipped out and it was time to cut more. It was easier to live and keep clean and go the lake to wash. The forest became greener. The leaves sprouted on the birches. The forest was coming alive. The ground was full of green moss and we discovered a new kind of nutrition. One of the Russians showed us how to cut into a birch tree with an axe. Right beneath the bark was a sap that poured out profusely. We put our mouth at the bottom and sucked the flowing sweetness.

The flow only lasted a few weeks but than the berries and mushrooms were abundant.

I received my permit to go to Juryna a few times, but there was only a little food to be bought. Only in the fall could we expect better trading when they harvested the small plots behind their homes.

Every couple of months some kind of commission, sometimes in NKWD uniforms, sometimes in civilian clothes. would arrive to Niuziary. They would ask us occasionally if we had any complaints. But if we were to ask them how long we were to stay here, or have any complaints about food and clothing they would smile and say "Everything will be alright." They looked over the camp, in the company of the commandant, and later locked themselves up in his office for food and drink.

The commandant knew when they were going to arrive and usually before their arrival, the food was better and the commissary had extra tobacco. They knew what they are doing, having lots of experience since the revolution. One thing I have to say, they listened politely to what we said and never showed us any contempt or hostility. We were the cheapest labor force in the world and as long as we didn't give them any problem, everything was fine.

What would await us — our families, friends and the life we left behind. We hated to think about it all the time. but this was the topic of conversation with everyone.

May was a beautiful month. The temperatures were comfortable. On Sundays, I started to take the boat out on the lake. The sun was shining, the day was warm, and I paddled to the tiny island in the middle of the lake. I would browse around and take a walk.It was my sanctuary, my retreat from reality. I would sit down on a rock and enjoy the warmth of the sun. I daydreamed of my happy youth at home and I dreamed about the future.

It was so good to be able to wash now every day in the lake. Working during the warm weather was also easier, especially the walk to and from work. Besides this the mosquitoes weren't bothering us yet. At work, when you got tired you could sit down, roll a smoke of mahorka. Ishkakov and the others trusted us to do the job and left us mostly alone a whole day. They would come before we finished and measured the amount we cut that day. This allowed us to work at the pace we chose. When we felt like laying down for a while we did without any permission. When we felt like smoking we did also. It made us more relaxed and comfortable. Sometimes we worked hard in the morning and in the afternoon we took it a little easier.

Occasionally, I would look up at the tall, beautiful trees that we were about to cut down and think about myself. In no time, without warning it is going to fall down with a great thump. How many years did it take to grow so tall? I would think about the few minutes it took me and Father to make a decision on my 17th birthday, Sept. 1939. On the road running away from Krakow, we separated from Mother and Niusia. Is this going to be forever?

We took advantage to stay outside as long as possible. We knew that soon the mosquitoes will take over and we'll have to hide inside. When I was not too tired, I would take a stroll with Cyla around the lake. There was not too much to talk about, unless to reminisce about days gone by. It was easier for her to bear because she was with her mother and brother. Of course, they had left many others behind. I worried and longed so much for Mother and Niusia.

The Red Army was pictured in the newspapers as an invincible guardian of the borders and ensuring the safety and freedom of the citizens of the Soviet Union. The tanks and airplane factories were producing improved tanks and airplanes. I knew that it was mostly propaganda, but sometimes we thought some of it must be partially true.

I had collected all the bits of foreign news and I realized all of Europe, except England, was in Hitler's hands. When I read that France had fallen and Hitler had visited Paris, my hopes took a real dive. Who was going to stop the Germans? Who was going to defeat them — only the USA and England could save us. I doubted if they could defeat Germany. I realized that with every country they conquered they took more arms, more booty, more military supplies and people to work cheaply for the super nation. yet, sometimes I hoped something would happen.

So, I tried not to lose hope. I think without this, life there would have been unbearable. Logic doesn't always reign. We heard about the atrocities committed by the Germans, while we were in Lvov. But there was absolutely no mention of anything in the Soviet newspapers. There was never a word about Jews being badly treated by the Germans. It seemed the Russians didn't want to express anything against the Germans. Somehow we thought the Russians were afraid of the Germans.

They were such enemies before the war, it was hard to believe they were truly friends.

One day we were told to come to the warehouse because new clothing had arrived. It was a big surprise. We were issued brand new quilted pants, jackets and warm hats . It was almost funny. In the winter when we needed them so badly, we didn't get anything. Now, we were being outfitted for the winter that had just finished. In a way, it was an assurance we would still be here next winter but at least we would be better protected from the bitter cold.

The weather was getting warmer by the day. Everything turned green. The birch trees were covered with leaves and the bushes sprouted. Here and there, little white flowers bloomed.The birds returned to the forest and all signs showed summer was coming soon. Soon we would have berries of all kinds.

Sam, mother and sister Niusia, 1926

Rose and Leon Honig, parents of Sam

Author with parents
Krakow, 1928

Sam with Uncle Henry
Cieszyn, 1933

Sam Honig and family

Sam's Bar-Mitzvah 1935

Sam, 1935

Family with Uncle Jerry – Krakow, 1933

Author's mother – 1937

Sam in paramilitary, 1938

Sam, 1938

Last picture of mother and sister, smuggled to Lwov, in 1940. Notice the arm bands with the Star of David.

Father and author, Chorzow 1946

Sam before his departure to Canada, Prague, Czechoslovakia, 1947

# TWELVE

On June 22, 1941, we ate in our lunch room with some people working inside the camp. Something odd was going on. The commandant, Poldek, another guard, Zina and a couple Russians were in the office all day. Not once had they left. Something was different, something was in the air. We had no clue what was happening.

The following morning we went to work as usual. We cut our norm, had our lunch, drank our *kipiatok* and sat a little longer. There was nobody to oversee us. Iskakov didn't show up and we didn't see any other Russians. We tried to do most of our work in the morning. In the afternoon we took it easy. Sometimes I would wander around the forest and go closer to the other part where another brigade was cutting trees. There, we had a smoke and chatted a little. On this day, for some reason the man who stamped the logs didn't show up. It was getting late and we didn't see anybody, so we picked up our tools and started on our way back to the camp. We met some more people on the way from the forest, but no Russians. Everybody asked if we had seen Iskakov or the others, but nobody had seen a soul. It had never happened before.

The minute we got to the barracks, I  found out something unusual was going to happen. A meeting of everyone in the camp was called for 8 p.m. in The Club. All kinds of rumors  spread about us being transferred, about a change in commandants, even about freedom.

By 7 p.m. The Club was full. There was no room for everyone and people were standing outside near the entrance and around the open windows. Promptly, at 8 p.m. the commandant appeared with his small entourage and marched straight to the podium Without any delay he started his speech. Everybody was spellbound, expecting  some big news. The air was full of electricity. Everybody was stunned. In the first sentence he broke the unexpected and dreaded news. On June 22, the Germans callously and without warning attacked the Soviet Union. They crossed the border and bombed several cities, including Kiev. The war for Mother Russia was on. Most of the people didn't quite understand or hear what he said.

The speech was interrupted. People started to talk to each other and asked all kinds of questions. The commandant summoned Mr. Garber to the podium to explain to everyone what he had said. After he translated, the reaction was mixed. Some started to cry, some saw this as a good sign. Everybody got quiet again. The speaker now started to talk again about how the mighty Soviet Union would crush the enemy. As for us, nothing was going to change. We were expected to work even harder and help in the war effort.

The speech was short. No questions were allowed. Probably, the commandant didn't know much more than he had told us. Slowly, we drifted into small groups to the barracks. People huddled together to talk about the new war. We stayed up very late, Father, Uncle Marian, Treister and I, trying to assess the consequences the war would have on us. I wasn't very optimistic. I could remember the recent Russian-Finnish war and how long it took the powerful Russian Army to subdue this little country. I couldn't understand why they were attacking Russia. Apparently, Hitler wanted to conquer the world. There was nobody to stand in his way, only the Soviet Union. This was going to be the make or break situation. I knew well, that if he succeeded there would be no room for Jewish people in this world. Now we prayed for our captors and our jailers.

We wondered what was going to happen now to our friends, the Shicklers and the others who helped us with parcels and kept our spirits up with their letters. How was this going to affect my mother and sister and the rest of the family we left behind? Thousands of unanswered questions filled our heads.

God help the Russians. On this we all agreed. That was our only chance. I was sure Dr. Kaminski and the few other Poles in our camp thought differently. We Jews had to think of ourselves. Maybe now the USA and England would join the war seriously and help Russia defeat the common enemy and free us and the whole world from our oppressors. I felt more and more like praying and pray I did, whatever prayers I remembered, or others I invented.

We went to work the next day very tired. We had gone to bed late. When we arrived at our workplace I could barely get our job done. My thoughts were on anything but the job, and. I almost got crushed by a falling tree.It was close, but though I was badly scraped and cut, I was lucky and didn't break anything.

It took about 10 days before we got the first papers announcing the outbreak of the war. There were huge headlines, but only a few details. All the papers accused Hitler for his breach of the agreement and the treaty and his callousness and treachery. They praised our great Red Army and promised to chase the enemy out of Mother Russia. The papers carried a great picture of Stalin at his speech, calling the war undeclared, a sneaky attack, breaking all the signed treaties without warning.

They mentioned air attacks on several Ukrainian cities but nothing about damage or casualties. As the newspapers arrived, at best weekly, there was nothing but to wait for the next batch. We'd only be 10 days behind.

The relative calm in the camp disappeared. People became edgy and nervous. Until now, we felt we were in a holding pattern, waiting for the war to wind down, while we were living in a country at peace. I received an old letter from the Shicklers in Lvov. There was no clue of any danger or war approaching. We never heard from the Shicklers again. They perished like most of the people who stayed on the Eastern territories of former Poland, taken over in 1939 by the Russians.

We were more worried now about the family we left behind. I still hung around with Cyla and spent a little time with her. There were lots of young women in the camp, married, some unattached, some separated by circumstances from their husbands. Often, I was invited to their little cubicles. I was tempted, but I knew it was impossible to keep it secret in the camp.

The NKWD that ran our camp looked quite unhappy and more serious than before. They avoided any questions connected in anyway to the Germans or the war. I had a feeling things were not going great. On the other hand, Iskakov and other Russians didn't seem worried. We knew they were confined here unwillingly.

The next batch of newspapers confirmed my feelings. They were full of optimistic articles, describing the courage of the Red Army, the invincible army of Russia, inflicting terrible losses on the Germans. But on the other hand, the newscasts were the ones that worried me the most. That's how they were always worded. After a fierce battle, inflicting terrible losses on our enemy, our army retreated to a new strategic position. It didn't take long to realize those new strategies and positions, were deeper and deeper in the Soviet Union.

It looked as if the Germans were just rolling through the Ukraine and Byeloruss without too much opposition. Sometimes, on the back pages of the newspapers there would be short dispatches about the English air force bombing Germany, and a few words about material help from the USA, coming to Britain. This was all we knew about the war while confined in the camp. It was maybe better not to know too much, because there was no encouraging news. Since the outbreak of the war, I just couldn't find peace. I was not able to relax. Now, even on Sundays, when I took the little boat and rowed to my little retreat on the island, it just wasn't the same. When I closed my eyes, I couldn't daydream, like I did before.

If the Germans were going to win the war with the Soviet Union, there was no question they were going to rule the world. The fate of the Jewish people would be sealed. If they lose and start to retreat, surely they would blame the Jews. Didn't they always, in their propaganda, call all Jews Communists? It was so hard to find a spark of hope. I did not share all my thoughts with father and the others. It wouldn't do any good. They surely were thinking the same.

My only hope was that the Russian winter would stop the Germans. They would meet the same fate that Napoleon did. It didn't take long for Hitler to conquer all of Europe with France's Maginot Line. It was only the beginning of July and the Germans already occupied so much territory. Yet, this unrealistic and only spark of optimism proved to be right, at least to a certain extent.

Our Polish friends kept very much to themselves. I'm sure they preferred fascism to Communism.

It is not to say that they liked the Germans. On the contrary. They hated them. But more than them, they hated Communism. One ugly incident in April cooled our relations with the Poles. Several of us got a permit one Sunday to go to Juryna for our usual bartering for food.

It was a nice sunny day when we approached the village. Usually the kids would play outside their homes. Their doors would be open and there was life in the streets. The women did some chores, like laundry, and they were busy in their little plots around their homes. Those were their future gardens that supplied them with food for the winter.

When we approached, the women called their children took them in and locked their doors. The street became dead with nobody in sight. I was with my friend Treister and we couldn't understand what had happened. I decided to knock on the door of the woman I always visited and bartered with. I knew her children quite well and she knew my name was Sasha. After quite a few knocks on the door and mentioning my name, she opened the door a crack and told me she was sorry she had nothing to sell. I said, fine. Why don't you let me in? I could use a glass of water. She came out with a steel cup of water, but was reluctant to let me in. I asked her what had happened in the village.

She was reluctant to say anything. I told her I would find out from the NKWD outpost on the way back to Niuziary. After I said this to her, she said she'd tell me, but I'd have to promise that I wouldn't mention her name to anybody.

They had heard from other people that the festival of Passover was approaching and the Jews in the camps were going to kidnap some children and kill them to have Christian blood to bake their Passover bread. This had apparently happened already in the city of Kozmiedomask, which is about 50 km from there.

I was dumbfounded and left immediately. I went to see the commandant, to have him help clear our names, and he listened to the story carefully.

A huge NKWD investigation followed and many people were interrogated. It had been disseminated by some Poles, but we never found out from which camp. Apparently, not from ours because nobody was arrested and taken away.

It didn't take long to see the results. Next time we came to the village, everything was back to normal. Even better than normal. It looked like the NKWD did a fast and thorough job. Nobody bothered or interrogated the woman that told me the story. However, this left bad feelings between us and the few Poles in our camp.

***

The Germans continued to carve up chunks of the Soviet Union, from the far north to the deep south. In the back of the papers, I found a few short dispatches that said the French liberation army was being organized in England and taking volunteers from all over the world.

A week later, the papers said the Polish government in exile was organizing a Polish army under the command of General Anders. Polish citizens all over the world were welcome to join. Well, here we were Polish citizens How about us?

A week later, there was a similar announcement for Czech citizens. Later, I read that all these governments in exile were signing agreements with the Soviet Union to co-operate and defeat the common enemy — Hitler and the Germans.

Soon, the papers were documenting the terrible atrocities committed by the Germans all over the occupied territories, including Poland. It was hard to believe these stories. I half believed this was mere propaganda and overstated. We found out later such stories were not only truthful, but underestimated.

I was bewildered. One day I would be hopeful and grateful the war started and this is the only chance we had to see Germany beaten. Deep down, I was more worried about our dear ones at home.

A majority of the people in the camp didn't know how to read Russian. Whatever they learned of the war was by word of mouth. To find out the truth one had to study the Russian newspapers. I say study because the Russian newspapers we received were published by the government, the mouthpiece of the Communist Party. The whole newspaper was propaganda. You had to read between the lines.

How can you win a war by losing city after city while your enemy is gaining more and more territory? They never announced their own losses. If they mentioned British air raids on Germany, it was a few insignificant lines. It was their motherland's war and that was the truth. There were fathers and children being killed, their land ravaged and raped. Now, I knew that they were right in the way they handled it, including the propaganda. What other way could they win the war, by telling the population about deserting armies by the thousands and losses of life, cities, horrendous losses both military and civilian? It would have destroyed the will of the population to resist and fight back.

So we were retreating strategically, our armies were fighting bravely our factories were working 24 hours a day, producing more and more war material — thousands of tanks, airplanes and artillery. Our collective farms produced more food and everything was being done to defeat the enemy. Mother Russia had to be defended and our enemies had to be destroyed. From all this I tried to sort out the facts as best I could.

The summer months were flying by. And even though everything was green and lush in the forest, we knew that in a few short months, the harsh winter would set in. The only consolation was that we'd have warm clothing.

The news about the war wasn't any more encouraging. The Germans were still forging ahead, possibly at a little slower pace. The newspapers started to list German losses in equipment and people. The papers wrote about the heroism of the Russian army and the terrible atrocities committed by the Germans, who were burning cities and villages and committing gruesome killings.

132

Apparently, people were hiding in the forest and organizing an underground army, called the Partisans, to fight the Germans. In time, they became a strong force in the war. At night they fought against the Germans, mostly disrupting their supplies and communications, by derailing trains and blowing up bridges. Every delay in the German offensive was meaningful because it stalled the blitzkrieg strategy and helped the Russians, who were awaiting the onset of winter.

There were short dispatches in the newspaper about our now so-called Allies, about the bombing of Germany, the war in North Africa and the landing in Sicily. The Russians hoped the Allies would open a second front in Europe and for this they waited a long time. By the time it came, the backbone of the German army was broken and the Germans lost the war. The Allies did help to shorten the war, and by doing this, saved many lives, many of them Jewish. At least 28 million Soviet people died in this cruel war.

In the camp, the atmosphere had changed greatly. The commandant and his lieutenants had become more friendly. They felt anxious about the war, and worried about their relatives.The camp rules were bent and the discipline lax.We still worked and made our norms, but we felt less pressure. The Russians had their own problems.

It was still warm, making life easier. After work I washed myself in the lake or took a short swim.

Soon it would be two years since the day that we lost our normal, civilized life. Soon, the high holidays would arrive and this time surely we'd have to go to work. The Russians wouldn't allow us to repeat our disobedience again. The war was on and they wouldn't tolerate this.

August came and went and we didn't hear from anybody, nor did we hear any encouraging news.

Then, one day the commandant announced an important meeting and everybody was urged to attend. The meeting started the same way as the previous ones. The house was full. The Culture Club was filled to capacity and the rest of the people, as usual, stood outside the doors and windows listening. I could not imagine what the meeting was going to be about. I had a feeling it had something to do with the war. I was afraid we might have to move to another location. That worried me. We had become accustomed to this place and the next one would surely be worse.

The commandant went to the podium and started his speech. It was something I never expected. It was unbelievable. The government of the Soviet Union had signed a pact with the Polish government in London. Therefore all Polish citizens were going to be free in a short time. We would soon be released from our camp  and we could travel to any destination in the Soviet Union.

There was a stunned silence, then pandemonium broke out, full of cheers, questions, tears and laughter.

I wanted to go to my barracks to digest the news and its implications. We talked for hours, Father, Uncle Marian, his wife, Hela and I, mainly about where should we go. With the Germans advancing, it was impossible to go west. They probably wouldn't let us go east and travelling north meant colder winters. Our only alternative was to go south, or southeast, but where? We decided I would talk to Zina, who would know more about the Russian geography.

Over the next few days, people became more and more confused. Everybody was seeking a destination. The authorities didn't  want to advise anyone and people became secretive about their plans.

We went to work as usual but with little enthusiasm, though work helped pass time more quickly while we waited for more information. I never stopped thinking about where we should go, where we would live and work while this bloody war continued.

The work camp had, up until now,  sheltered us from the war and our captors had done all our thinking for us. We only had to take orders and work. It seemed logical that after signing the treaty with Poland, to fight the Germans, we would be able to join some kind of army. According the the newspapers, the Germans were still advancing.

My knowledge of USSR geography was limited to the European part and a little about Siberia and the north up to the Arctic Circle. I had spoken to Zina but she was not much help.

One day, an idea struck me. Why not go to Volga, which was not far? I recalled that the towns of  Kozmiedomansk and Czuboksary, which weren't that far away, we could take a passenger boat and travel all the way to Astrachan. I remembered from school,  that between Astrachan and the Caspian Sea, the Volga created a huge delta of 10 main rivers  and the richest fish estuary in the world.  At least food would be plentiful there. It would also bring us far enough south to travel to the eastern republic of the Soviet Union.

I shared my idea with father and Uncle Marian. We debated and finally decided it was a sound travel plan. It was unlikely anyone from the camp would take this route. Most people had never heard of Astrachan. We felt more relaxed now that we'd made a decision. It seemed impossible that the Russians  would ever allow the Germans to cross the Volga, because if they did, the war would be lost.

We started preparing for our journey and tried to save as many rubles as possible. Freedom meant we'd need more money.  We made sturdy knapsacks using strong rope. We had accumulated a few more belongings, such as our new winter clothing, which might be worth money for trading. Now, all we needed were our papers from the commission.

We would be travelling through a strange, world in a country besieged by war. Krakow seemed more remote, now. How I envied the few people who were with their families, and more than ever, I longed for mother, Niusia and the rest of the family. It had been two years since we'd been separated. I was sure they were struggling. We would have no idea for a couple of years how bad it really was.

The papers were not interested in what was happening in occupied Poland. All of Europe was occupied. Everyone had their own problems to worry about. Occasionally, the newspapers mentioned the Partisans who had organized, fighting and hiding in the forests in eastern Polish territory. Apparently, in Poland itself, many other groups were being organized to fight in the war. Later, we would find out that these renegade armies had a serious impact on the outcome of the war in successful sabotage campaigns against the Germans.

Finally, the day we had been waiting for arrived — the commission arrived and they started to process our papers. They worked in alphabetical order so Uncle Marian Berkovitz with his wife were one of the first to be processed. It didn't take long and they didn't ask many questions. They already knew enough about us. They approved our destination of Astrachan without any problems.

We were issued papers stating we were free Polish citizens, living temporarily in the Soviet Union. This meant we had full rights and freedom and all courtesies should be granted to us. It all seemed so unbelievable. Only a few months ago freedom was just a dream. The camp paid us our outstanding money and bread cards were also issued to everyone.

We didn't want to waste any time. Soon it would be October and the weather would turn cold. We had no idea how long the journey to Astrachan was going to take. First, we had to get to Juryna our little trading town, located on the shores of the Veluga River. From there, we had to take a small boat to Kozmiedumnsk on the Volga and from there to Czuboksary where we had disembarked from the trains on our way to the camp. From Czuboksary, regular passenger boats traveled the Volga from the north, all the way from Astrachan.

Our day of freedom arrived. We finished packing our belongings into our now bulky knapsacks, stuffed with extra food and provisions. We hitched a ride on a truck to Juryna and suddenly became

135

foreigners, as Polish citizens, in this huge, unknown country. It seemed like a dream.

I was nearly fluent in Russian and my knowledge of the language made me feel a little more comfortable about travelling. But I didn't know much about the Russian system and how it worked.

*** 

The journey to Czuboksary, the capitol of the Czuwasz, USSR, was uneventful. Our biggest problem was finding overnight accommodations. There were no scheduled departures or arrivals from Kozmiedomask. The first trip we could get out was for the next day.

The city of Czuboksary, located on a steep shore of the Volga, was busy, with narrow cobblestone roads flanked by multi-colored homes with little gardens in the back. The side streets were dirt-covered. The population consisted of Czuwasz people and a sizable Russian minority. The Czuwasz were similar to the Maryjcy people and I had a difficult time distinguishing between them. Of course, they had their own language.

When you arrived in any city in the Soviet Union the first order of business was to find out where the free market was. They called it the bazaar. By the amount of food and merchandise at the bazaar, you could easily judge the supply situation. We found the market well-stocked and we allowed ourselves the luxury of buying a loaf of white bread, which we hadn't tasted for a long time.

By the time we got back to the port, many more people had arrived. Most people were sitting on wooden benches, watching the Volga which was heavy with boat traffic. As I sat and watched the the river, a group of people walked by and one of them tapped me on the shoulder. I turned to see my friend and classmate from Krakow, Zygmund Buchester with his parents, brothers and sister. I was amazed to see them. The last time we'd seen each other was in Lvov, where Zygmund and I had taken English classes together.

Zygmund's and I found some newspapers and scanned them together. The news was depressing as usual. Apparently, the Germans sustaining terrible losses, yet they were moving deeper into Russia, both north and south.

The Germans were continuing their scorched land policy, burning down cities and villages. The Russians were withdrawing, also burning everything they left behind. People were hiding in the forest where they would join the Partisans.

Even here, waiting for the boat on the Volga it was apparent there was a war going on. Soldiers by the hundreds, in a variety of uniforms, came and went on the boats from Czuboksary. Whole families stood on the shore saying goodbye to their sons, mothers and sweethearts, some crying or looking sad. As well, there were wounded soldiers with bandaged hands or some limping.

That evening, we found some space in a warehouse, where we settled in with the Buchesters for the night. Zygmund and I stayed up most of the night outside, talking about the good times at home, our school and our friends. It was close to dawn before Zygmund and I finally laid down to sleep for a couple of hours. Many people were just getting up, bringing in buckets with boiled water and eating their breakfast.

With all the commotion, I only slept for a couple of hours. When I awoke and walked outside, I saw the sun coming up from the east, illuminating the powerful Volga. I stood and admired the awesome sight and the beauty and serenity of this scene calmed me down. I started to think about the adventure that awaited us.

I went to the shore of the river to shave and wash myself. I spotted some kind of cafeteria down at the pier, which, of course, had a huge lineup. Me, father, Uncle Marian and Hela stood in line talking with Zygmund. After a couple of hours in line, we were finally served a delicious and hearty fish soup, a little bread and we got a piece of sugar for our tea. It was the best meal we'd had in a long time.

After lunch it got quite warm outside. The sun rose high in the sky and we went back to the port and sat on the benches awaiting our boat. It was supposed to arrive around noon but it was late.

Around two o'clock, the crowd at the port broke into a pandemonium. The boat had arrived and everyone gathered their belongings and stood up to get in line around the building leading to the boarding dock. We said goodbye to Zygmund and his family, whose boat wasn't to arrive for a couple more days.

We ended up at nearly at the the end of the line and stood to watch our boat dock and the colorful array of people disembarking.

It finally came time for us to board our boat. With our third-class tickets, we were put on the bottom of the boat in a huge room, which contained two-level bunks with thin mattresses. We were used to these kinds of accommodations.

There was a cafeteria on the boat to purchase bread. They also had some simple pastry and a couple of soups, *kwas,* which was like a sour borscht and a fish soup they called *ucha.*

In the evenings, the boat came alive with drinking and accordion playing by some soldiers on board. They sang and played songs about love, war and sacrifice. Even the patriotic songs were sometimes sad. They reminded me of the gypsy music I'd heard and always loved back in Krakow. From time to time, they would switch to a quick-paced Ukrainian dance melody, which they called a *hopak*. Some of the drunken soldiers would attempt to dance, which was a funny sight. Very often their eyes were full of tears. They were away from their homes and dear ones. Despite the hardships of the war, they appeared to love their land and country.

Our boat stopped in every big city for a few hours to pick up and let off passengers. Some stops were longer when they picked up fuel and other supplies.

People on board were friendly and conversations flowed easily. My accent always sparked curiosity about where I was from. I spoke with them gladly, learning lots of geography but tried to stay away from political talk or news of the war. When they asked me directly about the war I told them what I wished would happen: That Hitler would lose the war and the Soviet Union would be victorious.

The farther south we went, the wider the Volga became. Only on very clear days could you see both shores. When we stopped we were not allowed to leave the boat, so I stood on deck watch all the activity on shore.

On one of the longer stops, I think it was Saratow, a group of people in uniform emerged from the port building and boarded the boat. Two of them stood on the plank not letting anybody in or out. The others immediately started to check everybody, papers and identities. Our papers seemed to be in order. But after the thorough search of the boat, they took several people with them. This incident shook me up a bit and it emphasized the need to have your papers with you at all times.

As we got closer to Astrachan, I became more nervous. This boat trip had been something of a vacation, but now, I felt we'd soon be entering a different chapter of our life in Russia. We'd have to find a place to live and work and build some kind of existence.

They announced that we soon would approach Astrachan. The weather had become cloudy and gloomy with an intermittent rain. From afar, the city looked grey and unfriendly. When we approached the port it didn't look any more inviting.

## THIRTEEN

Docking into pier 14 took hours and upon disembarking, our papers were thoroughly checked by the NKWD.

I didn't like what I saw when we stepped on Astrachan soil. We were overwhelmed by crowds of people laying on the ground in a sort of encampment in around a building on the pier. I became disoriented. It was getting late. Where should we go, who should we ask? We found a little space on a cement floor, between thousands of other people. It seemed this pier area had been their home for quite some time.

They were all refugees from the Ukraine, some even from White Russia, but mostly from the southern part. They spoke about the atrocities committed by the Germans — murder, torture. Their cities and homes and villages had been burned and destroyed. Most of them were older women and children. Their stories were similar to ours. They had run to the east and now they believed that the Volga was going to protect them from the German onslaught.

More refugees streamed into port every day. The stories were all the same. Apparently, the Germans had broken through the front near Voronez and were again moving in fast on all fronts. We felt we were in a desperate situation. I now felt that my decision to come to Astrachan was bad one. But, how could I have foreseen this situation from Niuziary?

Space at Pier 14 was getting tighter and I ventured out to another part of the port. Everywhere it was the same. I tried to find out about taking a boat to the Caspian Sea, but it was impossible because all the ships had been assigned to the military. It was the same situation with the railroad. There were tens of thousands of people in the city with the same problems.

We didn't know what was going to happen next and meanwhile our little spot on the cement floor, was becoming our home. Slowly our food supply was running out and finding more food was next to impossible. We were plagued by petty thieves and had to sleep on our belongings, guarding them every moment. Even that didn't help. They cut a hole in father's bag and stole some of his clothing while he slept with his head on the bag. I tried to stay awake all night and rested a little during the day. I was afraid to lose anything. The only way to get food was to trade some of our belongings.

After two weeks our chances of leaving looked slim. Few refugees were leaving, and thousands more were coming. It seemed we were stuck here and were destined to wait here until the end of the war.

One day I decided to venture deeper into the city, hearing that in some places you could line up for bread. I hesitated to leave everything behind. I decided to get dressed in my best clothing, which I had brought from home. I wanted to stand out in the sea of refugees by looking different.

I shaved myself with a straight razor and combed my hair. When I came back from the washroom, everyone looked at me as if I was crazy. I told Father and Uncle Marian I was going to the city to see if I could get some help. It wouldn't be long before the cold weather would be here, and I didn't want to be still living on our piece of cement.

I walked deep into the city. It was drab and unfriendly, teeming with civilians, soldiers and trucks. Refugees were everywhere, some on foot with bundles going in every direction. Others walked with wooden carts, carrying children and bundles. I asked for directions to the railway station and was told it was quite a distance.

I turned the corner to go to the station and noticed a long line of people against the buildings. Apparently, this was the bread line. I was rather hungry so I joined the endless queue into a store, but I couldn't even see the entrance.

People looked at me strangely. I guess because of the way I was dressed. The longer I stood, the more disappointed and depressed I became. As I watched the passersby, I noticed in the distance an elegantly dressed lady walking in my direction. She wore a dark coat and a hat and stood out from the others. As she got a little closer, she resembled my mother. I started to tremble and tears welled up in my eyes. She must have noticed me looking at her. I couldn't take my eyes off of her as she passed by. I wiped my eyes and when I opened them again, I saw her turning around and, looking in my direction. She was coming towards me. I stood like a statue, following her every move. She came to me, looked at my face and without saying a word pointed her finger, beckoning me to leave the line and follow her. Dreamlike, I did so.

She stopped and asked why I had been staring so sadly and intensely I explained, and she wanted to know everything about me. We stood for awhile on the sidewalk as she listened to everything I had to say. I was talking to her about myself. I was sure she was Jewish and I mentioned that I was Jewish, too. She started to walk, listening to my story and asking more questions. She started to walk a little faster and told me we were going to her apartment. I didn't ask any questions, I just followed her.

The apartment was on the main floor of a big complex. The building looked shabby and old. It was a dark apartment, consisting of a big kitchen and another room. She invited me to sit at the kitchen table, took off her coat and hat and started to put all kinds of food on the table. I hadn't seen this kind of food since leaving Lvov — white rolls, bread, butter cheese and milk. I was stunned. She sat at the table and invited me to eat.

"Don't be ashamed. Eat as much as you want," she said. "I know you are hungry."

She had some milk and a small roll while she talked to me and told me she would eat when her husband got home. Now I knew she had a husband, and I imagined, a family.

She told me she and her family had been evacuated from the Ukraine, a few months ago. Her son was in the army and her husband was an engineer working here.

I probably could have eaten everything she put on the table but I restrained myself. I finished eating and we talked a little more. I didn't want to leave this haven, but I felt it was time to go and thanked her for her hospitality. As I got up from the chair, ready to say goodbye with a heavy heart she detected my move and said: "I want you to stay until my husband comes back. Maybe he will be able to help you in your situation."

It sounded more like an order, but what a sweet order it was. Finally, I asked her name and she told me it was Alina Axelrod. I told her the story about my name and how it had been changed in Russian from Samuel Honig to Sasha Gonig.

I was tired from all this excitement and hoped her husband would come home soon. I wanted to believe she had some connection with my mother. I couldn't take my eyes off her. Every move she made reminded me of my Mother. My thoughts were a mixture of reality and fantasy. Then, as the time kept passing slowly, I thought of Father and Pier 14. He might think I had been arrested or deported.

The door opened and a tall, well dressed man entered the apartment. He had a limp and made a few steps towards me at the table. He wore glasses and had a full head of hair, sprinkled with white. I got up to greet him and I could see how surprised he was to find me here. Alina kissed him on the cheek and introduced me. We shook hands and immediately Mrs. Axelrod took her husband to another room. They spoke for quite a while and I knew she was explaining my presence and the circumstances that brought me here. I sat excited and impatient, feeling the conversation might have an impact on my future. They emerged from the room and I was relieved to see Mrs. Axelrod had a smile on her face.

Mr. Axelrod wanted more information about me and what kind of documentation I had. He told me his parents were born near Lvov and had moved to the Soviet Union after the First World War.

He was a forthright man who spoke with authority. He told me to come back the next day about the same time and he would try to do something for me. I practically begged him to try and help all four of us — Father, my uncle and his wife. I told him they were all the family I had and we would like to remain together. He understood and assured me he do his best. As I got up to leave Mrs. Axelrod gave me a bundle of food and a slip of paper with their address.

With tears in my eyes I hurried back to Pier 14. I practically ran, but I was afraid to cause suspicion.

It was getting dark when I found Father on the pier. He was frantic and crying. I tried to tell him what happened but I stopped and opened the bundle. Then slowly I told them every detail about my day. They listened in disbelief with tears in their eyes.

I told them I hoped and prayed this would be the answer to our prayers, saving us from this hopeless and impossible situation.

I was to arrive at the Axelrods at 5:30 p.m., but was so anxious I left way ahead of time. I had no trouble finding their street and passed the time by walking in the neighborhood, counting every minute. Every minute seemed like an hour. I was beside myself with anxiety by the time I knocked on the door

Mrs. Axelrod promptly answered with her friendly smile. It gave me some assurance. She noticed I was anxious and nervous and told me not to worry. "Everything is going to turn out alright, " she said.

Mr. Axelrod walked in. He invited me to join them for supper. It was another royal meal for me, including some meat, which I hadn't tasted in a long time. He told me he was going to send us by boat the next morning to a fish processing plant, located on an island between Astrachan and the Caspian Sea. He would give us the proper papers to show the director of Orajeryjny Combinat who was going to provide us with employment. He also said the director, Mr. Shramko, was his friend and we had nothing to worry about. I was overjoyed.

While I ate he gave me more details. We were to meet him the next morning at at 7:00 a.m. They would take us to a small pier nearby, where we would be taken to a boat that would bring us to our new destination. I was so happy I didn't know how to thank them. I couldn't wait to share these good tidings with Father and Uncle Marian, waiting at the pier impatiently.

I thanked them again and with a bundle of food I was on my way. I wanted to kiss and hug Mrs. Axelrod, but I was afraid I would offend them. I only said, thanks, and promised never to forget their kindness. I hoped to see them again.

I raced back to the pier to tell the news to everyone. They found it hard to believe that in a few hours we would be leaving this God-forsaken Pier 14. We kissed and hugged and finished everything in the bundle.

We packed our backpacks and waited for the dawn. Around 5 a.m. I went to get some kipiatok. One at a time we went to wash up and left much earlier than necessary. The streets were deserted. The sky was cloudy and it looked like rain. When we got to the apartment it was only a few minutes after six. The four of us leaning against the wall, reminded me of pictures I had seen of wandering beggars and gypsies.

Promptly at 7:00 a.m., Mr. Axelrod emerged from the building, and greeted us warmly. A few minutes later, we heard a truck approaching. The driver, who knew Mr. Axelrod, jumped out of the cab. He opened the gate for us and we threw our belongings in.

We descended towards Volga, and stopped in front of a small pier, with a small tugboat moored to it. While Axelrod exchanged some words with the captain, we boarded the boat. He gave us a sealed envelope which we were to present to the director of the Orajeryjny Combinat upon our arrival. We bid him goodbye and thanked him for everything. He promised to be in touch with us.

We were on a small tugboat with a crew of three. We found out it belonged to the Combinat. The captain was a middle-aged man, who was friendly and talkative. They offered us some bread, butter and cheese. In the past three days, I had eaten better than in the past two years.

The tugboat motor was slow and easy as we headed downstream. It was windy and cloudy and the Volga didn't look like a river, more like an endless sea. I stood close to the man steering the boat, trying to find out how long and far away our destination was. He told me it would take e a few hours but it all depended on the number of stops we had to make. The tug also carried mail and supplies to the island. Within an hour, we entered a wide river and the man

143

explained to me that at this point the Volga split into several rivers, before flowing into the Caspian Sea. This was the notorious mighty delta of the Volga. It was an exotic place, one which I never dreamed I would travel through.

The river narrowed and we could see both banks easily. The mighty Volga was gone. There was a map of the delta on the door of the steering room and I looked at it with curiosity. It showed the main rivers flowing to the Caspian Sea. I was amazed at the little rivers between them. The map looked like a net. The captain explained the map and showed me a spot where the Orajeryjny Combinat was located and where we were going to arrive in a few hours. The estuary of the Volga has hundreds of small rivers between the 10 main ones. We could see some of them from the boat and hundreds of small islands in between.

A few hours later, we approached a big island. We could see sand-bars at its tip and as we cruised closer to the shore, we could see many buildings in the distance. This was our destination.

Those buildings we saw were really individual homes, dotting the shore. Inland, on a little higher elevation, I could see larger buildings and some warehouses. We docked at a good-sized pier and picked up our belongings. Our captain instructed us where to go, pointing to a large three-storey building where we were to report. We walked around among many people on the streets. They looked Asiatic. I found out later they were called Kalmuks from the republic close by.

The building we approached turned out to be an administration building. As we entered, I handed the guard the letter we had from Mr. Axelrod It was addressed to the director Shramko. He led us to a large waiting room and entered inside with our letter. When he emerged, he told us we'd have to wait awhile because the director was busy. After a long wait, a good-looking woman emerged from the office and called us in. We entered, carrying all our belongings. At a huge desk stood a tall, elegantly dressed man. He had a delicate smile on his face. He was extremely good looking and his appearance and manner struck me as quite different from people we'd met since our deportation. He told us to leave our bundles at the door and invited us to sit down on the chairs. He had read the letter from his friend Mr. Axelrod, explaining our situation.

He told us he was glad we were here and we would be assigned to suitable employment. He then instructed us to wait outside and soon we would be taken care of. A man greeted us and we were told to follow him. We were led down a road to a small, white house on the shore of the river. The house was empty when we walked in. The floor was made of clay and a few pieces of old furniture were in the room — a table with a few chairs and around the wall were narrow, wooden beds and some wooden benches. One-third of the room was taken up by a clay oven, with two openings covered with steel plates. It needed some cleaning and fixing up but it was quite livable. We were issued a ticket to a dining room and coupons for bread. The job assignments would come in a couple of days, giving us a chance to get acquainted with our new home.

We cleaned the house and divided the room by hanging a sheet for privacy. While the others continued cleaning, I went to find the dining room and a store to get our bread rations. Around six, we went to the eating hall, the *stolowa*. Of course, we stood in line to get our portions. The menu was simple — fish soup and a doughy soup called *zateruha*, made by dropping dark flour in boiling water and mixing it. It created a dark soup, with a few flour balls in it. The food didn't' satisfy me for long and most of the time I felt hungry.

The weather was getting progressively colder. The rains fell often and the mornings were foggy and damp. We had little wood to burn in our oven, just enough to boil water. I assumed we'd gone far enough south on the Volga so I expected milder weather. I soon learned how bitter cold the winters could be here.

The store in the Combinat didn't offer much in the way of merchandise. Most of the time they were out of tobacco, or *mahorka*. We learned many supplies were available on the black market, but we didn't have much money and we weren't willing to trade what little we had left.

The man that brought us to our new home, appeared two days later and took us to a small building called the *Otdel Kadrow* or the employment office. We spent all day there being interviewed. In the Soviet Union, whenever you went to apply for a job, an apartment, to travel or anything having to do with the government, you had to endure an interrogation.

We were assigned simple, menial jobs, but they had to know everyone's life story first. Father and Uncle Marian got jobs as watchmen. Hela got a cleaning job and, I being the youngest and educated, was to be trained as an engineer in a steam-generating facility.

There was a big demand for watchmen at every factory or facility. Stealing was a fact of survival in the Soviet Union, because there was a shortage of everything. The authorities called it stealing, but they were guilty of the same crime, only they did it officially by issuing requests and falsifying papers. An ordinary Russian didn't call it stealing. They called it organizing. If you worked in a store you stole whatever merchandise you could get away with. If you worked in a bakery you stole bread or flour. If you worked with lumber, you stole lumber.

Most things that you "organized," you actually needed and couldn't buy. It was the way of life. The authorities knew about those petty thefts, but in order to prevent breaking and entering, especially at night, they needed watchmen for every facility, building or store.

We got our papers and information about where to report for work the next day. I was directed to go to the fish plant, which was quite a long way from the settlement. It was a huge complex, consisting of several buildings, warehouses and barracks. In the centre, was a clean-looking smaller building built of solid concrete. This was my workplace, a power plant that supplied hot steam for cooking the fish before canning. It also supplied heat to some of the surrounding buildings.

I was to become an apprentice, learning the trade, called a *koczegar*, similar to foreman. The inside of the building was sparkling clean. Everything was painted white, except the floor which was blue. The entire building, except for a passageway, was taken up by a huge cistern. The huge tank was filled with water. Underneath was a furnace, that heated the water and created steam. There were pipes, gauges and hoses everywhere. The fuel used in the furnace was a byproduct of refining oil. It was a thick, dark fluid called *mazut*, which was piped from an outside tank, attached to the building and flowed freely to the furnace. The man that I was assigned to on the daily shift was a Korean. He was a quiet and private man. He never spoke of anything except work. But his assistant Lova made up for the silence.

Outside, the weather was colder but the plant was nice and warm. I was happier to be here than in our damp house. The work was easy. I only had to watch the steam, supply the mazut, clean the burners and watch the pipes. Everything depended on the fuel. The fuel we used, sometimes had dirt or pieces of asphalt, which could cause the furnace to shut off and plug the pipes. Then we'd have to clean the furnace, open the tank and clean the filters. This had to be done fast or the water would cool and the pressure would go down. Then there would be no steam for production and the plant would come to a halt. All the foremen from the fish plant would come running to see what happened. We worked frantically to repair the system, but the blockages happened all too often. We had no control over the fuel that was sent to us. Not to fulfill the quota in the Soviet Union was serious business. I was happy to be only an apprentice.

It didn't take long to learn this new trade. In about six weeks, I was sent to another steam plant in the centre, where they were short one person. This power plant was a little smaller, but the building was much roomier than the other. The plant supplied steam to the eating room and hot water to the inhabitants. There were two 12-hour shifts, daily and nightly. I was posted to the day shift under the supervision of a foreman. This man was responsible for all the steam plants in the Combinat. He showed me all the intricacies of the plant, which was similar to the one I had been trained in.

Soon, I was on my own, with the foreman checking in on me periodically. It was the same story here. If the fuel was clean, there wasn't a problem, but if there was a disruption the cooks in the eating room were in trouble. All the cooking was done in steam kettles. I tried my best to keep the steam running smoothly, because if the cooks were satisfied I got better portions.

One of the cooks, an elderly woman, named Aunt Dunia, took a liking to me. Whenever she could, she gave me an extra thick soup and cereal. Everyone lined up with their own pots and was served a certain portion upon presenting their coupon. Usually, Dunia saw to it that I got a good portion. This was the bonus for working a day shift.

The night shift had its pluses, too. It became quiet and the job consisted of more cleaning and polishing. There wasn't much else to do and it was easy to keep the steam pressure at the prescribed level, because the steam didn't go anywhere until very early in the morning, around 4 a.m. I usually found time for a nap. The only danger at night was if a problem arose, you were on your own.

\*\*\*

One night around 10 p.m., I heard a knock at the door and a woman came in. She was dressed like a typical Russian, wearing a winter coat and thick shawl over her shoulders. It was extremely cold outside and she asked if she could come in to warm up. She took off her shawl. She had long dark hair and a lovely face. She was a little older than me, probably in her late 20s. She was a widow who had got into the habit of stopping here to visit her friend, my predecesor at the plant for a few hours. That's how my friendship with Marusia began. She would come every night when I worked the night shift. She knew the furnace and my work better than me. When a problem occurred she would help me.

We became friends and later lovers. She didn't expect anything. We were both lonesome, unsettled and waiting for the end of the war. She liked me and my stories of the west. She listened, quietly and anxiously. If I had seen her walking on the street in the Compinat, I probably wouldn't have taken notice of her, being dressed like all the locals with this drab uniform-like clothing. Yet, she was beautiful with her long, black hair, white skin and dark eyes.

It was an unusual relationship. When I worked the day shift,  , I hardly saw her. Once or twice, I spent a couple of early evening hours in her house. Nobody knew about my affair. There was no place to go, no movies, or concerts. So, most of the time we spent together was on my night shift. Marusia understood our relationship.

The night shift had another benefit. We were the sole distributor of the hot boiled water in the southern part of the island. Around five in the morning I adjusted the furnace to the highest burning capacity, because at six we began to dole out the rationed hot water to the local people waiting

Father's job as a watchmen, meant working the night shift, too. So we spent the day together. I liked when he was home. I would have someone to talk to and we would prepare a good meal. I would always get fresh fish from the fisherman working nearby, sometimes for nothing, sometimes for a cigarette or a little tobacco.

Every few weeks a different kind of fish was caught. The biggest prize were beluga and  sevriuga fish. The fisherman would steal one and sell small pieces, take some for themselves and the rest they peddled around.  I would buy fresh caviar,  sometimes black and sometimes red, which was not a favorite with the locals. Father would fry it  with onions, and if we had an egg we'd throw one in with a little flour, which made a delicious dish. Some belugas weighed 50-60 kg, or more and would bring in about 20-30 lbs of caviar.

This island sometimes seemed like a dream. The news from the outside world was sketchy and outdated. Newspapers were hard to get and I knew even less about the war, now. It was dangerous to get into conversations about it. We heard rumors and the less you spoke about the situation, the better.  Although radios were not common in the Soviet Union, the Combinat piped in a government radio sta-

148

tion into people's homes aired from the office complex. The little news they broadcast was not encouraging.

I never expected the winter to be so cold here. It was getting worse by the day. The winds blew incessantly. Marusia told me soon the frost would arrive and the scores of rivers and channels we were surrounded by would freeze so hard that they become roads for transportation. In December, the weather turned ugly. The area was flat with no trees at all. The winds howled non-stop.

Soon, the water froze and sleds became the main form of transportation. A few weeks later, trucks and tractors appeared and the river became a regular highway.

Getting fuel for heating and cooking became our main concern that winter. As soon as the river froze hundreds of people could be seen pulling their sleds up the river to nearby islands covered by thick bamboo-like grass called *kamycz*. They cut it, tied it in bundles and brought it home to burn in their ovens.

Between me, Father and Uncle Marian we were able to scrounge used lumber and I would bring a can of oil from our workplace to burn in our oven. Even with all the fuel we had we were still cold. We slept completely dressed and washed once a week in a public bath — for which you needed a coupon. It was a bleak winter — work, sleep, cold, no social life — except my meetings with Marusia. And even she didn't come regularly because of the wind and cold.

Our three winters spent in Russia were taking it toll on us, physically and emotionally. Uncle Marian's wife Hela wasn't feeling well, but no one told me what was wrong with her. She went to the hospital on the island several times. Dr. Czubarowski, of Polish descent, was the only doctor. He took care of Aunt Helen and late that winter she underwent an operation. She returned home very weak and never went back to work.

*** 

In early spring, I got permission to go for a couple of days to Astrachan, where there was a Polish government office. I spent one day with the Axelrods and found out, through them, the location of the Polish office. We talked very little about the war but almost always about Poland. I had kept in touch with Mr. Axelrod, who sometimes came to the Combinat to see the director, Mr. Shramko.

The following day, I went to the office of the Polish representatives. They took my family history and I registered the four of us. I was told there were plans to organize a Polish army in Russia and that someone would contact us.Whenever we are here we should stop and update, I was told. The man who helped me left the room and came back with a few packages of cigarettes, a few cans of meats, two bags of sugar and a Polish newspaper

I thanked him and left for home. I hadn't read in Polish for about three years. I read how the Polish air force was fighting along with the English air force and how the Polish army was being organized all over Europe. It appeared the Germans were still advancing, but on a much smaller scale.

We felt more  now that we were  registered in Astrachan. At least somebody knew  where we were, what our situation was,  that we had names and actually existed.

That spring, I was called to the head office of the Combinat. I didn't know why, but those calls usually meant bad news. I was brought to Director Shramko's office, and an assistant came in. He looked at some papers and told me I had a reputation for being a  good, dependable *koczegar*. I was recommended by him to work on a boat for two weeks, because one of the foremen was going away on sick leave. The boat was to travel all over the delta, down to the Caspian Sea. I wasn't thrilled with my new assignment. I was worried about being separated from Father.  But I couldn't refuse the assignment.

The boat, the Red Star, was a little freighter that took supplies from one depot to another, mainly salt and fish and also brought back other foodstuffs. I was introduced to the main engineer and was told I would be working the 12-hour night shift  with another foreman. He was a Cossack and his Russian was very poor. But we got along well.

I was assigned a small cubicle on the bottom of the boat where I would sleep. It was a harder job than steam production. It was hot and smelly on the freighter and there was no ventilation. Every chance I had I would run to take a deep breath on the deck. The food was plentiful, though, with lots of bread, fish and even some meat. Nothing was rationed. There was plenty of vodka and cigarettes.

Most of my free time, I spent on the deck, even on the cold days. I went to my cubicle only when I really had to go to sleep.  If it was warm enough I would sleep on the deck.

We stopped in Astrachan for a day which gave me a chance to go to the Polish office. They wanted to give me some food, but this time I didn't need it. They promised we would hear from them soon. A few weeks passed and I became worried. I asked the engineer when I would get back to my Combinat and he promised the next time we stopped there, the man I was replacing would be ready to come back to work.

In the third week we arrived and I was told to disembark. It was early in the morning so I went straight to the office to report that I was discharged and to find out when I could go back to work. It took a long time to straighten everything out. I got paid for my time on the boat, which was higher than I expected, and to my surprise, I got three days free time, before I went back to my factory job..

I was looking forward to seeing my family. When I came to our little house, only Auntie Helen was there. Father and Uncle Marian were at work. Nothing had changed. Helen told me she wasn't working yet, but felt a little better. I was happy to be able to sleep in my own bed.

I was tired after three weeks on the boat. Father and Uncle Marian returned home and I told them all about my trip over one of Father's gourmet meals. He was an expert cook. He could improvise with the least amount of food. If you gave him a little piece of black bread and flour, he could make meat balls. You could swear you were eating ground beef. With fish, a few drops of oil and a little seasoning, he would prepare a dozen different fish dishes.

I told Father and Marian about my visit to the Polish representative in Astrachan, and that they promised to supply us with necessary papers and get us in the Polish army soon. We enjoyed the cigarettes I had brought home, a welcome change from the *mahorka* cigarettes rolled in newspaper.

The next day I went to see Marusia at her home. We were happy to see each other. I told her I had three days off and she asked me to spend the night at her house. I accepted her offer. I went home first, and pretended I was getting ready to go to work. I could never tell my father where I was going, and I felt bad about lying to him.

Her house was very simply furnished, but sparkling clean. Homes on this side of the river were built of some kind of clay. No lumber was available. It was the first time I had spent the whole night with a woman. I was happy in a clean bed, covered with a soft, down blanket. The only thing that disturbed me as I lay there with Marusia, was that her husband lay dead some place on the front in Ukraine. She lay quietly for a while and it seemed to me she was thinking the same.

On a visit to Astrachan once, I checked to see, if by chance, the Axelrods were still there. But they were gone. Now, my only hope to get out of here was the Polish government in exile.

We became more anxious. The war was dragging on and there was no end in sight.

During the summer it was unbearable in the boiler room, but the job of keeping the pressure up for the steam was easy. Marusia visits broke up the monotony. I was still optimistic we would survive the war and return home to find some of our dear ones.

In my spare time I walked along the river and watched the fishermen. They threw their nets in a half circle from a boat, and within a half an hour, they pulled the net toward the shore. Sometimes they used a small tractor. It is impossible to describe how rich in fish of all kinds this area was. Every few weeks a different species was caught. The fish came in waves. When the water was warm, you could wade, and catch them with your bare hands. Fresh herring was my favorite. After scaling and cleaning them, I would cut them in pieces, put them in a frying pan in their own fat.

I watched every day for the letter carrier, but he never stopped at our home. We were still waiting for some news from the Polish representative.

One beautiful sunny afternoon I was sitting outside our home, as usual watching the river. The postman was coming along the shore as usual, but this time he was coming straight towards me. He asked me my name, because we never got mail. He handed me two letters, one for Father and I and the other for Uncle Marian. The envelope had the emblem of the Polish government on it. My hands trembled as I tore open the letter. It read we should come as soon as possible to Astrachan to receive our proper papers and instructions. I felt a new will and energy and I couldn't wait until Father came home to share the news. I pictured myself in the Polish army uniform, fighting the Germans, taking my revenge until victory and eventually returning home. This seemed the only way we'd get out of this place.

Father and Uncle Marian, though excited about the news, became worried about Aunt Helen's health.

We decided Father and I would go to Astrachan and get more details, but we needed official permission from Director Shramko. I showed him the paper from the Polish government, requesting me to come to their office as soon as possible. I was given permission to go, but I didn't mention anything about going in the army.

\*\*\*

Father and I boarded the boat to Astrachan full of anticipation. When we arrived, we hurried to the Polish office. We were welcomed at the commission, and our papers were ready. We were accepted into the Polish army and were to travel north to the city of Saratov, along the Volga, where the army was organizing. There were a bunch of documents for the Polish authorities and travel permits. We were given money to purchase tickets and some papers telling our workplace we were going into the Polish army and should be released as soon as possible. They gave us more canned meats and a few packages of cigarettes.

We were advised not to delay going to Saratov. We asked about the state of the war and they sounded upbeat. The Allies were organizing in seriousness. The Russian front wasn't in great shape, but Saratov seemed safer than here. It's going to be a long war, they said, but Germany will be defeated.

We caught a boat back to the Combinat and when we arrived, it was getting dark. We didn't talk much. We were engrossed in our own thoughts. We didn't go to work the next day and stayed home to discuss our future. Uncle Marian was worried. He didn't think Helen was ready to travel. Dr. Czubarowsk agreed. It was a sad day. We didn't know what to do. Uncle Marian insisted father and I  go. It was logical for us to move, he said,  even though it would be difficult to separate.

We got the go ahead from Director Shramko, without any problem. I told him we wanted to join the Polish army to fight the Nazis, together with the Allies.  He told me we'd be released within a week, as soon as they found a foreman to replace me.

We started to pack our belongings. I cleaned, washed and pressed my clothes. I  still had two pair of good pants, a navy blue sport jacket, a few shirts, socks underwear, two ties, two pair of shoes, two fountain pens a few handkerchiefs and a few other trinkets. I treasured those belongings from home with a passion. They were always hidden in a safe place, so they couldn't be damaged or stolen. I also treasured and still carried  my last school report card from 1939.

I broke the news of my departure to Marusia. I told her I was being drafted into the army. She cried terribly and came to my work place every night and stayed till I went home.

A terrible sadness came over Father and I when we had to part with Uncle Marian and Aunt Helen. We said goodbye, promising to write and hoped they'd be able to join us soon.  They were the only family we knew we had. I could not help but cry.

# FOURTEEN

We arrived in Astrachan, and without any trouble, got tickets. I decided to wear my good suit. I felt lucky wearing it. To my surprise, the Polish representative let us sleep in his office. He loaded us with more cigarettes and a few chocolate bars.

The boat to Stalingrad was a good size and terribly crowded with people. — peasants, soldiers, some of them wounded, and recruits going to the army led by military personnel. As far as languages , it was a tower of Babel — Tartars, Cossacks, Kalmuks, Uzbeks, Russians and others. Some I couldn't distinguish.

I started to think about going into the army. I had some military training and had attended a couple of military camps, but that was the extent of my experience. The last one I attended was a month before the war in 1939. I knew how to shoot a rifle, throw grenades, march for hours and sustain on army food and rations. I didn't crave for the war and fighting, but this time I had a purpose.

The journey to Stalingrad, which was halfway to our destination of Saratov, lasted about three days. It was around noon when we docked in Stalingrad, a large, bustling port.As I went up on deck, the line for disembarking had already begun. We noticed NKWD agents everywhere. They closed the gate and started to check everybody's papers. They were looking for deserters from the army or people avoiding the draft and maybe even for some black marketeers. We watched this scene with fascination and could see some people being let through to disembark, mostly women and older people. But, quite a few were led back to the boat downstairs. They were apparently looking for men of military age.

I wasn't worried. We had all the necessary papers and we were foreign citizens. Our tickets were legally purchased. But I still didn't like what I'd seen, the way they pushed people, not even looking closely at their papers and not listening to their explanations. When our turn came, I tried to act confident. I handed our papers to the NKWD man. I could see he was not familiar with this type of document. I explained everything to him, stating I was a Polish citizen. The other document explained we were going into the Polish army. He seemed suspicious. He told me to go on board so the superior officer could look at our papers.

We were ushered to a room, where an NKWD officer was sitting at a table with two men. I presented our paper and asked them to let

154

us go, because our boat to Saratov would be leaving soon. Take your time, they said, there are lots of boats leaving to Saratov. They looked at our papers and the interrogation began.

They asked hundreds of questions, wanting to know everything about us from the time we'd been born. We answered all their questions, and the higher ranking officer made a speech and a quick decision. Our country, he said is locked in a terrible war with Nazi Germany. They are our enemy and yours so it doesn't make any difference with whom you fight our common enemy. We need you now and so you will help us.

I argued we were foreign citizens and explained our situation again, but it didn't matter. They took our papers away and a guard took us upstairs. We left the boat and joined another group of detainees and under the watchful eye of a guard we sat on the ground.

It was late afternoon when they led us to the city. I was so worried and disappointed and didn't even look around. It took about an hour before we got to a large, grey numbered warehouse. It was a military recruiting station.

We were led through a gate into a huge yard, where we were ordered to sit on the ground. There were other groups of people nearby, who told me they'd been there for two days. We were given hot water, bread and salted fish for supper. I drank my water with a piece of sugar and finished the bread.

I was terribly depressed. I took our new situation harder than Father. He tried to cheer me up and told me we had to stay calm and survive.

We spent a sleepless night outside, like prisoners under guard. I awoke bitter and angry — angry with myself. We were fed some cereal and then ushered into small groups into the building, where some more interrogation took place, this time by the military authorities.

When our turn came, we were again in front of another trio of officers. I complained bitterly about the treatment we received, as Polish citizens and foreigners trying to fight with the Polish Army. I told them what they were doing was illegal. They smiled and politely told us the same line we'd heard from the NKWD. I realized no argument would help us. We were in their hands. We were led back to the yard again and waited. Most of the people in the yard were close to my father's age and older. Not many looked like army recruits . We slept another night outside. We found out we would be joining a working battalion to help build the defenses for the heroic Red Army.

We were the working battalion under the direction and supervision of the army. We also found out the reason we were taken off the boat — the German army had broken through the lines endangering Stalingrad.

We were loaded onto open trucks and driven west of Stalingrad, away from the Volga. We drove for several hours on bumpy side roads, until we arrived to a settlement and led to a huge barn that was to be our home. There were probably close to a hundred men in my battalion. Later, more arrived and were stationed in another barn. They gave us some straw for a bed on the floor, and that was all. Everything seemed to be done in a hurry, without order or organization.

We were later in so many places, I don't' remember their names. But I remember our first stop was called Cybinka. It was a small village that grew mostly cabbage. I remember the cabbage because I ate it raw by the ton, to supplement our meager rations.

The next morning we were led several kilometres from Cybinka, to a place in the middle of nowhere. I could not understand what we were doing here. Around noon, we saw several military vehicles approaching, a car and two trucks.

They unloaded shovels, steel rods and other tools. We were assigned to a division and were told to start digging trenches. Everybody was required to do so many metres per day. Father and I had never worked with shovels or the other tools. We worked so hard, I thought this was the end of us. The days were hot, the terrain stony and dry. My hands became painfully blistered and our shoes fell apart from pressing on the shovels. When we returned to the barracks, I was so exhausted I couldn't eat.

The name of the Russian man in charge of our division was Starczyna.

From the beginning, Father and I had trouble finishing our assigned length of trenches to be dug. We tried, but often Starczyna and some other men had to help us finish. Surprisingly, everyone was friendly and helpful and within a short time, we improved and were able to finish our assignments.

Everyone began to get infested with lice. I tried to wash myself often, but soap was in short supply. I even tried rubbing kerosene or gasoline on my skin, but it was a losing battle.

One Sunday, I walked to a nearby cabbage patch and laid down between two rows for a nap and some fresh air. I cut down two small, young cabbages and started to eat them. I had a little pocketknife, one of my treasures. I was enjoying the sweetness and tenderness of their leaves. The weather was beautiful, the sky blue and clear. Suddenly, I heard an airplane coming close. I didn't pay too much attention because it sounded like one of the small, low-flying biplanes that were quite common. I could hear the roar of the engines and I saw two planes streaking from behind a cloud towards the slow biplane. I heard the tick-tock of the machine guns and saw the plane being attacked. It caught fire and crashed, not far from where I was laying. I looked again towards the sky and I could see a parachute drifting slowly downwards and the military planes circling around. As the parachutist came lower, I could see the pilot with a revolver in his hand.

I ran toward the barn and reported what I'd seen to Starczyna. We found out later the German pilot was killed. It was the first time I'd seen a German plane shot down by Russians. We were all happy about the outcome of this dogfight, but it made us realize the Germans were not far away.

Starczyna was moved to another battalion and we got a new leader, who was a Romanian. Since we'd been inducted into the work battalions, we had no idea how the war was going.

We became nervous after the German plane was shot down. For more than a week nothing special happened and we returned to our normal routine. The work was backbreaking, the food meager. The heat during the day was atrocious and there was not enough water to drink, never mind for washing. I could hardly speak with Father or anybody else, because of all the work. All I could think about was food, finishing the work and sleep. We didn't talk about the war or home. My mind became blank, busy only with surviving the day. I had a feeling the Germans were catching up with us.

We were told we were leaving Cybinka. The battalion stretched in a long line with horse-drawn wagons and a couple of officers on horses. We didn't know where we were going, but I could see we were going east, towards Stalingrad. The area was flat with a few withered trees and seemed not to be inhabited. We walked along a dirt road that hadn't been used for awhile. In some places there was no road at all. The soil was dry and stony, apparently not fit for cultivation.

We made short rest stops along the way, only to take a drink and quickly resume our march. I liked to march at the back of line and as I did, we looked like a haggard bunch of prisoners, not an army. Everybody was dressed differently, some with caps, some without. Everybody's shoes were different. We got a pair of army shoes because our own had fallen apart.

It was late afternoon and everyone was anxious to stop for the night, for food and sleep. Out of the blue, we heard a roar of airplanes and in seconds could see them diving towards us, heading to the front of our battalion. Before we had a chance to get a good look at them, we heard the staccato of machine guns and cannon fire. I instantly recognized the German Stukas.

The front of the battalion became bedlam. It seemed a few of them had been sprayed by bullets. Everyone started running. The horses bolted and ran wild pulling the wagons in all directions. I grabbed Father and we ran to the side of the road. Strangely, I didn't panic. I had been through this in 1939 in Poland. But, here there were no trees to protect us.

We threw ourselves on the ground and crawled to a small depression at the roadside. We laid down for a few minutes until the plane departed. There were scores of wounded and dead. People were moaning and crying. We were ordered to line up and continue to march. A couple of army officers were running back and forth on their horses, issuing orders. We started to march again while a few men were left behind to help the wounded. Everything was in disarray.

We marched not more than 15 minutes, when we heard the roar of airplanes again. We realized they were heading toward us again. Everybody started to run in every direction. I noticed a few trees nearby, but first we dropped to the ground and as soon as the planes turned around we ran to the trees. This time, they made several passes and flew so low we could see the pilots. The machine guns strafed in every direction. We hid under the withered trees and as soon as we had a chance, we ran far from the road. The Germans were playing cat and mouse with us, taking their time, playing it safe, without any opposition. It was dark when the planes disappeared, but I didn't want to go back towards the road. Slowly, people came out of hiding and we decided to sleep where we were. There were about 15 or 20 men, all of us frightened and exhausted. The sky was starless and the moon disappeared. We couldn't see anything.

We must have been close to the front. The war was catching up with us. Who knew what awaited us the next day.

We got up to a chilly and damp dawn. There were no signs of anybody looking for us. We discussed what to do and where to go. Everyone had a different opinion. In our group were Russian, Ukrainians, Poles and a couple of Tartars. The first concern of the Russians was finding food and water, which I didn't disagree with.

One of them was a cheerful, middle-aged man named Vania, a farmer from this part of Russia. We let Vania lead us. I'm sure he did not know where to go, but we had to follow somebody. I decided to depend on him. We knew it was better to go east than west. At least we would be going away from the front. I shared my view with Vania but first in his opinion we couldn't go anywhere without eating or drinking.

We walked for hours without finding anything. Maybe we were going in circles. Finally, we came across a small patch of harvested cabbages. The roots were our meal. I had a piece of bread that I had stashed away. I took it out and told Vania to divide it. There was one bite for everybody. Vania asked if anybody else had anything. A few had some.

We got up to march farther to the east. But we needed water. It was a hot day and we were thirsty. A few men became sick and unable to walk. We rested more and more often. Vania was optimistic we'd find water soon. The people who had planted this cabbage must live close by. But in what direction? The landscape here was flat and empty. Exhausted, we didn't walk close together, but tried not to lose sight of our leader Vania.

We were losing our confidence. Our situation was becoming desperate. We couldn't think of anything but water. Walking became unbearable. We hadn't had a drink for more than 24 hours and the heat was unbearable.

As we came across a few tiny trees and a few bushes, we sat down and waited for the stragglers. Vania, with a couple of healthy, young men, were way ahead of us. Suddenly, we saw some of the men running towards us, gesturing and hollering. Had they come across some Germans? Vania was hollering "Rybiata! Woda! Rybiata Woda! Boys, water!" Like an electrical shock it hit everybody and we started running towards him. I looked ahead and couldn't see anything, except the same flat, empty steppes, like the day before and the day before. I became suspicious that Vania was crazy from the heat. He was ahead of us about 200 to 300 metres, and we followed his every move. Suddenly, he disappeared, like the earth had swallowed him. We started to run faster. An unbelievable sight awaited us. I almost fell down a huge steep ravine. I stopped in time at the edge, trying not to fall down from the impact of the sudden stop. It looked like a huge crack in the steppe and down at the bottom flowed a river.

Everybody was running down, taking off their shoes, pants and underwear, leaving them where they fell and going straight into the river. And we drank without stopping. We rested a minute and drank again.

We decided to stay here in proximity to the river overnight. Now the hunger wouldn't let us rest. Vania picked up some dry grass and we boiled some water. He also showed us some grass containing little seeds in it. We chewed this and drank our hot *kipiatok* and felt better. I fell asleep, exhausted. In the middle of the night I woke up feeling cold.

Everybody was asleep. I laid down, but I couldn't sleep. What a mess I had gotten Father and myself in. Where would we go in the morning? What if we didn't find any food. I fell asleep and dreamed of fish soup and white bread at the Combinat. It seemed such a long time since we'd left Krakow. How much longer would this last? We were in the war zone and the Germans had not stopped advancing. They were close to the Volga and if they crossed that mighty river, there was no chance to beat them back. For us, there would be no place to run.

Dawn was upon us and the huge red sun appeared on the horizon. I walked to the river and watched her murky water flowing slowly. There was complete stillness in the air. It was going to be another hot day. I looked in the direction where I'd seen a blinking light the night before, but now I couldn't see anything.

We boiled some water and repeated our last evening's meal, chewing on the grass and drinking the hot water before setting out.

We walked almost all day, stopping often to drink and wade in the river. By late afternoon we heard the airplanes again. They were quite high and didn't attack. The sun was nearing the horizon when the river turned sharply to the left. We followed it and Vania pointed to a dark dot in the distance. He predicted we would arrive there in about an hour. The dot became buildings that looked like silos.

As we came closer, we saw cultivated land with cabbage an sugar beets still in the field. We couldn't resist taking some as we walked along. We entered the village and headed towards the centre. It was late and the road was deserted. Vania and myself were in front, trying to figure out where we were, but nobody was on the street. We were about to enter one of the homes, when a few soldiers appeared out of nowhere, pointing their guns at us and hollering for us to put our arms up. We froze. When they came closer, they saw we were unarmed. They led us to a larger building, with a big yard surrounded by a wooden fence which turned out to be a military stockade.

There was a group of people sitting on the ground, some of them from our battalion and we were told to sit with them. Our

160

escorts went inside the building and we were given a meager meal. Some of the men, who had been here for a couple of days, told us they had been interrogated every day and that we should expect the same.

Three of us were called into the building. We didn't have our papers, because our Polish documents were taken from us and new ones not issued.

They asked why we had deserted the battalion. I knew they were suspicious and were indirectly calling us deserters. I became worried. I knew what desertion meant in the Russian army, especially during a war. After a few hours of questioning we were let go.

Father and I discussed how no matter how many interrogations we were put through, our stories should never differ and we should be careful of any attempt to sway us. We were interrogated longer than the others. I felt they were more suspicious because we were foreigners.

Every day we had a different interrogator. On the third day, my interrogator was a friendly officer who seemed more interested in my life story, my family and life before the war. When I told him about how we were separated and everything that had happened to us, he became sad. He treated me politely and handed me an almost full pack of cigarettes, a small treasure, which I immediately hid under my shirt. This was my last interrogation. The same for father.

Every day more people were brought into the yard. We were here about 10 days, doing nothing. The food was poor and meager, but we had a chance to rest. We slept outside at night and during the day,we tried to avoid the heat by sitting under a few trees in the yard.

Rumors started to circulate. We would be tried as deserters. We'd be sent to the Gulag. The optimists thought we'd be inducted into a special penal battalion of the army. When I looked at those people surrounding me, they didn't look like front line material. The majority, especially the Russians and Ukrainians were older. Some were even sick, coughing all the time.

One day, open trucks started to arrive. It was getting dark and we were loaded tightly into the trucks and headed east. Apparently, the trucks waited with the departure, to avoid attacks by the German air force. The drivers knew their way in the darkness.. The headlights were dim and they kept quite a distance from each other. I had a feeling we were going back towards the Volga.

From now on, I cannot tell my story in order. Things changed so quickly, sometimes every few days, sometime every few hours.

161

We arrived to a small city, called Dubowka. We got out of the trucks and entered a yard between several barracks. We laid down to rest, guarded by soldiers.

When morning arrived, we lined up for bread and hot water. They started to call us in and we were led into one of these buildings. The place was full of people. It looked more like a military headquarters, with officers and soldiers everywhere. Our papers must have arrived with us, probably a result of the interrogation. There were no more questions. We were being organized in work battalions again. This time, I could see everything was more organized. We became more connected to the army and were treated differently. There were army officers, army political officers and engineers connected with the battalion. We were again divided into platoons, about 25-30 men.

We stayed another few days and were issued army shirts, trousers and shoes. I determined we were being prepared for a German attack on the Volga.

We were loaded onto the trucks again with the tools of our trade we were driven away from the headquarters. Several hours later, we were dropped off near a an abandoned barn. We spent the night there packed inside like sardines. I slept outside.

Early the next morning we were woken up and given only hot water and a piece of bread. There was no civilian population in sight, only a few bombed out barns. They must have been evacuated long ago. If nothing else, we realized we were in the war zone.

The work was similar to what we had done before, digging trenches and bunkers, some prepared especially for machine guns and one large one for the military headquarters. This time, all the work was supervised by the army and every day they inspected to make sure the work was done to their specifications.

We were treated fairly and with respect. Quite often, some independent officer would leave us some cigarettes, an extra piece of bread or a can of food.

Once we finished the job, we were moved to a new location, sometimes only a few kilometres away. In many locations, we slept in the partially finished bunkers to keep us protected from the wind.

We worked rain or shine. When it rained, we shivered all night, hoping the sun would come out the next day. We learned not to light fires, for fear of German attacks. Food was brought to us, in the evening by horse-drawn wagon.

The action in the air increased by the day. The German bombers were flying towards Stalingrad overhead, quite high, and then returned west. Most of the time they ignored us. Maybe they didn't see us because they flew too high. Only rarely the Stuka would attack us, machine gunning us from the air. Now, we had more experience to avoid being hit. We witnessed several dogfights between the Russians and Germans, but to our great disappointment, the German Messerschmidts always won. We felt terrible watching our planes being shot down. Sometimes we could see a pilot bailing out.

I was probably the youngest man in the platoon. There were mostly older people in their 40s and many, who for medical or political reasons, were not acceptable for the Red Army.

Autumn was approaching, the days were getting shorter and it rained often. We were working closer to Stalingrad, but we couldn't see the city, only the Germans bombers returning from their missions faster than before. Our work became more and more chaotic. We were moved more often, sometimes leaving the trenches half done, and then marching for a few hours and only to start digging again.

We never knew exactly where we were. Most of the information we got was hearsay or plain guessing. Nobody dared to ask our leaders questions. It was too dangerous. Everybody was suspicious, especially when you asked for information.

One evening we were getting ready to go to sleep after a back-breaking day. We found an area with some trees, which always made us more comfortable than sleeping in the open spaces.

Suddenly, we heard a very different shrieking noise, which was slowly becoming louder and more frightening by the second. We were petrified. The noise disappeared only to be repeated a few minutes later, again and again. We asked our platoon leader and the others in charge for an explanation, but nobody knew the source of this noise until later.

The German airplanes, sometimes when flying very high, dropped empty steel drums, which fell very slowly. When they fell they made this terrible noise. It had a terrifying effect.

*** 

I was sure we would soon be in Stalingrad, but I was wrong. We skirted Stalingrad moving south of the city.

Early one evening, we came up to the shore of the Volga and upon seeing the mighty river, I had a feeling I had some connection with this river and would always return to it.

That night, we slept in some buildings on the outskirts of the town, where we had a longer rest and were given water and porridge. There was no question by now, that Stalingrad was under siege. And if it fell, the Soviet Union would be in mortal danger. If the Germans crossed the Volga, there was no natural barrier to stop them, only maybe the Ural mountains.

It was our job to build defenses on the flanks of Stalingrad. Daily, it became more dangerous. On one occasion, we were taken to retrieve huge logs, anchored at the shore of the Volga. We dragged the logs ashore and had to cut them to a length needed for reinforcing bunkers. But, the saws and axes were dull and not suitable. It was a difficult job.

We worked there a couple of days until we were discovered by a German Luftwaffe, which attacked us one afternoon.It swooped so low without warning and with a frightening noise as I was chopping with my axe. I looked up to the sky and dropped the axe on my finger. Some men were hit and laying on the ground, dead, other were wounded I started to run towards an embankment. Father was there already. I tore a sleeve of my shirt and bandaged my finger. Luckily, it was only a flesh wound. The bone wasn't touched. The planes made a few swoops, strafing our area and flew away.

It took until night before help arrived to clear the dead and wounded. A medic bandaged my hand and I put it in a sling. There was nobody to stitch it. There was no free time, to rest. I went to work with my right hand, keeping my left in the sling. The job had to be done and the next day we were at work again as if nothing had happened.

They gave us extra men to finish the job faster. I scouted out a hole in the bank, very close to our place of work and prepared to hide there when attacked again. And they did. This time we had a little warning because they came flying parallel with the river. We all ran towards the steep embankment. The casualties were much smaller than the first attack. Now, we were getting more medical help from the army.

It was decided we should work that night and at dawn we marched away from this dangerous spot. Food distribution was terrible, probably because we were constantly on the move.

We were always hungry, even after we ate our rations, when we got them.

This time, we marched for about 48 hours, close to the banks of the Volga. We passed villages, but everything was deserted.

Sometimes we passed fields of overgrown cabbage, which the people left unharvested. We would grab some leaves and chewed them on the way. The leaves were sweet and helped stave off our hunger a little. Our rations were long gone.

The evenings were getting cooler, especially being so close to the river and the night dampness contributed to the chill.

There were a few men in my platoon, who had a constant cough. Some of them spitting blood. Surely they had tuberculosis, yet they were not discharged and had to work just like the rest of us. I was worried about TB

When we woke in the morning we could see in the distance, some buildings. It must have been a collective farm. We didn't get our rations that morning.

We waited a while and then descended to the river, washed and filled our kettles with water. We started a little fire under the trees to boil the water. Our fellow Russians went to the nearby pumpkin field and brought back some for everyone. After boiling them for a few minutes in the kettle, and stirring with a spoon, it became a sweet thick paste. We spent all day cooking and eating the pumpkins. But no matter how much we ate, it didn't satisfy our hunger.

After sitting without orders for days, we realized our platoon was lost in the maze of military movement.

We were frightened. There was no communication with anybody. We could see our leaders were totally confused. They came to the conclusion we marched in the wrong directions. The platoon commander decided to scout inland to communicate with somebody. He chose a few of us to go with him. After a few hours, we came upon the building that we'd seen in the distance. It was an abandoned collective farm, except for a few old men and lots of dogs that barked and tried to attack us. They told us that the order to evacuate came quite awhile ago. Men were taken into the army and the rest were taken across the Volga to the east. They had little food, some flour and barley. They gave us bread.

We were still far from Stalingrad and we knew the direction of the city from the German bombers flying their daily missions. After a few hours, we decided to go back. I was worried about losing our way and Father was not with us.

A few days passed and still nobody showed up. It was somewhat like a vacation, a reprieve from our hard work. All we did was collect twigs, dry grass and cook our pumpkins all day, but we started to worry about falling into the hands of the Germans. Again,the platoon leaders scouted around in several directions, but without ever contacting the proper authorities. On the last try, towards Stalingrad, following the Volga, they finally found our battalion.

We were given some rations, and they tasted terrific. The place was abandoned and badly bombed. It seemed to have a railroad station with quite a few sets of tracks leading south and north. The rest of our badly depleted battalion was at work on the fortification.

They had been caught in a town, when suddenly at dusk, the German bombers attacked them and killed a lot of men. They were happy to see us but they envied our vacation in the pumpkin field.

\*\*\*

I was sure the battle for Stalingrad would decide the outcome of the war. I was so busy with daily work and survival that my mind was too numb to think about other problems. Our home in Poland and the people we left behind became so distant, as if it had never existed. Only in my dreams could I remember them.

We were on the go again. We started when the sun went down, marching all night. We were going southeast. It started to drizzle, it was cold and the ground was muddy. Lots of men took their shoes off and walked barefoot.

In the early morning, we came to the shore of the Volga. Three days later we marched downstream, all the time along the shore of the river for a few hours, until we came to a wider beach. We were ordered to rest and try to camouflage ourselves. The Volga flowed quietly and in the distance I could see a good size island, or maybe a huge sandbar. By late afternoon, a small armada of boats docked in front of our position. It was quite obvious they came for us. It was an array of boats, all shapes and sizes. It appeared we were going cross the Volga on our new assignment. We were loaded on the boats quickly. Our boat took about 10 people, including my father and of course the barber, Vania and a few Uzbeks.

It was still light outside. The water was calm and our boat moved quietly downstream. As we neared the island, with the rest of the boats following, we were in the open water without protection. I had a feeling of nakedness in this area dominated by German Luftwaffe. I scouted the sky, but couldn't see anything. We were floating slowly to the island's shore with a few other boats , but most of them were still in the middle of the channel, when I heard the familiar noise of approaching German planes. They swooped so low we could

166

see the fliers. First, they concentrated their attack on the boats in the centre of the channel. Some men were hit on board and others were jumping into the river as some of the other boats began to sink. We were the lucky ones. Our boat was so close to the island that we all jumped into the shallow water and ran towards the sandbar. At least we were on solid ground. There was tall grass and some bushes nearby and we ran for cover. Nobody on our boat was hit.

We could see the stukas swooping back and forth machine gunning the boats at will. In a few minutes, they were gone. We crawled out to assess the damage. Almost all of the boats were gone. We were not the only ones on the island. A few more people had swam from the boats in the shallow water and joined us. The casualties were high. It only took a few bullets to hit the wooden boats and sink them.

I took a walk on the shore and found some more survivors. The others did the same. When we gathered together, there were about 25 of us. One had a flesh wound bleeding profusely. I took both the sleeves of his shirt and bandaged him.

We were sure that the next day we would be picked up and given food and another assignment. We were tired and laid down to sleep and only then did I begin to think how lucky we were to survive.

I fell soundly asleep. The Volga flowing a few feet from us with its tranquilizing whisper.

We woke up in a thick, white fog, barely able to see a few feet in front of us. I couldn't see if our boat was still there.

The boatmen waded into the water to get our boat, but couldn't find it. It had probably drifted away during the night. Here we were again, a group of survivors, without a leader. The mist lifted and we all stood on the beach looking toward the distant shore. We couldn't see any movement as we signalled with our hands, hollering and screaming, to no avail.

All we could do was wait and drink the Volga water without any food. The gloomy, cold day passed, without any sign of rescuers. A few of them men had some mahorka, and we rolled some smokes in the newspaper, sharing a puff or two. Vania decided that in the morning he would go around the island, toward the eastern shore to see what was there. We spent another cold, miserable night

The next morning the fog persisted. It was not safe, but we decided to take a chance on a fire and boil some water. It was a great feeling to drink something warm. Vania, with two others, disappeared in the mist. They would travel along the water to see what they could find.

167

We sat awaiting the return of Vania. Around noon the weather cleared up and we heard shouts from Vania. We could see all three of them carrying boxes on their shoulders. They looked happy. They dropped the boxes in front of us, with the cry of victory: "Let us eat," they said.

The boxes were full of ripe red tomatoes. They told us, not far from here, they noticed on the tip of our island, close to shore, was a partly submerged barge. After shouting and getting no answer, they waded towards the boat, where they found the treasure. It had probably been sunk during the air attack by the German planes. They didn't find anybody, only the boxes of tomatoes.

Another few days passed by. We knew we were lost and forgotten. and decided we would have to take a chance and set up some bonfires at night. In the evening, we prepared everything on a clear spot of the beach, closest to the shore. We set the fire and moved away as far as possible, in case of an attack. We kept going back and forth to the boat, bringing more tomatoes We kept busy with bonfires.

The next morning, one of our men came running from the beach, to tell us a boat was coming in our direction. It was a small boat with two people, both in military uniform. We embraced them a they stepped on the shore. They had heard about the attack on our battalion, but didn't expect to find so many survivors. If not for the fires they would not have come.

They had no food with them, but we were happy they had cigarettes. They updated us on the Stalingrad situation, telling us the Red Army was heroically defending Stalingrad. The German army had been cut off from its lines. This was fantastic news.

They stayed with us a few hours and promised to make arrangements to be picked up shortly. It took another two days before this happened. Everybody was quiet and weak. But I was encouraged there was no German air activity.

A tugboat finally showed up to rescue us. We had to wade quite far in the cold water to get to it. We were given hot tea, bread and a good chunk of sugar.

The tug skirted the island and turned toward the eastern shore. We went to the opposite shore of the Volga and disembarked in a small fishing village. We marched to the outskirts and were led to a compound with a couple of houses and a large barrack. It turned out to be an assembly place for people being drafted into work battalions and the army. We found some remnants of our people who survived. Everybody had a horror story to tell.

The courtyard was filled with Russians, Uzbeks, Tartars and Kirgiz.

We stayed there for a week. We were assigned a political officer and had to listen to his stories about Communism, Stalin, the Red Army and the war we were winning. We are going to destroy the enemy, he would say. From their lectures, I found a trace of more reassurance about the fate of the war than I had heard before. Their task was propaganda. Yet, between the lines you could find some truth.

It was quieter on this side of the Volga and seemed to be unaffected by the war. We were being organized again in platoons and battalions. All the island survivors were kept together, with a few new men added.

It was almost impossible to sleep outside anymore with the cold and frost. As our march progressed, we started to hear artillery in the distance. It was obvious we were getting closer to Stalingrad. Soon, we could not only hear but see the light of the shells tracing the sky and exploding. We were still quite a distance away. Our route, so far, was close to the river, but later we reached the road, running a little farther inland. We were skirting Stalingrad.

The rumble of the artillery continued to get louder. We were not far from the river on the opposite side of Stalingrad. In some openings, we could see fires. We marched all night, without a stop.

At dawn, a place of rest was prepared for us in some abandoned factory, where we lay on the floor, completely exhausted. Being so close to the Stalingrad front petrified all of us.

We were again close to the Volga and settled for a while near a small pier. It was around November. We were waiting for transportation to take us across to the western shore.

We started the journey across, landing downstream on a sandy beach, next to a steep bank. We climbed the steep, narrow track and came out on the banks of the powerful, majestic Volga. We could see for miles in both directions. We were assigned to a barrack. I occupied a cubicle with Father.

We were north of Stalingrad and were being sent wherever we were needed most, digging fortifications and anti-tank trenches.We were close to Stalingrad, in the immediate war zone and often found ourselves digging and being shelled by both sides while the Russians and Germans exchanged artillery fire.

The current rumors was the Germans around Stalingrad were surrounded by the Red Army. Several times we noticed, especially when we were on higher elevation, German planes circling and going down slowly for a landing, not far away. They were not dropping bombs, which was their usual purpose, but were going in to resupply the German army. The other odd thing was the absence of Stukas attacking us in this vicinity. Maybe they were attacking Stalingrad, but we didn't see them. I started to believe the powerful German army was in trouble in Stalingrad.

We had no idea what was happening on the other fronts. One thing we knew for sure —the Germans were deep in Russia and another winter was coming. When I thought about the Russian winters, I thought about Napoleon's defeat in Russia and hoped history would repeat itself.

***

One evening around bedtime, came a cry for help. I got up to see what was happening and saw a young Uzbeck having a seizure. The nearest army doctor was a few kilometres away so I asked a couple men to help me pin the man down while I pried open his mouth. I inserted my wooden spoon handle into his mouth and was able by twisting it to pull out his tongue. The convulsion ceased and he started to breathe normally. His comrades thanks me and rewarded me with dried fruit.

Two days later, I was ordered to report to the station. I didn't know what to expect. I entered a building, where I was greeted by a woman soldier. She had heard the story and expected a full report from me. I was ushered to a large, bright office and introduced to Dr. Rosa. She wore a uniform with the rank of a major. From her name and looks I was sure Rosa was Jewish. She began to interrogate me, questioning my childhood, education and medical knowledge. When we finished, I was sure she knew I was Jewish, but she didn't acknowledge it. She left and returned with another soldier, bringing in coffee and a cake. In few words, she told me to come back tomorrow to learn about my new assignment.

Back in the barracks, I lay there wondering what tomorrow's meeting with Dr. Rosa would bring. I was happy to get away from the outdoor, back-breaking work. I didn't expect drastic changes, but I had a good feeling about Dr. Rosa.

When I entered the compound, the next morning, I was told to wait. She came in and began asking me more questions, this time more personal.She asked where I came from, about my family, school and the family I left behind. She was polite as I answered and apologized for asking me so many questions. She told me she was from Ukraine and was evacuated just before the outbreak of the war. Then, she got down to business.

She had presented my case to the medical commission and they decided to make me a san-instructor, which is similar to a medic in the American army. I would be responsible for minor cases in our platoon and the surrounding ones. I would answer to Dr. Rosa and could not act alone. I was to consult with her weekly and would also be responsible for the cleanliness of the barracks and the people living there. I could not excuse anyone from work for more than a day.

A girl then entered the office and brought in a canvas bag, containing a first-aid kit. Rosa opened it and explained each item. There were all kinds of bandages, tape, aspirin, iodine, peroxide and antacids. I was responsible for all of the contents and was to use them wisely.

I left for the barracks with my new Red Cross arm band, which I was to wear on my sleeve from now on. Father was happy to see me as I told him about my new job. He was happy for me, but warned me about the dangers of my new responsibility.

When winter set in and the Uzbeks suffered the most. I tried to be compassionate, letting them stay in the barracks for a few hours or a day, to warm up and rest. I left with my first-aid satchel every morning with my platoons, staying close by in case of any medical problems. I set up a small office in a nearby building and spent my day visiting the various platoons, attending to minor problems, mostly cuts, bruises, infections, boils and blisters. I did what I could and the more serious cases I sent to Rosa and her assistants.

Quite often, I had spare time so I made friends with some of the villagers and gave them leftover aspirin and antacids. They repaid me with bread, fish and tea.

We didn't know how the war was going, and in the rare meeting that the political officers held, they only talked about victories. They added that soon we would witness the greatest victory of all.

Our platoon was sent on an assignment north to Dubowka, where our battalion had its headquarters. We were just outside of the town but we saw columns of tanks, moving south towards Stalingrad. It gave us confidence looking at them, more hope than any political speech. We also noticed the Katiuszas, which were powerful mine throwers used by the Russians, and the arsenal being pulled by strange, powerful trucks — American trucks. They were Dodges and Studebakers. This was the first time I saw a sign of American help. I was starting to believe in victory.

In my eyes, the omni-powerful Americans were on our side and I started to believe firmly the Nazis would be defeated.

## FIFTEEN

Winter was in full force and we began to feel true hardship. We had better information from the war from Stalingrad and knew the German armies were surrounded. The German Junkers and Henkels were no longer flying in supplies to the German army, only para-chuting them in. Though I wasn't toiling in physical work anymore, the cold made me miserable. The winter here was worse than in the camp at Niuziary. The temperatures were warmer, but the wind fac-tor was tremendous. It was too cold to build trenches so now we were building all kinds of fortifications from lumber and underground shelters, called *ziemlankas*, for the army to rest and live there.

Time and again these forays brought us right to the front. The fight was not on a regular front now, it was all over, in the city itself and in the suburbs. My job as a medic became more realistic and dangerous — tending to casualties from shrapnel and artillery fire. I would have to get the wounded when the others stayed undercover. There were quite a few close calls, but fortunately, we only stayed there for a few days.

The Volga was frozen solid. In many places there was a large amount of lumber tied together and frozen in the river. The army needed the lumber and our job was to get it out from the frozen water. It was a backbreaking job. The men trying to extricate the lumber, used sharpened steel rods and axes and anything they could hold on to. After long, and in some cases, whole trees, were freed from the ice, they had to be dragged out on to a steep, slippery, snow-covered bank with ropes.

I had my office on the top on the shore, in a little hut with a fire going constantly. I felt terrible about Father working outside with the others, while I was in a warm hut. But I couldn't do anything about it. I was busy with the soldiers and their many ailments.

Our food now consisted of frozen bread. It was frozen so hard we had to use a saw to cut it evenly in rations. Occasionally, we got dried fish or a piece of salt pork. Everybody was weak and malnour-ished. Many people developed boils and carbuncles, including myself, which didn't heal for months. To this very day, my neck is full of scars from them.

The barracks were frigid, with one small stove in each corner. Everybody tried to huddle around them. The walls and windows of the barracks were completely covered with frost. The only light in the barrack was from the stove .With no washing facilities, we all became infested with lice.

I saw Dr. Rosa often, when I had a report to make or when I brought someone in. She was official, yet I felt she had a certain sentiment for me. I wasn't sure if it was sympathy or kindness. She would speak only of business, yet she always gave me a few cigarettes, some bread or tea and a newspaper.

Here and there, in the back of the paper, I would find an article about the involvement of the Allies in the war. The politicians were optimistic and I became a believer in victory at Stalingrad. The soldiers were mostly farmers and workers. They only wanted the war to end so they could go home. I was sure some of them didn't care who won, as long as it ended. The few of us from Poland had another wish and opinions. We had heard about the atrocities committed by the Germans to the prisoners of war and the civilian population, but never specifically against the Jews.

The long, bitter winter affected everyone. More men became sick and unable to work. I was doing my best with the little supplies that I had. At times, 30 per cent of the people were not able to work and I tried to hide them in the barracks. But I had to report all the cases, and some had to be sent to the medical station just to prove what was going on. They were often sent back the next day, with a little medication. Some didn't return at all and we would get replacements, but less often, now. It was a sign the Stalingrad campaign was winding up. We were still retrieving the logs from the frozen Volga and piling them up on the shore. But they stayed there for a long time, before they were picked up. The urgency was over and we were allowed to use a log or two to burn in our stove. At least now we could keep the fire in our barracks going all night.

We received orders to march to a new assignment, for a few days. We had no idea where we were going. Until now, we would have been afraid to walk out in the open, but we felt the war in Stalingrad was in a different phase. We weren't afraid of the German Stukas, which hadn't been seen for a long time. They were all gone. Only once in a while would we see the Junkers that flew in supplies to the apparently surrounded German army. The situation had changed drastically.

After an all-day march, we could see from afar, a huge complex of buildings. It looked like a castle with tall stone, fences. The area, closer to the buildings, was teeming with military vehicles. It was the headquarters of some unit or division. The buildings must have served as a monastery before the Revolution. We slept in a shabby building, which probably served as a stable years ago. There was a stove and lots of straw to sleep on. The best thing about this assignment was the decent food we received. We were led to a mess hall and were given an ample portion of a thick soup with a few pieces of meat in it, bread and hot tea with a piece of sugar.

With a full stomach, feeling good and tired, I fell asleep. The hour was early and it was cold and the snow fell steadily. I didn't sleep long when I was awakened by singing. I was sure I was dreaming. But the singing got louder. I went outside to investigate and to my astonishment, there were many people outside listening. The singers were Italian prisoners of war, brought in earlier that day. The army men, all well dressed, mostly officers, stood outside smoking their cigarettes and listening until the singing died down.

We stayed at the headquarters for few days. Our work consisted of cleaning, shovelling the snow and cutting logs for firewood to supply the kitchen. We received warm soup or hot cereal every day. Boiled water was always available. Often we were treated by the army boys with cigarettes. The place was also a processing area for prisoners of war. Some were marching out of the compound and more were brought in daily. The majority of the ones I saw there were Italians and Romanians. A few German officers were mixed with them. I was amazed the way the army treated them, especially the Italians. They were happy the war was over for them. I could see with my own eyes that the battle of Stalingrad was going well. You could feel victory in the air. You could see it in the faces of the officers and military personnel. They were all in a good mood

We were sorry to leave this place. Not far from the headquarters, as we marched back to our barracks, we came across a huge column of German prisoners of war, marching north. They certainly didn't look like the conquerors of Europe. They dragged themselves, in complete silence. You could only hear the shuffling of their feet in the snow. They were unshaven and bundled in tattered clothing and didn't resemble an army. They had babushkas on their heads and shawls around their shoulders, not proper attire in the Stalingrad winter. Even the officers that walked in front were shabbily dressed.

Back in the barracks we found everything as before. Everyone felt better, having eaten nourishing food for a few days, and just seeing the upbeat mood of the headquarters, lightened everyone's spirits. The urgency in our work was gone.

The winter dragged on and the  sunny days were few and far

174

between. The days grew longer and we waited for the warm weather. Around this time, Father started to complain about his feet swelling and the fact he couldn't put his boots on. It was a common complaint, caused by hard work, but mainly it was malnutrition. I tried to arrange for him to stay in the barracks as much as possible and do some light chores. But I couldn't do this too often. There were others in worse shape and I had to rotate them.

I noticed Father's swelling was getting worse and reached up to his knee. I was worried and took him to the medical station to have Dr. Rosa examine him.

She looked at Father's legs and didn't say much. She gave him some pills, that looked like vitamins, and written permission to stay in the barracks for four days. I didn't question her. I knew she wanted to help me and I was happy she let Father get some time off.

THe rest helped the swelling go down and I tried to get extra food for him, but most of the time there was nothing available. As soon as Father went back to work, the swelling flared up and got worse. At work, I tried to keep him on the top of the shore so he would not have to climb the steep banks, dragging the heavy logs with the ropes. He looked much older than his age.

The day came when the political officer entered our barrack and without any preliminaries, raised his hands and announced the German army had capitulated.

He said: " Thanks to our Father Stalin and our unbeatable Red Army, victory is ours! We will chase them now until we get to Berlin!"

This time, we believed him and a shouts of joy and hurrahs went out. Too bad there was nothing to celebrate with, but the officer promised supplies would get better. Nothing changed for us. We still worked our hours, but we got a day off to celebrate.

The next day, we went on an assignment to clear a road that was blocked with debris, closer to Stalingrad. We witnessed thousands and thousands of German soldiers being led by the Red Army troops. They were in terrible shape. They walked in silence with their heads down

Father's legs were getting worse so I spoke to Rosa about it. She told me it might be possible to arrange a longer sick leave or a furlough. But she gave no details. It had to be organized and a medical commission would have to deal with the decision.

The days, though longer, were uneventful. It was still cold, but life seemed more bearable without the German threat. I went to my friends, the villagers and was the first to bring them news of the victory in Stalingrad. They found a drink of vodka and a piece of bread to celebrate the occasion, giving me a little to take home.

When the war began, many Russians including some of the autonomic republics, secretly wished for a German victory. They hoped to gain independence and get rid of Stalin's cruel dictatorship. Whole armies surrendered. But as the war progressed, the news of German ruthlessness, murder and burning became known and verified, including the horrible treatment and eventual death of thousands of prisoners of war. Their opinion changed drastically and the war became a war for Mother Russia. This strong sense of nationality was the biggest factor in the defeat of Germany.

I went to the medical station with a report and to get some supplies. Rosa told me a commission would be organized, soon to arrange furloughs and temporary releases for the sick. Father would be one of the many candidates. I didn't say anything to Father, because I didn't want to build up his hopes.

Now that the Stalingrad campaign was finished, all kinds of rumors started about our future assignments. Some said we were going to be transferred to other fronts, others said we were going to the heart of Stalingrad, where there was lots of work. Some even dreamed we would be demobilized and go home.

We still didn't know how the war was progressing on other fronts. Were the Germans retreating? Was the victory of Stalingrad just a local victory?

One day, we were taken by truck to a town called Dubowka. It was better than marching. We were to clean some warehouses where thousands of German uniforms, boots and other clothing were taken as booty. Some were blood-stained and had bullet holes in them. We found German pamphlets and letters and photographs from home in the pockets. We met thousands of prisoners of war on the road, being led toward Dubowka. Long columns of motorized divisions passed us, too. It felt good to see the military power.

Father, who served in the Austro-Hungarian Army, had told me about the misery he saw in the First World War. The peace treaty was to end all wars, and here, after a few years of peace, another war, much more deadly, was raging. Who was going to win? And what were they going to win? Who was going to pay for the waste of young lives? Who was going to pay for the grief of their families, their bombed homes, villages and cities.

176

# Sixteen

In a few days I was given a list of men eligible for sick leave including Father. In the evening, I told the men who were going to be checked by the commission. I thought Father would be happy, but instead, he looked sad and showed little emotion. I understood his sadness. Suppose he got the furlough or release. We would have to separate. Where would he go? Other people had relatives' homes to go to. But where would he go?

Father was one of the first to get a furlough. The commission, chaired by Rosa and two other women doctors and a couple of medical officer, took one look at Father's legs and approved a six-week leave. I could see Father was worried. He refused to go anywhere without me. We discussed many scenarios, but Father wouldn't consider any of them. Deep down, I was worried about separation, too. Where would he go? How would he return? Logically, I knew once we separated, God knows when or if we would even meet again.

Father repeated the last words my mother said to him and I had never forgotten. On the road out of Krakow in 1939, when we decided Mother and Niusia should go home and we would go to the east, we kissed and hugged and Mother said to Father: "Leon, take care of him, he is only a child." My eyes filled with tears then.

Father said with tears in his eyes, "I promised to your mother I will bring you home with me." I had to do something about this.

To whom could I talk about this dilemma? Maybe Father could not accept the furlough and things could be as before. Even if this was possible, his feet were still swollen and he was quite sick. I decided the only person who could help me was Dr. Rosa. She knew a little about our ordeal, but this was war and millions of people had problems like ours and many were worse off. The only way to solve the problem was for me to get a similar furlough as Father and this way we could go together.

I had nothing to lose by asking her. She was my only hope. I devised a plan and as an additional bribe, I dug out my carefully hidden treasure — my gold Waterman fountain pen that I had received as a Bar Mitzvah gift. I wrapped it in a beautiful handkerchief and went to see Rosa. I wasn't sure what I was going to do. I had to find a way to see her alone.

I chose late afternoon and I was lucky to find her alone in her office. The night before I went to her office I tied up my legs, just below the knees. I wanted to see if they would swell and, surely, they did. I kept the strings on all day, not allowing the swelling to go down.

I entered Rosa's office and sat down in front of her desk. I was so nervous, I was shaking. She asked me what was wrong and I told her about my problem. I told her about Father and me, about the talk I had with him. At the end of my story, I told her my legs were also swollen. I lifted my trousers and showed them to her. She only glanced at my legs. I understood that she realized what I was doing. I asked her with a pleading voice to help me. I took out the handkerchief and unwrapped my beautiful Waterman pen and put it on her desk, telling her to take it. I'd had it for a long time, I said, and was afraid it would get stolen.

My eyes filled with tears. I said goodbye and walked out. I painfully left behind the only memento of my Bar Mitzvah.

In a few days, I was notified to come to the medical centre. I tied my legs every night and sometimes during the day, until I had to appear before the commission. I didn't shave so I would look older and haggard.

I went before the commission and was told to show my legs. They examined them and told me to go. I was sure I would get my furlough. Rosa had accepted my gift and I was called to an abbreviated commission, soon after my meeting with her. When I told Father about it, he cheered up. It would take a few days to get medical approval from the commission.

We started to discuss where we should go. Once we received approval, we would get a travel permit and list our destination, which the army also had to approve. The only place we could think to go was back to Astrachan and the fish factory. But we didn't want to go there, even if it was possible.

We finally agreed to go to Kuibyszow, where we knew the Polish government in exile had an embassy. We considered ourselves Polish citizens, but our documents were taken away from us illegally on the boat in Stalingrad. When Moscow was in danger of falling to the Germans, all foreign embassies and the Russian government and important defense factories were relocated in the vicinity of Kuibyszow, on the Volga.

Quite a few other men were expecting to be discharged or transferred to other locations or get furloughs like us. Our barber was also expecting to be released. He was planning to go to a collective farm where he worked before.

I was busy arranging and managing the delousing station and tried to get more time for people to wash themselves.

One day a terrible thing happened that frightened me more than any of the German bombings. I took a platoon to the delousing station. Everything was routine, the clothing was bundled up and my helper hung the clothing to be deloused. The men were washing themselves and I was waiting to do the same. As I sat smoking a cigarette, my assistant ran in to tell me smoke was coming from the delousing chamber, where the clothing was hanging. I opened the door and the room, with the men's clothing in it, was in flames. We desperately tried to rescue them, but couldn't. It was a disaster. Now, 20 men in the middle of winter were practically all naked. I sent my helpers to the station for help. A few bundles of clothing were probably placed too close to the drum.

Later, I found out, that in some spots, the drum was pierced, or had a burn hole. Whatever happened, I knew I would be blamed for it. The delousing station was my responsibility. I didn't need this only a few days before I was expected to leave. I was devastated.

Father and I nervously waited a few days to hear the outcome of the investigation. The following week, I was called to the medical station and ordered to bring the men who had applied for discharge or or medical furlough. Everybody, except me, was given their papers, including Father. They were ordered to leave as soon as possible to army headquarters, where travel permits would be issued.

I waited until everybody left and I entered the office, where Rosa was. I could see by the look on her face that something was wrong. I asked for my papers, but I couldn't see any on her desk. I knew that I was in trouble.

Rosa explained. I was approved for a six-week furlough, like Father, but because of the incident that destroyed the clothing of my "fighters," as she called them, my papers would be sent to headquarters with an explanation as to what happened. They would make the final decision. She said if there was another way to help me, she would, but her hands were tied.

I was told to go with the others and wait for the courier to bring my papers. I explained to Father it was a formality, because of my position as a medic. My papers would be brought to headquarters I told him.

Back in the barracks we packed our belongings and started on our way. Everyone was happy and in a great mood, except for the two of us.

We walked quickly down the familiar road and in a few hours we saw the outline of the headquarters. Once inside, we were led in by a sentry and walked upstairs to the administration building on the third floor. It was a long corridor with doors to offices on both sides.

We lined up near the office and the process began. Everyone's travel papers were ready. They filled out the destination, time of furlough, were issued a permit to go downstairs for two loaves of bread and their discharges were final.

While everybody was getting their papers, including Father, I waited next to the door for the courier to bring my papers. Father didn't want to go, but I persuaded him to go downstairs and get his ration of bread. I sat there alone waiting. I had a feeling I would have great difficulty once the papers arrived and deep down I felt that I would get punished in some way.

I was sitting next to the door, destitute, frightened and depressed when suddenly I heard the heavy footsteps of a man coming to our floor. It was the courier, heavily dressed in quilted pants and a jacket. He'd probably arrived by sled. He looked cold. In his hand was a satchel. He passed by me and turned to an office just opposite to where I was sitting. As he made the turn to the office, a little bundle of papers fell out of his quilted jacket. The papers were a little wet on the outside. I grabbed this bundle, unrolled it and I couldn't believe what I held in my hand — my papers!

Attached to my papers was the report about the fire which occurred under my supervision at the delousing stations and caused the destruction of the clothing of a whole platoon. I was thankful I could read Russian fluently. I removed the report, put it in my pocket, took the papers and entered the room where I was processed quickly, without any questioning.

I quickly ran downstairs to meet Father. He had his two loaves of bread in his hand. I didn't say a word and grabbed him, leading him outside. I told him we had to leave immediately—and fast! We caught up with the others from our platoon and came to a crowded road with people and military equipment travelling in all directions.Evening was approaching so we started to look for a place to sleep. We found a barn and decided to stay for the night. We made a small fire, melted snow to boil water, but it was too cold to lay down and sleep.

In the quiet of the night, I took Father aside and for the first time told him what really happened with my papers at the headquarters. He uttered a prayer and said somebody was watching over me. I was trembling at the thought of what could have happened if they read the attached report. I took the report out my pocket and put it in the fire.

180

It was cold, we were freezing, but I felt happy and sure of myself. I dozed off around the fire. I went outside, it was crisp and cold. The sky was studded with millions of stars. There was a full moon. The combination of the sky and the white snow made it look like it was day. Traffic was as heavy as during the day. I decided to get up and move. There was no use sitting here and freezing. We walked to the railroad station.

I don't remember the name of the station, but we knew it was a good two days' walk. We had little food. Occasionally, we came across an army vehicles parked on the side of the road and ask them for a smoke. They would treat us to a gulp of vodka and sometimes a piece of bread. I think the soldiers took pity on us . We looked cold and poorly dressed. So sometimes they would give us some extra food.

The third day, we approached a little town and asked some civilians for directions to the railroad station. When we entered the station, I became scared. It reminded me of Pier 14 in Astrachan. People were all over the floor, civilian and military. There was no room to sit but at least it was warm with all the bodies around.

Nobody knew when the train was going to arrive or where they were going, but they didn't care. Nearly everyone wanted to go northeast. Our plan was to go north to Kuibyszow, a city on the Volga.

The train arrived and everyone ran out of the station, trying to get on. The trains consisted of boxcars with very few passenger cars. They were overcrowded, mainly with soldiers.Some trains didn't even stop at the station, they just slowed down. People, in desperation, jumped on the stairs and hung on the outside. Many had to walk back after freezing while hanging on for a few kilometers.

We spent almost 10 days at the station without getting on a train. As people left to find food, more people came to take their place. We were unable to board any of the trains. We became desperate. Food was running out, there was no place to wash and we were infested with lice. We lost our space on the floor in the station. every time we tried to get on another train.

I studied the boxcars and noticed that between some of them there was a little platform with a door opening into the cars. I decided it might be possible to jump on one of the platforms and at least get to the next stop.

This plan succeeded after several unsuccessful attempts. The three of us stood on one of these little platform, waiting for the train to move. I banged on the door to the car, hoping somebody would let us in. The train began to move, first slowly and then it picked up speed. The faster it went, the colder it got. The wind was terrible and we knew we wouldn't last very long on the platform.

I started to bang on the door and in desperation started to holler and begged them to let us in. I told them we were freezing and couldn't hang on much longer. Somebody took pity on us and opened the door. It was warm inside. In the centre of the car, was a red, hot stove and soldiers, only in their shirts were standing around the stove, smoking cigarettes. They looked at us, standing like frozen mummies. One after the other started to offer, at first a little vodka, then a cigarette. Once one started helping, the other tried to outdo them. They even gave us salted pork with a piece of bread. We came to ourselves quickly.

The car was crowded with soldiers but away from the stove we found a place to sit. When the train stopped, a couple of soldiers would leave the train and get more wood for the stove.

One of the soldiers approached me and politely asked my name. I introduced myself as Sasha and he said the next time we stop, it will be your turn to get the firewood. The train slowed down and came to a complete stop, the door was opened and another man and I stood in the middle of nowhere. A wooden fence was plainly visible from the tracks. The soldier in charge told us to break pieces of wood from the fence. The closer I got to the snow fence, the deeper the snow got. It was almost up to my chest. Finally, I got close enough to break off some planks, when I heard voices from the train: "Hurry up, we are moving!"

I turned and saw the other man running back to the moving train and being lifted up by four men. I dropped my booty and frantically tried to run, but the deep snow held me back. When I got back to the tracks, the train was gone and out of sight.

Here I was, alone, in the middle of the night, in a wasteland with nothing in sight but a white blanket of snow. It was close to dawn, but still completely dark, bitter cold, with the wind blowing towards the fence. I was without my jacket or hat and I had no documents or papers. What was I going to do? My eyes filled with tears in desperation. I sat down on the rails. My head was in my arms. I sat for a while. I would surely freeze to death. I had seen it happen to other people. If you sit down, at first you'll feel cold, slowly you get sleepy and when you fall asleep you freeze to death.

I jumped up and started to run between the tracks, , the only place clear of the deep snow. It was so many years ago, yet when I close my eyes, I recall every detail of the run for my life. How long and how fast I ran, I don't know, but I'm sure I set some long distance records. The hair on my eyelids froze. I had icicles from the tears on my face. I was tired and my feet hurt, hitting the wooden trestles on the tracks. But I ran and ran. I began to hallucinate. Every time I looked up I could see in the distance the rear of my train. This gave me the incentive to run faster. It was like running after something so close, yet so impossible to reach. All I could think of was running. I didn't feel the cold. I was sweating and my breathing was getting heavier.

Dawn was approaching. I cleared my eyes, stood for a moment and started to walk. I couldn't run anymore. I looked to my left and I could see the outline of a building. I started to run again. Was it just a vision? I ran faster than before and the buildings started to get closer. I could see the rear of a train standing on the tracks. Was this another illusion? I stopped looking at the building and looked only at the rear of the train. I kept my eyes low, just looking at the track. When I looked up I could see I was gaining on the train. When I saw the train slowly pulling away, it gave me strength to keep moving. In a couple of moments, I caught up. The platform of our car was within my reach and I jumped on it and banged on the door crying: "Father! Father! Open the door!"

The door opened and Father and the barber dragged me inside. The warm air hit me and I passed out. When I woke up, I was laying on the floor, next to the stove. I was so weak I could not talk. They gave me hot water with sugar and a potato, donated by one of the soldiers. I ate a little, drank the hot water and fell asleep again. It took a few days for me to recover.

When I told them what happened, they couldn't believe I survived. Even some boys from Siberia were in awe. They were careful now, not to jump out in the middle of nowhere for wood, but rather get it at the small stations when the train stopped.

Our journey was slow. Almost three weeks had passed and we were not even half way to our destination. The train stopped often, sometimes for days. Apparently, it was impossible to get enough coal to run the train. It crawled from station to station, trying to get more coal. We were afraid to leave the train, never knowing how long it would stay in the same place. Seldom did we get food, even though we were entitled to bread. The soldiers, the officers, got food more often and they often shared it with us.

Our beards were getting longer. I looked at my father and he was an old, unkept man. I didn't see myself so it didn't bother me. What worried me was the duration of our journey. We would arrive, using all six weeks of our furlough, travelling only one way. We were technically deserters. Fearful, we said our goodbyes and decided to seek out the Polish Embassy and get advice from them. The problem was how to find the embassy before being caught by the military patrol or local militia.

The street were full of people going to work. When we passed by a store with a good-sized mirror in the window, I stopped to look at myself. At first I thought a beggar was standing behind me or in front of me. I moved my arms and realized it was me. We looked terrible. We hadn't shaved for weeks and our clothing was a crumpled mess. I was afraid to be stopped by any patrol, just because of the way we looked.

I asked a few civilians for directions, but nobody had a clue. We came close to the centre of the city, but still couldn't find the embassy.I noticed a man in a different military uniform, with a beret on his head, coming toward us. I asked him where the Polish embassy was. He looked me over from head to toe and asked in Polish if I was from Poland. I said yes, and that I desperately needed help from the embassy. Not only did he tell me where it was, but he walked a couple of blocks with us and pointed out the way to go.

It was a quiet, well-kept residential street. On the left, there were a few buildings, which looked more like government offices. Some had foreign flags, indicating they were embassies. I went to the right side of the street, to be as far as possible from the militia patrolling the entrances to the embassies. Then, I noticed the Polish flag hanging in front of a huge building. The building had a high iron fence. To enter the building you had to go through the iron gate, and then toward a massive wooden front door.Out front, stood a militia man, walking from one end to the other. I was worried that we would be turned away once he saw our condition.

A few people approached the embassy, opened the gate, went to the wooden door and without a problem, opened it and went inside. The only obstacle might be the militia man, walking back and forth in front of the building. I chose a moment when he was as far as possible from the gate door and I grabbed Father. We ran across the street, opened the gate and entered the building through the main door.

We found ourselves in a vestibule with a high ceiling. There was another door, leading from the vestibule inside. How would we be treated? What could they do for us?

I tried to delay for a few moments our entrance through the glass door. What would I say? If they don't help us we'd have to give ourselves up to the military command and tell them our story. Who knows where they will send us or what they will do to us? Will they believe our story or treat us as deserters?

I closed my eyes, took a deep breath, opened the glass door and entered. It was warm and bright inside. I stopped for a moment, just to look around. I felt I didn't belong in this clean, beautiful place, I was so filthy.

I noticed a man and woman behind a desk, gesturing for us to approach them. The place was so quiet that it scared me. I was afraid to step on the carpets covering the marble floor. When we finally approached the desk, I froze, not knowing what to do or say.

I looked at the man dressed in a dark suit, with a tie, and the young woman behind the desk, who looked like someone out of a magazine. She had a beautiful face, long, blonde hair and she wore a crisp, white blouse with a dark ribbon around her neck.

I couldn't look at them. I put my head down, feeling very self-conscious. The girl noticed our confusion and started the conversation, asking what they could do for us. I didn't know where to begin and I was getting more nervous. She said it would be better if she asked the questions and we answered. This put me at ease. The questions concerned our origin an our names.

I was becoming more at ease. When she asked me about my formal education, I opened my bag and took out my 1939 school report from the Gymnasium in Krakow. They could not believe how in my circumstances I saved this document. They were flabbergasted. I saved this report, because it was the biggest treasure I possessed. From that moment on, they became more helpful and friendly.

Still I worried our Jewishness would affect their behaviour.

When we were almost done, she said it was time for tea. Out of nowhere appeared a girl with a tray holding a teapot and cups and she set it down on the table and disappeared, only to return with a couple trays of pastries. I didn't know what to do first. The young girl with the tray was about my age. She was wearing a short skirt, white blouse and white apron. She looked like an angel. She had a ribbon in her hair and a beautiful friendly smile on her face. Was I dreaming? I pinched myself.

We were invited to sit down and have tea. The girl sat down with us for a few minutes, encouraging us to eat and enjoy the food and she went back to her desk. I didn't know where to start.Everything was so beautiful, the silver tea set, the sugar and pastries. We devoured the delicate crepes and pastries. We could have finished everything and more, but we left a few pieces on each platter. I felt clumsy holding the small tea cup in my hand, afraid to drop it. When we finished, the girl called us back to the desk and asked us a few more questions.

The young man returned and sat next to us with a smile on his face. I could see he had good news. We had nothing to worry about, he said. Everything was going to be taken care of for us as rightful Polish citizens. He got up and told us to follow him.

We went to the back door of the main building, walked a few feet and entered several smaller buildings.

There was an entire compound, surrounded by a high fence. Our office leader, called in a strong voice into one of the small buildings: "Peter, Peter!" A large, middle-aged man emerged from one of the rooms. They spoke for a minute and he told us not to worry, as we would be in good hands.

We introduced ourselves to Peter. He was from a small town outside of Krakow. The conversation went smoothly and he turned out to be a friendly, jovial man. He told us, his orders were to turn us into normal looking human beings, who could call themselves Polish citizens.

The cleansing began in earnest. He led us to a warm room with wooden benches. It a *bania,* a typical Russian steam bath. We were flabbergasted by Peter's first order. Take off all of our clothing, which we'd been wearing for eight weeks, including the lice and our shoes. He put it all in a prepared sack, handling each piece of clothing with two fingers, careful not to get contaminated. He disposed of the clothing and opened the door to the steambath. We steamed ourselves for along time, washing with plenty of hot water and all the soap we wanted.

Peter came with scissors and a straight razor and began cutting our hair and shaving our faces. By the time he finished with us, we were sparkling clean. He disappeared again and Father and I sat in a room looking at each other in amazement. Father looked so young and different. I hadn't seen him this way in a very long time. We didn't talk to each other, sitting in silence, wondering what was going to happen next.

When Peter returned, we couldn't see his face because of the pile of clothing he was holding in his arms. Everything was brand new — underwear, uniform jackets, pants, winter jackets.and shoes. He had a good eye for sizes, because everything fit. We packed our sacks with spare underwear and socks.

He led us back to the main building. I felt like I was flying in all my new clothes. Everything was so comfortable. When I appeared at the desk, I was greeted by the girl with a broad smile. She couldn't believe the transformation in me. The waitress brought us lunch and when she saw us she almost fell over.

We were led upstairs to a large office and greeted by the secretary to the ambassador, Dr. Kot. This was where the decision about our future was to be made. He presented us with new papers, stating we were Polish citizens and foreigners in this country. He was very polite and asked many personal questions.

We were directed to go to a town named Kinelczerkasy, where the the Polish government had a representative who would help us. We were to take a local train to the station named Kinel, and from there it was a few more kilometres to Kinelczerkasy.

They allowed us also to sleep in one of the small buildings overnight. We received our new papers, a generous amount of rubles and food. We thank them and said goodbye

We left early the next morning, to the train station that would take us to Kinel. We had no problem, getting tickets and the next train was to leave later that afternoon.

Knowing about anti-Semitism in Poland, I had been apprehensive about the way we would be treated at the Polish embassy. We were amazed we received so much help and sympathy.

While waiting to buy our tickets, I struck up a conversation with one of the engineers and asked him if he knew where the Polish representative lived. He gave me directions without hesitation.

When we arrived we took a wide road leading to the town, and without difficulty found the Polish representative. He lived in a small house, on one of the side streets. We found him eating breakfast served by a Russian woman, which we later found out he was renting the place from. He invited us for tea and the woman brought some porridge and bread. Mr. Komorowski had a quick look at our papers and I got the impression he was not impressed by our Jewish names. But, he acted professional, and after a conversation, became more friendly. We needed to find lodging, he told us, and it wouldn't be a problem.

The Russian woman knew many people willing to take us in. Most households were without men, all serving in the army. They felt safer to have men in their homes, she said. The money we would pay for rent, would also come in handy.

We found ourselves in the home of a widow with two small children. Her husband had been killed in action the year before. The house was clean and built of logs, as all the homes in the area were.

We moved there almost immediately, after receiving from Mr. Komorowski, more rubles to last for a month and a few more cans of food. The next day we were to meet him to register with the local authorities. Mr. Komorowski then helped us get a job at the employment office. Our qualifications weren't in demand, but the local restaurant needed two men to chop wood to keep the place warm and the stoves burning.

With our experience, this was an easy task. They gave us a couple days to settle in. We had a job, a place to live, and we were presentable. The work was not hard and anytime we felt, we could take a break, go inside to warm up, smoke a cigarette and of course have a cup of tea. We got cabbage soup for lunch and our bread ration and cereal. Bread was strictly rationed at 400 grams per person.

We worked diligently but we were way ahead of the needed supply for the restaurant so we slowed down just enough to keep the place going, otherwise we'd be without a job.

We had Sundays off, and spent the day washing and cleaning. Sometimes we had the opportunity to go to the steambath but I didn't feel comfortable there, because of the resentful Anti-Semitic comments made by the old men.

We were approached once, by an elderly man, who brought a bag of flour for the restaurant. I unloaded the wagon and took the flour to the kitchen. His name was Gluskin and he asked me if we could come to his home and chop wood for him, from time to time. He would gladly pay us, so we accepted the offer.

He showed us his well-kept, home with a good-sized lot, located not far from the restaurant. Kinelczerkasy consisted of two wide streets with long rows of tiny log homes. One led from the railroad station and included larger buildings, the hospital and government regional offices. The other street was connected to the open market.

The following Sunday morning we went to his house to cut the wood.He asked us our names where we were from. I had a feeling Gluskin was Jewish. He was polite, neatly dressed and had a gentle smile, but despite the smile, I detected a sadness. He didn't look like the locals.

There was a lot of lumber and he told us we didn't have to finish it all in one day. We didn't ask how we would be paid. Whatever extra we would get would help. We worked for about three hours and the pile of wood grew higher and higher.

The door of the house opened and a matronly woman with a white apron came outside. She asked us to come in for a bite to eat. We entered a small vestibule in the house, where on a wooden bench was a pail of water and little soap. Mrs. Gluskin encouraged us to wash our hands. Their home looked like the majority of the other ones on the street, but not inside. It wasn't a peasant house. It was sparkling clean with freshly painted white walls. On the wooden floor there were rugs and the place was neatly and colorfully furnished. I hadn't seen a home like this in a long time.

We were invited to sit at the table and to our surprise there was an array of food — milk, eggs, cheese and a big loaf of white bread. This is all yours, she said, and there's more if you want. She said she would wait to eat when her husband returned. Mrs. Gluskin was more inquisitive than her husband and wanted to know everything about us, which we were glad to tell her. She told us they are Jewish and had been evacuated from Poltawa to the Ukraine, where here husband kept a high position in the flour industry.

She brought us two photographs of two handsome men in uniform and with a great sadness and tears in her eyes, told us these were her sons who were fighting in the war.

Only one had written to her quite often, but the younger one she hadn't heard from in a while. We could understand her anxiety.

We finished eating and she told us to clean the yard a little and go home to rest. Next Sunday, we could finish the wood-cutting job.

Our relationship with the Gluskins continued as long as we stayed in Kinel. Mr. Gluskin called on me often and always paid well. I helped him at the flour mill, loading flour on the horse-drawn cart.

Though I was very friendly with them, we never talked about politics or the war. We talked about the weather an our families. The Gluskins spread the word that we were good workers, and offers from women, whose husbands were at war, came to us. We were glad to get extra work which was usually paid in food.

The Polish office closed, as the Polish army had left Russia. No sooner had the office closed than we were notified to appear at the local military recruiting office. I knew they wouldn't leave us alone. A series of interrogations began. They offered us Soviet citizenship , telling us this would be an honor bestowed upon us. We explained to the interrogator we were Polish citizens and our families were in Poland. After the war end we wanted to be reunited with our families, so we couldn't accept this honour. None of our arguments were reasonable and the interrogation started in earnest. We'd been through this before.

The interrogation lasted for days with some breaks, and it seemed our peaceful days in Kinel would soon be over. The days dragged now in uncertainty and our spirits were getting low.

Winter would soon be here and the days were rainy. Even chopping wood became a chore. The woman we stayed with was saving the fuel for winter. We solved this problem by bringing a few logs from the restaurant, which was risky and illegal.

SIXTEEN

Before long, we received a notice to show up at the recruiting office. Without an explanation the officer in charge told us we were going to be mobilized. I told him we were Polish citizens. He smiled. We all had to fight the Germans, because they were our common enemy.

We were given a few days to wind up our affairs, and on a set day we were to present ourselves to the office. We started to pack our belongings into clean flour bags. We had no clue where we were going to be mobilized  We said goodbye to the Gluskins and thanked them for their help and kindness.

There were lots of other men being inducted, too, mostly middle-aged men and younger ones, just reaching the draft age.We were formed into columns and marched with a military escort to the rail-road station. Mothers and wives walked alongside us.  It was a sad picture. They wanted to stay with their loved ones for as long as they could. The few kilometres to the station seemed long. We were upset to leave this place. We had felt secure here, for the first time in years. But good times never lasted long in Russia.

There were more draftees waiting at the station. The war effort demanded more people. We were counted and recounted several times  and loaded into the boxcars. I hoped this time our journey would not last long. We were going to Kuibyszow, where our destination would be decided.

We sat on the floor, coasting slowly toward Kuibyszow, stopping at little stations. Our escort would open the door at longer stops. But we were not allowed to get out.  In a few hours, we arrived at Kuibyszow. The passengers disembarked, but not us. We waited about an hour until we felt the train moving again slowly. We could hear them detaching some of the boxcars and until there were two left. They finally opened the door and we could see we were far from the station.

We were ordered outside, formed in columns and marched toward the city. We entered a huge compound teeming with people. There were mostly civilians being inducted in the army,  and men in military uniform.

We were led to a barrack to sleep overnight on the floor.The next morning, we were lined up in front of a building to go through anoth-er interrogation and selection.  We waited in a long line until we

190

reached a desk with three men. A few question were asked and I told them we were Polish citizens, refugees in the USSR. They didn't say much and ordered us to go to a large room, where quite a few people were standing around. They were all Father's age and older.

When the room was nearly full, we were led back to the railroad siding and to the boxcars. More people came and boarded different cars. By the time they hooked up the locomotive it was dark. The short ride to Kuibyszow didn't take long. We were pushed out again to a siding and heard some of the cars being moved. Ours stayed put.

In the morning, the door opened and we could see only two cars were left. Finally, a locomotive arrived and we were moving again. We passed Kuibyszow station and the city. Within two hours we came to a stop. The doors were opened and in the distance we saw big factories surrounded by rows of new barracks as far as I could see.

We were being taken to an employment office, where we were to be screened and assigned to work in nearby factories. Father and I were relieved that we would be working and not sent to the front-lines. Maybe we would begin a real civilian life.

It was finally our turn and we were led to a huge room full of people, with women secretaries, handling papers. As we went up to the desk, we found two civilians and a uniformed army man. We gave our names and handed over our documents. The man in uniform didn't agree with the assignment we were about to be given. He asked a few more questions about our status as Polish refugees and sent us outside to wait. We were called back and told we were going to get a different assignment.

The room was empty except for Father and I and three middle-aged men. A civilian called our names and we were told to follow him. We followed him through some muddy streets, passing huge factories.Our guide was talkative and willingly answered some of our questions. He told us these factories produced the best aircraft in the world to fight Hitler's hordes.

We entered a small building and found ourselves in the factory director's spartan office. He introduced himself as Zajcew. He told us we were in *sapogo valalnycech*, a place that produced felt winter boots called Valinki. I had never owned a pair, but often dreamed of having Valinki boots. I had seen officers, directors and some Siberian army units wearing them. They were expensive, especially the ones of better quality. In a dry cold sub-zero climate they kept your feet warm.

Mr. Zajcew took us on a tour and showed us the beautiful finished product. Our guide and Mr. Zajcew finished up some paperwork. I looked around a bit. The place was full of huge vats, in which were funny looking    flat boots. A few people were working on machines. Our guide and Mr. Zajcew emerged from their meeting and announced we would start work at eight tomorrow morning. The guide would show us where we were to live, close to the factory.

We were disappointed with our living quarters — called ziemlanki — which were really underground earth shelters. I had seen them and we had built them in and around Stalingrad, as temporary shelters,  but I never expected to live in one. They were made by digging a ditch about six to seven feet deep and then covered with logs or boards and covered with dirt.

We were assigned bunks. The bunker was almost empty except for a few people who worked nights.  We were introduced to an elderly man, who was the caretaker of our new living quarters.  He was responsible for keeping the place clean.  There were outhouses, a little distance from the quarters and water was brought in pails and stored in steel drums inside. Strangely, the place had electricity. The lighting consisted of three dim and dirty bulbs in the centre, giving us light 24 hours a day. We were unhappy living in such primitive surroundings with no privacy.

It took a few days to find out where we really were.  The name of this huge complex of factories surrounded by small plants and little supply offices was Bezemianka, meaning a nameless place. A million people worked and lived here and they couldn't even give it a name. It was a huge tract of land about 80 km from Kuibyszow. Before the revolution, it was called Samara. It was unsuitable for agriculture, complete wasteland. When the German armies invaded Russia and were advancing quickly towards Moscow, endangering the heart and capitol of the USSR, Stalin decided to move all the foreign embassies and aviation factories and most of the government offices to Kuibyszow.  It was a gigantic undertaking and it was done by sheer force of masses of people, without any consideration of hardship, suffering misery and victims.

They built Bezemianka probably much like the pyramids of Egypt, only faster. Generally, people who came here didn't want to talk about it. It was an unbelievable undertaking in a short time period and something to marvel about.

They brought from the Gulags hundred of thousands of prisoners who levelled the land, practically by hand. They completed the rail line and started to build a gigantic coal-powered hydro station. Once the land was ready, they built the factories, from the bottom up. Most of the cement was mixed by hand, everything was  done in the open.

The factories were working before the walls and roofs were put on. They worked seven days a week, 24 hours a day. The prisoners lived in the ziemlanki we lived in, but more primitive and without electricity. Some of them were forced to sleep outside because it was so crowded. There were huge food shortages and no medical help. People died by thousands, not only prisoners but builders too. The people and specialists who operated the factories moved here from all over the country as far as Siberia and the Urels. Their families came with them unwillingly. It was a cruel unbelievable effort, but necessary with the Germans invading so quickly.

When we came to Bezemianka, the place had normalized. The prisoners were gone, many of them joining the army. The workers in Bezemianka went on producing the planes at full speed. The building continued, but it was mostly offices, living quarters and smaller feeding plants. There was already an electric train connecting the place to Kuibyszow.

The next morning we got up early to be at work for 8 a.m. We waited for Mr. Zajcew to assign us to our jobs He came in cheerfully and greeted us. Father was considered an older man so he was given a job with the women, cleaning grass and dirt from the huge bales of wool. They worked in a separate room, most of the time sitting. After this operation, the wool was taken to the next room to a huge machine called a *czoska,* a combing machine. The small batches of cleaned wool were brought here and put on a conveyor and fed to steel combs where it came out in long sheets. From there, it was rolled in bales, like carpet. It was very loose and easily taken apart.

It was an easy and monotonous job, to which my father was assigned. As the only man, the woman took good care of him and treated him to all kinds of goodies from their homes. Father was happy here and he was well-liked. He told the women stories of Poland, and about the First World War.

Mr. Zajcew called me to his office, where a man, probably in this 30s, was waiting. He introduced me and then Zajcew made a speech about the importance of supplying quality boots to keep the working people producing the best airplanes and army people warm in the winter. He decided that I should learn the tricks of the trade and I was to learn to make the boots from scratch.

I would be the master bootmaker Alexi's apprentice. If I followed his instructions, I could become a master and my future would be assured. I thanked Zajcew for the opportunity.

I followed Alexi to the room where he worked. It was neat, not very large, with only about 10 people worked there. There were tables and wooden benches, where the men worked. I was assigned an area about two metres wide, beside Alexi. As the master, he always got the best wool, snow white and delicate. His boots were masterpieces. Most of them were destined for the higher echelons, civil servants and military. He made them with great love and dedication. They were beautiful to look at. Most of those went to a special shoemaker to be fitted with leather soles. Of course, only a few could afford these.

Food was incredibly short. We found out there was a free market nearby, where you could buy tobacco and food, like pumpkins, potatoes and lamb fat. But we didn't have much money, or much left to trade. I hated to trade the little good clothing I still had.

The country was locked in a terrible war for a long time and shortages were part of life. Yet, the Russian always shared with us.

One day I met another Jew, a man named Mr. Lew, who was friendly, and he helped make arrangements to move us into his barracks. Father and I went to our dugout, packed up our few bundles and quickly left. On the way, we hardly spoke a word, both of us nervous about our new living arrangements.

It was dark when we entered the barrack, but we walked into a well-lit room. The place was alive with activity. Women were cooking delicious smelling food around a couple of stoves. Around a long wooden table, People were eating. A radio was blasting the news. Everybody was listening with attention to the reports, describing the action on the fronts. We stood at the entrance without being noticed.

We went farther inside to ask for Mr. Lew. A few women were around and knew we were coming because the decision to let us live with them was decided by consensus. Everybody welcomed us and stated asking us questions. Mr. Lew arrived and showed us our living space — if you want to call it that. It didn't look much different than the other barracks we had seen before. It was the third bunk from the door, one up for me, down for my father. There were a couple of straw sacks on them and that's all. Yet, we were happy to be here. It was a different atmosphere, reminding me a little of our barracks in Niuziary.

Most of the inhabitants were women. They knew each other from their former homes in Ukraine. There were grandparents widows, mothers, teenage girls and children and a few men. Most of them were in the army. We put our bundles in the bunks and were invited to sit down and eat. We brought our bread to the table and were treated to a few potatoes, a piece of salted fish and good tea with a small piece of sugar. We told them about our home in Krakow and how we came to the Soviet Union.

194

They were patriotic and excited  the Red Army was liberating Ukraine. Soon, they said, the heroic Red Army will liberate Poland. They cheered us up, telling us we would soon be able to return home to our families.

There were a few girls my age or a little older. I noticed they were examining me quite closely, offering me more tea and sugar, trying to keep me a little longer at the table. It made me happy. I hadn't dated anybody since the camp in Niuziary a few years ago. I often dreamed of the girls I went out with at home.

I was already in my 20s and my body demanded contact with the opposite sex. Here, it seemed would be my first real opportunity  to have a relationship. That night I had very sexual dreams.

Families in the barracks lived in improvised rooms, created around their bunks with bedsheets, cardboard and blankets. The floor of the barrack was covered with wooden boards and was kept clean

There were two teenage girls in our barrack who took an interest in me. One lived with her sister, mother and grandmother. She was tall, good-looking but a little chubby. I noticed right away her  mother and grandmother had serious marriage plans for me and this scared me. Besides,  what kind of relationship could we have when they watched us constantly?  I couldn't  even sit with her at the table without being spied on, so I lost interest in her.

I was serious about finding a girlfriend, and began to take great care in my appearance. I felt safe enough to bring my treasured bundles of clothing from Zajcew's office to our barrack. I found out that following Sunday an American movie was playing at the workers' theatre. I asked the people in the barrack if they were interested, because I was going.

The results were astonishing. Five women and several younger girls wanted to go with me.  I got dressed in my best clothes, pressed to perfections and took my harem to the movie. The whole barracks watched me leave,impressed with the way I looked and the way the women followed me.

The movie was a smash hit. It was Midnight Serenade, with Sonia Henie and John Payne. The movies setting was Lake Placid, New.York What a pleasure it was to watch a beautiful location,in the winter with  happy, singing people. I closed and opened my eyes just to make sure that I am not dreaming, this was only a movie.

Zina, the Russian girl in our barrack, moved very close to me and started kissing and hugging me. I felt embarrassed and tried delicately to cool  off the situation. This scene convinced me that I should forget dating the women from the barracks. Sooner or later, it could cause some trouble. A few married army wives, with children, started to pay too much attention to me. It always started with an invitation for a piece of cake and tea. These were tempting offers because there was never enough food to satisfy my hunger.

When I went to a movie, or later to the dances that were held in the social club, I would invite several people. This way I didn't have to get involved with anybody personally. We went as a group and always had a good time.

There was a radio in the barrack, more like a loud speaker. The programs were piped in all the barracks in throughout the neighborhood. There was only one station, the government-controlled media. Every hour it broadcast news from the front.

The news was getting encouraging. The Red Army was advancing rapidly, every day closer to the 1939 Polish/ Russian border. Everyone was excited about it. We were convinced the war was going well and the Nazis were going to be destroyed soon. We would return home to Mother and Niusia and the rest of our family and friends.

The radio also broadcast reports about the atrocities committed by the Germans, but they never mentioned Jews, in particular. Once in a while, they mentioned some of the accomplishments of the Allies in the war.

At work, I was advancing rapidly, under the guidance of Alexi and Mr. Zajcew. I was becoming a master valinki maker. I learned the process from beginning to end. I could make a pair of valinki by hand, from the raw material to ready to wear. I became a spare, substituting workers who didn't show up for work. I also learned little by little how to make a few extra rubles. By making the valinki I would save small amounts of wool. When I had enough I would make a small pair of boots for youngsters or children. The following Sunday, I went to the bazaar and traded them for bread, maybe a pumpkin or half a glass of tobacco.

If you couldn't sell for money, you bartered for services or something else. Of course, during the war the premium jobs were connected with food, because it was the easiest item to sell, especially at the bazaar, but this was dangerous. Often, without notice, the police would surround the market and check everybody's papers. They checked for deserters from the army and the merchandise people sold. Anybody they didn't like, or what they were selling could disappear, God knows where. Once you got into the hands of the NKWD, it was impossible to predict where you would wind up.

196

Whenever I had to go to the bazaar, I tried to stay only for a short time. I sold whatever I could at the going price and purchased what I needed without haggling, just to try to get out of there fast.

I had papers stating I was a Polish refugee and that I was excused from military service for six months. After six months, the military exemption had to be renewed. Here, I encountered an officer who became my enemy. His name I'll never forget. It was Epstein. He was Jewish, bald, short and wore glasses. He dressed in an immaculate uniform with shiny leather boots. When I presented my papers to him, he gave me an unfriendly look.

"I'll extend your papers for only three months," he said. "You westerners don't like to go to the army to defend our Motherland."

That was always his speech. I'm sure he had never seen the front and he knew damn well we were on the frontlines all through the Stalingrad campaign.

After three months, Epstein called us again. This time he gave us seven days to settle our affairs, because we were going to be mobilized. My explanation that I was a Polish citizen, didn't impress him. I returned to the shop upset and told Zajcew all about my meeting with Epstein. He swore with Russian intensity and said that I was not going anywhere. He made a few phonecalls and the next day set up a meeting with General Ivanov, who was in charge of our factory, No. 24.

I told General Ivanov what happened. I had a feeling that Ivanov knew Epstein well and didn't like him either. He called him and they had a disagreement and a long discussion. I heard General Ivanov on the phone say this phrase: "Till the end of the war." At the time, I didn't understand what he meant, but when I went to Epstein's recruitment office, it became clear.

I didn't see him personally. My papers were handed to me by a secretary and she said goodbye with a smile on her lips. I left, opened the papers on the street and read that I was not to be mobilized till the end of the war.

The next day, the armistice was declared and the war was over. Epstein called me to his recruiting office but I didn't bother going. I had official papers and I was a Polish citizen of the new Polish Communist government of Wanda Wasilewska.

Most of the Jewish people I met during my years in Russia were friendly, especially the older generation. People who lived before the revolution, understood us better than the younger ones. Stalin's regime taught people to distrust each other. Spies and informers were everywhere. Parents were careful what they said in front of their children.

During my stay in Kuibyszow, as the Jewish New Year, Rosh Hashanah, was approaching, I decided to find out if the city had a synagogue. I went to Kuibyszow a week ahead of time to find it and had great difficulty. Early on the morning of Rosh Hashanah, we left for Kuibyszow. We walked the distance from the station to the synagogue, which was situated in the back of an old apartment building, facing a huge courtyard, enclosed by more dilapidated apartment buildings. There was only a handful of people there when we arrived. They greeted us with a warm welcome of "Good Yom Tov."

Father and I introduced ourselves and they asked where we were from. There were few prayer books, but they gave us one. Slowly the place filled up, mostly with older people, some in military uniforms. There was a small divider with partitions for the few women that showed up. The services were short, with no speeches or singing, yet, I felt some joy being in the synagogue after so many years. Hearing and reading the familiar prayers, my eyes filled with tears. I wondered whether we would celebrate the holidays with our family again.

When the service ended, the elders produced a couple bottles of vodka and cake. In complete silence, we took a drink and said goodbye. We exchanged Good Year greetings. Everybody seemed to want to leave in a hurry. . The younger people just minutes before the services ended. It was not a popular place to be found in the Soviet Union.

## SEVENTEEN

Word spread of the new Polish government being organized and that an office was opening, not far from where we lived. At the first opportunity we went to register. After a short interview, we got new papers, stating we were citizens of Poland.

The new government was on a much smaller scale than the previous government, with representatives in exile in England. We all knew it was a puppet of the Communist party of the Soviet Union. I wasn't interested in politics or the leanings of the government.

We were interested in only one thing, returning to Poland at the end of the war as soon as possible. We didn't want to get stuck somewhere in Russia.

Every Sunday, there were meetings, speeches and lectures. To my surprise, I found out there were hundreds of people from Poland in the similar situations as ours, all around Kuibyszow, probably in a 100-150-km radius. The news from the front through the Polish organization was more detailed than I'd ever heard before, and about the current situation on the western front and in occupied Poland.

We realized there was a lot to worry about, especially about our loved ones we'd left behind. There were all kinds of opportunities to be active in the new government and in the offices here. But, I didn't want to get too involved.

Life became more normal and predictable, as far as work and our conditions were concerned. Some advantages came our way, like extra food and occasionally some underwear or winter clothing from the new Polish government..

During the meetings at our new Polish offices, I met quite a few refugees like myself. A majority of them were Jewish. Two of them were intelligent and well informed about everything. I've forgotten many of the names of people I met in Russia 50 years ago. but them, I remembered quite well.

These two Jews, Rubenson and Blatt were brothers-in-law. Their wives were with them. The Rubensons had a baby boy. They lived together, not very far from me in a tiny, two-room, tiny flat. They invited me for tea after meetings. Both were much older than me but I found their story fascinating and hard to believe. Later, I discovered it to be very common.

In pre-war Poland, all four of them were active members of the underground Communist party. I say underground because the

Communist party was illegal in Poland and any activities were severely punished. All of them were caught by the Polish police, tried and sentenced to long terms. The husbands were sent to notorious concentration camps in Bereza Kartuska and the women to women's prisons, called Fordon.

The Rubensons spent most of their youth in Polish jails for being devoted Communists. When the Germans attacked Poland they were released from jails, reunited and ran to their beloved Communist country, USSR. They fought and suffered all their young lives. When their dreams to reach this heaven was fulfilled, they expected to be welcomed as heroes and rewarded as dedicated communists. But it didn't work out that way.

Stalin had no use for idealistic western communists. For him, they were useful as the fifth column in the west. With their lofty, idealistic ideas in the USSR, they were considered a hindrance to Stalins' dictatorship. I don't know what happened to them, but by now they surely had been "cured" of their idealism. They were treated harshly with suspicion and now they registered like everybody else to return to Poland,as soon as possible.

Later, I found out most Polish communists fared the same way in Stalin's Russia. Most of them hated Stalin and became bitter enemies of his regime.

On one of my trips to Kinel, I stopped in the local hospital to see the director I knew well. He had been waiting to see me, and ask my help with a problem. His hospital was filthy and in desperate need of a paint job, but there was no paint to be had. He offered to pay me well in money and food if I could find some for him. I knew it would be dangerous to try to get the paint, as it would have to be bought on the Black Market, but I agreed to try.

It took several weeks to put the whole plan together. I had managed to locate some paint on the Black Market, a light, silvery paint that I was sure must have been stolen from the airplane factory. I was quoted a very high price, but was told I could get a better deal if I bought a larger quantity. I managed to convince some fellow refugees to go in on the purchase with me, and finally one day the deal was made and we were on our way home, three of us, each with five cans of paint in our sacks.

The weight was terrible, as I was carrying the paint only in an old flour sack on my back. Soon after we set off, it was all I could do not to simply throw it off the train, I was so sick of holding it. I prayed instead that we would reach our next stop where I could set the sack down and rest. But when we got to the station, we saw that it was surrounded by the militia. I feared at once that we would be caught. My companions simply abandoned their packs and denied any knowledge of their contents. I kept my sack, and was detained, taken into custody. It was several hours before we reached Kuibyszow, where we disembarked, and I was left with all three sacks of paint, despite having denied responsibility for the other two.

I was questioned at length by a NKWD officer, and frightened though I was, I believed I detected some sympathy in him. He asked me a lot about my background and the circumstances surrounding the paint, and finally checked my story with the director of the hospital. After a seemingly endless period of time, he returned, told me what a serious crime I was guilty of, and that I was lucky the director of the hospital had confirmed my story. I was to be let off with a warning, and was even to be permitted to take the paint.

I could scarcely believe my luck. With help, I managed to reach the station and finally to deliver the paint to the hospital, where I was well-paid by a very grateful director. I was more than a day late returning home, and had been unable to get word to my father, who had been worried sick. I never told him exactly what had happened.

I was progressing well in the valinki shop and had learned all of the operations, production and distribution of the factory. Mr. Zajcew called me to his office one day, offered me a smoke, told me to sit down and asked me some questions. He wanted to know more about my education, specifically my knowledge of math, and if I could read and write Russian. I couldn't understand his curiosity. Then, he dropped the bombshell. The warehouse manager, Stephanov, was leaving and Zajcew was considering me for the job. He would let me know soon, he said.

I was a little apprehensive because it was a lot of repsonsibility. It paid better, but had many dangers. I would be responsible for receiving the raw materials, turning in the finished product, receiving it from the shop and shipping it from the shop. I wasn't sure though, if offered the job, I could refuse such an honor, especially because the shop guaranteed me a position and protected me from being mobilized into the army.

In a couple of days, Zajcew called me to his office and told me I had the job.. I would start the next day. I would become Stephanov's apprentice until it was time for him to leave. He wasn't happy about leaving. He was being transferred to the territories retaken by the Soviet army and his job would be to reorganize the new administration.

My apprenticeship lasted almost a month and I learned fast. Everybody was on the take he said, and he instructed me as to who got what. He always received a few extra pair of boots or gloves and a few bottles of vodka. You had to shmire to pay off all the inspectors.

There was a girl in the office that I had daily business with.Her name was Mura. She was a stunning woman, a wholesome Russian girl. She was always smiling. She recognized I was a Westerner and we spoke often about all kinds of topics, not connected with business. She was from Moscow and longed for the city and the family she'd left behind. She wanted to know more about me, so I told her a little about myself. I wanted to ask her out on a date, but simply didn't know how to approach her. I didn't know where to take her.

Once she asked me out on a date at the Soc-gorodok, but while we were there, a friend told me Mura was soon to be married. Surprised and disappointed, I never accepted another of her invitations to go out.

***

Production in the shop went smoothly and I kept my office tidy and orderly. I was always prepared for the surprise inspections. Zajcew, thankfully told me a bigshot from the ORS was coming soon for a visit. It gave me time to prepare and stock up on vodka, beer and snacks.

The bigshot, Ivan Ivanowich Lunin was a cheerful, middle-aged man, balding with a smiling face and sparkling blue eyes. He came to my office with Zajcew who introduced me and left us alone. I showed Lunin the combing operation and the warehouse. He was impressed with my innovations. I had organized the stock shelves by numbers, sorted out by quantity, sizes, men and women. Everything was sparkling clean, including the cement floor that shined. When I took over, I was sure the floor had never been washed before.

After the tour we returned to my modest office, where I expected him to check my books and ledgers. I offered him a drink and we had a smoke. I put the goodies I prepared on the table. In no time, we finished a bottle and started to wash it down with beer. I tried to pour myself a little less because I didn't want to get too dunk. Lunin's tongue got loose after a few drinks and he started to tell me about his personal life. He began singing melancholy Russian melodies. His family was in Moscow and for some reason couldn't join him. He was lonely and was pouring out his heart. He forgot his

202

whole purpose of coming to the factory. Then he stood up, looked around with glassy eyes and said: "Sasha, I don't like your office."

He finally spelled out the reason. "How can you run an office without a secretary? It is a dull, lonely place."

It told him I had taken over the office without a secretary and I handle the job myself. Ivan was adamant. You need one, you will get one and I will pick her out personally. I finally agreed.

We had another couple of drinks and he dozed off in his chair. I waited until he woke up after dark and everybody had gone home. I sent him on his way and I returned to my barrack.

The next day, Zacjew came to my office and told me Lunin had called to tell him my warehouse was the most orderly he'd ever seen. He was impressed my first inspection went so well.

About a week after the inspection, by Ivan, Mr. Zacjew appeared at my office accompanied by a young, good-looking woman. I was sure this was a new employee for the combing room. He introduced me to Natasha, and announced Lunin had sent her to be my secretary to ease my heavy workload. I was surprised Lunin remembered his promise.

When he left the office, Natasha and I stood alone in my tiny cubicle office. She had auburn hair and a pleasant smile She was 20 years old, from the city of Tver, north of Moscow. She had worked in a factory there and was later transferred here with many others. My first assignment for her was to clean up the desk near the window, that I never used. I left for a couple of hours and upon my return, I found my office clean, with the floor and windows washed and the desk organized. I shared my lunch with her because she didn't bring anything and we had a long conversation.

She came from a poor family who worked in a co-op. The soil north of Moscow was not very productive and the growing season was short. Her father was an alcoholic, had been arrested several times and was presently serving time. She also had relatives in Twer, where she attended school, until the war broke out and then she was transferred to the factory in Moscow. She had been happy there trying to build her life, until the move to Bezemianka, where she worked on a grinding machine. She showed me her hands to prove it. They were scarred and chipped. When I asked her if she had ever worked as a secretary, she blushed, and started to cry. She hadn't done this kind of work and had no idea what it was all about. I told her not to worry. I would teach her.

There was not much for her to do in the office, so I had her working in the warehouse, keeping it clean and orderly. She would do anything, she said, to stay away from the hard and noisy job in the factory. She begged me with her eyes not to reject her and send her away.

After lunch, I sent her home to rest and come back the next morning. When she showed up the next morning, she was neatly dressed. I liked her for her down-to-earth thinking and simplicity. She was eager to learn and in a couple of weeks she became more sure of herself.

In time, she became more confident and began to show an interest in me. But our relationship was confined to work. We didn't date and neither of us expected any commitments.

The war was going better than we expected with victory after victory for the Red Army. When I went to sleep, especially after the late newscast, I was overwhelmed by the fear and uncertainty awaiting us after the war. I often looked at the only picture I had of my mother and sister Nusia, from 1940. I kept it in my desk, under lock and key because I was afraid someone would steal it. When I was by myself after work or on Sundays, I would stare at this picture for a long time, sometimes sobbing uncontrollably. I closed my eyes for awhile and thought about the days gone by. I didn't talk to Father too much about my thoughts. I didn't want to upset him, although I knew he felt the same way.

Father had not been feeling well lately. He coughed and had a temperature. He went to the policlinic to see a doctor, got some aspirins and was sent home to rest for three days. This happened several times until, finally, the doctor sent him to the local hospital. He was diagnosed with a touch of pneumonia and was admitted into a ward with several other patients. The doctor told me father should stay a while. He needed mediation and better nourishment to help fight of the sickness.

I visited Father every day and to ensure he got the best care, I gave the head nurse a pair of children's boots. After a few days, he seemed to improve. By the end of the week, father was released with permission to stay off work for a few extra days.

I decided to go to Kinel to buy some extra supplies for Father to help him get well — things like sugar, eggs and cheese. When I got there, I got the supplies, and also some Mahorka, which was sold and traded by the glass. The food helped Father, and by the end of the week he was released, though still unable to return to work for a few days. The Mahorka I took to the bazaar to try to sell. It promptly got me in trouble. After selling a few glasses of it, I was approached by two men who claimed I had just cheated them in giving change.

204

It was a con job, and I refused to give them any money. A fight was inevitable, but I was lucky. When I swung my sack at him, I somehow got dust from the tobacco inside into his eyes. He was unable to fight, and I fled. About a week later I saw the men again, but they bore me no ill-will, indeed invited me to join their gang. I declined, but saw them often, and occasionally had tradings with them.

I continued to attend the meetings of the Polish citizens. It was obvious this leftist government, with the support of the Russian Army, was going to be the leading force in Post-war Poland. The speaker had harsh words for the Polish pre-war government and the government in exile in London. Every day we were one step closer to winning the war. Preparations for the return of people to their homes, was getting more serious. People were showing up to register and keep in touch with the post.

Everybody in our barrack was excited because Ukraine was being liberated, but news started to trickle in that they would have to wait until the end of the war, and maybe later, before being able to go home.

Later, they found out their homes were destroyed. The whole town needed to be rebuilt. This dampened their spirits and some questioning whether they should return at all.

One day I had to go to the offices of the ORS to see Mura. It was a regular business visit. I was on friendly terms with her and she always helped me get the supplies I needed for the plant.

I knocked on her door and walked in. A woman with her back to me sat on the edge of the desk talking to Mura. Her long, blonde hair covered the collar of her sable fur coat. She didn't even turn her head to see who entered and continued the conversation with Mura. They finished their conversation and I went around to Mura's desk. I could finally see the person sitting on her desk. I almost froze. I had never seen a beauty like her, only in American movies. She was dressed so elegantly. Her coat was open and I could see a beautiful white blouse with a scarf. She had a beautiful, delicate face. Her lips were covered with a light-colored lipstick. She wore red nail polish on her exquisite hands.

We exchanged first names and I couldn't say another word. I must have looked stupid, ogling at her, speechless. She stepped down from the desk, said goodbye and briskly left the office. For a moment, I forgot what I came for. I had never seen a woman like this, especially in drab and damp Bezemianka. She was totally out of place.

I came to myself and presented some papers to Mura. I hoped that she would say something. But Mura didn't say anything. I wasn't going to leave her office without learning more about her. I had no choice but to ask. Mura revealed that Claudia, a chemical engineer, was married. She was from Moscow and was in charge of a food laboratory inside plant 24. I was disappointed and didn't ask anymore questions.

I returned to my shop but I couldn't forget Claudia. She seemed too young to be married. It was unlikely I would get to meet her socially considering her position.

I never discussed girls with my father, but I had to tell him about Claudia. Then, I told myself, I'd better forget her.

Every time I went to Mura's office, I hoped to see her again. I even tried going there, neatly dressed but I never met her in her office again, nor did I dare ask Mura about her.

Father was feeling better but then I got a bad cold and developed a cough with a temperature. I had no medication and decided to see the doctor at the policlinic. After a lengthy wait, I was checked by a young doctor, given aspirin treatment and was told to drink plenty of liquids and get some rest. The doctor asked me where I worked and when I told him I was a warehouse manager at the valinki shop, he became more interested in me. He told me his boots were worn out. Would it be possible for me to get him a pair? I said yes and he wrote on a paper that I was to have three days off. He also inferred that if I didn't improve, he would send me to a rest home for a mandatory vacation. This sounded like a good deal.

We settled on a price for the boots and I asked him what size and the color he preferred. In about a week, I had his boots ready and dropped by the clinic to set up a drop-off time. We set a date for a week later, giving him enough time to organize the necessary paper for the rest home. Everything worked out perfectly, and to my surprise, I got two weeks approved.

I had heard our factory had rest homes, but mainly for the bigger bosses. They also had room for workers in dormitories.

To get there, I had to go to Kuibyszow and take a coastal steamer. Everybody in the barrack was surprised I was going. They speculated I had tuberculosis from working around the wool dust. I needed to breathe fresh air for awhile.

The ride on the boat was pleasant and was well supplied with soft drinks, ice cream and snacks. The steamer sailed close to shore upstream on the Volga and made frequent stops, where people embarked and disembarked.

When we arrived I walked with a few other people toward the rest home. It was a short, pleasant walk on a dirt road, cutting

206

through a forest. The fresh air smelled of pines. We came to an area covered with one-floor buildings, neatly painted in bright colors. In one of the buildings was a reception office where we registered. I showed my papers and a woman led me to the building where I was going to stay for the two weeks. She opened the door to a large room, containing 10 beds, five on each side. My bed was neatly made up. At the end of the room was a large closet for hanging clothes. A few men were sitting at a table in the room and I was introduced to them.

In the middle of the compound, was a large dining room where the meals were served at different times. There were separate larger dining rooms for the upper class, who ate at different hours. The food was plentiful and compared to my regular diet it was fantastic. Bread was not rationed. It was white and tasted like cake. There was a little milk occasionally and a little fat in the porridge. Sometimes we got a small piece of meat or fish, often sugar with our tea, sometimes even a small piece of cake.

The rest home also had a library with a record player and a good supply of records. For the first couple of days I took long walks in the surrounding woods, around the shore of the Volga, enjoying the beauty and the freshness of the air. The feeling of being satisfied with a full stomach and not to having to worry about my next meal brought me serenity and peace, I hadn't felt this way in years. I tried not to think about the past or the future.

The men in my room were friendly. We talked a lot and played dominoes. Lights went out at 11 o'clock because we had to get to breakfast early. If you wanted, you could stay in bed all day.

I visited the library and took out a few books. I listened to music, mostly Russian classics, Tchaichovsky, Borodin, Mussegorski and my favorite Amar Khachaturian.

In a separate compartment were records for dancing, including tangoes, foxtrots, waltzes, slow waltzes and of course Russian national dances. Every evening dances were held as part of the entertainment and exercise.

After resting and taking walks, it was a good way to meet people. I would put on my good clothes and shoes. Usually the women only danced while the men sat around talking. I waited for the tangoes and waltzes to begin because I knew them well. I asked one of the girls who worked in the library to dance. It was a familiar tango and we did quite well. It didn't take long before many other women started to ask me to dance. I became popular at the dances, because the women seemed to like my Western accent and dancing skills.

Before I had come to the rest home, I was feeling nervous. All the talk about the end of the war and what the future held for us was stressful. But here, I tried to chase away those thoughts as hard as I could. I didn't want to listen to the daily news from the front, that were piped into most of the rooms on the radios. Physically I felt better,and gained some weight.

The days became routine, but pleasant and restful. I was not used to so much free time and it gave me ample opportunity to think.

But all this was suddenly about to change.

On the fourth day of my stay at the rest home, it was a Sunday, and I was getting ready to go to the dance.

The attendance was better because most of the employees, who had the day off , came. All men in my room were getting their best Sunday clothes on.

I put on a tie, and the men laughed at me, telling me I looked like a big boss. I kept it on anyway.

I got to the dance a little later and everyone was there.The dancing was in full swing and soon the women were asking me to dance. I took a break and sat down, when the door opened and in walked an elegantly dressed woman. Behind her was another woman and a well-dressed man escorted them in. They came closer to where I was sitting and I lifted my eyes to have a closer look at them. I couldn't believe my eyes. It was the gorgeous and elegant Claudia that I had met at Mura's office.

My eyes wandered over to her and another girl sitting with me asked if I knew this trio. I was overwhelmed. I didn't know what to do or say. As soon as the music started I began to to dance, although my legs were trembling. I tried to dance my best, hoping it would get Claudia's attention.

I realized this was my opportunity to make a move on her by asking her to dance. Maybe I could get to know her. But, I kept postponing dance after dance. I didn't have enough guts to ask her. I looked at the clock. It was getting late. It was now or never.

One of my favorite tangoes began to play and I crossed the floor, trying to pull myself together to approach Claudia and I asked her to dance. Without hesitation, she got up and danced with me. I was concentrating on doing my best. My throat was so tight I could hardly speak. She followed my steps effortlessly and gracefully. Her delicate, slim body seemed to float. How different she was from all the other women I knew.

After a few minutes, I asked her if she remembered me from the meeting in Mura's office. She didn't recognize me. The music stopped and I took her to her seat and thanked her. When they started another record, I danced with another girl. About two dances later, I pulled myself together and asked Claudia to dance again. She got up with a trace of hesitation. It was a slower dance and she told me that if I wanted to dance with her, than I better not dance with anyone else. I was startled to hear these words. It sounded a little like an order, which I was glad to oblige.

When the dance ended, she grabbed my hand and led me to the corner to introduce me to her companions. I was nervous, but in seventh heaven. We spoke a little, dancing almost every dance. It would be over soon, because it was getting late. I planned to ask her for a date or at least come to the next dance with me. Then, I recalled Claudia was married. This confused me.

When we got up to leave, she asked me very naturally if I would escort her to the building she lived in. It was a beautiful evening with thousands of stars flickering the sky. The air was still and the aroma of the woods was intoxicating. After a short walk, we separated from the other couple. We walked slowly and came closeto her building and she suddenly suggested we take a short walk to the river. It was too nice to go inside and sleep, she said. I couldn't have been happier. We walked slowly, holding hands, along the shores of the mighty Volga. I wanted to grab her in my arms, but I couldn't make myself do it.

We found a small bench near the rest home. I put my arm around her and she cuddled closeto me. For a while, we sat quietly, our faces toward the river, then we started to talk. She wanted to know everything about me. She showed an interest in everything I said, always posing questions. She wanted to know about life in Poland and in the west before the war, nothing political, only details about people, how they lived and dressed.. The time flew by quickly when we realized dawn was approaching.

We walked back to her building and she ask me to come in. Her room was small, neat but sparsely furnished, but it had lots of potted flowers. It was late and I wanted to go back to my room. But she put her arms around me and we kissed passionately for a long time. My knees almost buckled from the excitement. Finally, she let go and I said goodbye. She said goodnight, until tomorrow, and I left.

I could not fall asleep for a long time. When everyone left the room to have breakfast, I finally fell asleep until lunch. I looked for Claudia that afternoon, but couldn't find her until evening, when she came to the library and later to dance.

209

She suggested we leave and while everyone was dancing, we quietly disappeared. It started to dawn on me that all the decisions and suggestions were coming from Claudia. I was just a follower. She must have been here before, knowing every road, every bench, every trail. I felt completely under her spell. I was falling deeply in love. I knew so little about her, because she hadn't said anything about herself. I don't think she knew Mura had told me she was married. We took another walk and sat on the same bench as the night before. We kissed and embraced again. When she started to ask more about me, I answered her, but I said I would like to know about her, too.

She found it difficult to begin. But after a brief silence, this was the story she told me.

Her grandparents and parents were wealthy landowners in the Ukraine, where they lived for generations. When the Bolshevik Revolution broke out, during the First World War, everything was taken from them. They were deported deep into Siberia. Her grandfather died on the train from cold and malnutrition and a few years later, her father in some remote settlement from hard work and unbearable elements died, too. Her grandmother, mother and herself were moved to a small village, to stay forever. She moved to a small town nearby, went to a government school, which separated her completely from the remaining family. She was allowed to see them only during vacation. She did well and finished high school.

Then she was sent to university in Irkutzk, still farther away from her grandmother and mother. She studied organic chemistry and did well, but was lonesome for her mother. Again, she could see them only seldom. The government wouldn't allow her mother and grandmother to visit her in Irkutzk. She tried very hard, but to no avail. Pressing too hard would put her in peril.

She finally got a job in a food laboratory, and a part-time job in a factory. The extra income allowed her to send parcels to her mother and grandmother. While working there, she met the chief engineer of the factory and they began to date. She was much younger than him, and impressed by his high position. He helped her earn more on her job.

The courtship lasted a few months and he asked her to marry him. He was Jewish. His name was Berezowski. She refused because her mother was in exile and unable to get out. Brezowski was a party member and quite influential. It took him a few months to get her grandmother and mother to Irkutz.

He found a place for them to live and he supported them. Shortly after they got married, her grandmother died in Irkutzk. The war broke out and after the evacuation of the plane factories to Kuibyszov from Moscow, her husband was transferred to Beziemenka to help with the establishment and organization of the plants.

He left Claudia alone. She was pregnant and their daughter was born in Irkutzk. She joined him later when the apartments in Soc-Gorodok were ready. They lived with her mother and Claudia got a position in charge of the food laboratory of Plant #24.

This was the story Claudia told me on this bench facing the Volga. She looked straight ahead and when she turned to me her eyes were shining with tears. She put her hand on my shoulders and gently cried. After a few minutes, she wiped her tears and her composure returned. Now, I knew her story and she knew mine.

We sat a little longer, embracing, not exchanging a word. When we came to her building, she led me to her room and closed the door.

She spent her days with her friends from Soc-Gorodok, but practically all the evening with me.

I was happy and in love and didn't want to know how this was all going to end. About three days before Claudia's return to work, we were as usual in her room. I snuck out of her room. I went around the barracks, down the narrow, winding road and turned toward my building. It was always quiet. I never met anyone on my way. But this time, when I left her building and entered the little trail, I noticed somebody moving quickly, straight towards me. He stopped and asked me if I knew where building #4 was. I showed him and he left in a hurry, practically running. He was well dressed, but I couldn't see his face, because of the darkness. I had a funny feeling. What would he be doing running towards Claudia's barrack.

I went back to my bed, but I was the first up when the sun rose. I didn't see Claudia all day and in the evening she didn't show up in the library. I knew something was wrong. I met the couple Claudia came with to the dance and asked them where Claudia was. They told me Claudia's husband arrived last night. I noticed a smirk on the face of the men. Now, I was sure the man I met last night running towards the building was her husband.

I stayed in the library all day an evening, waiting for Claudia, but she didn't show up. I was devastated. Is this the end of our affair? Am I going to see her again? I had to.

The next day I didn't know what to do. Should I see her or her friends? I was sure she had left with her husband. We had a fling and it was over.

After supper I went again for a walk and soon wound up on my favorite bench. I didn't feel like talking to anyone and was looking forward to the end of my vacation. I would find out from Mura how to get in touch with Claudia. The evening was peaceful, the river covered by a delicate mist. I could hear someone's footsteps. I jumped and hid behind a tree trunk. After a moment, I peeked from behind, Claudia was sitting alone on the bench.

I didn't want to scare her. I waited for a couple of minutes and called her name quietly, approaching the bench. We embraced and stood motionless, both with tears in our eyes. She was leaving the next day. Her husband had left. I told her about meeting him on the way from her apartment, and how lucky we were not to get caught. Somebody squealed on us and he came to nail me in her room that night. We sat there till very late. The river was completely shrouded in mist. It became chilly and damp. She told me how to get in touch with her, by calling her lab from the offices of the ORS. I could also call her from Zajcew's office. This was an internal telephone between factories. We kissed goodbye.

The last few days at the rest home seemed to last forever. I was anxious to go home.

***

I was welcomed back to the barrack with open arms. Father was happy to see me. He always worried even when we were separated even for a day.

The war was still going on. How long would it last? The news of the German atrocities against Jews started to filter in. We didn't know how much to believe. We hoped it was propaganda.

After a couple of days, I got in touch with Claudia. She was delighted to hear from me. The distance from my place to her plant gate was a five or six-minute walk. I waited outside, because I had no clearance to enter the huge factory. I was anxious to see her.

She came out, as always, nicely dressed with her proud and sure walk. We greeted each other rather officially. We had to be careful. We walked slowly towards the Soc-Gorodok, where she lived. By the time we were close to her building, it was dark. We stayed there for awhile and then I took her to the entrance of her building.

This is the way our romance continued for the first few weeks. We would meet three or four times a week. Father became anxious about my long disappearances in the evenings. I had to tell him something.

212

I told him I had met Claudia at the rest home and we were dating, but I didn't mention she was married. I tried assure him it was nothing serious. As usual, he warned me not to get involved because soon we would be returning home. Why complicate your life, he said.

But I couldn't listen to his advice. She was like a magnet to me. I waited for my next meeting with her. I lost interest in the other girls. Claudia was so different, beautiful beyond words, intelligent, well-dressed and informed.

On one of our meetings, late in the fall, with the snow starting to fall occasionally, she said she had good news for us. Her husband was leaving for Moscow on business, for about a month. We would have more time together. I was delighted.

Two days after his departure, I picked up Claudia at the gate and briskly walked towards her home. The weather was ugly. Snow was falling and the wind made it worse. When we came close to her place, without stopping, Claudia announced with a smile. You are coming upstairs to meet my family. I was hesitant, though I was happy. My feeble resistance melted in a second. She took my hand and led me to her apartment.

She opened the door and her mother was standing there with a little girl in her arms. She greeted me by my first name. This made me feel at ease. Claudia had told her all about me. She was happy to meet me. She was a tall woman, elegantly dressed and had an aristocratic look. Later, when we sat at the table, I realized she was also a very good looking lady. The little girl was sweet, blonde and had a tiny nose and beautiful eyes.

The apartment of the Russian war standard, had two tiny bedrooms, a small living room and kitchen. But what struck me the most was the flushing toilet. Everything was clean, but simply furnished.

We had a delicious meal together and soon after her mother with the baby, retired to the another room. While her husband was on vacation, I spent nearly every evening with Claudia returning to my barrack late. I always tried to sneak in, so not to wake up Father, but I seldom succeeded.

When Claudia's husband returned from Moscow, Father was happy I was home more regularly.

One day Claudia obtained a pass for me to come into the plant for a few hours. She waited for me at the entrance and led me to her laboratory, where the girls prepared a delicious dinner. It was a birthday party for one of her closest co-workers.

I was introduced as a close friend from the ORS. The food was great and with a little vodka, the time passed quickly. Suddenly, a man entered the plant. I recognized him immediately. It was the man who asked me on my vacation at the rest home how to get to Claudia's building. Sure enough, Claudia introduced me to her husband. He was stout  much older than her. I was formerly introduced as a warehouse manager in one of the sections of the ÓRS. He had a few drinks with us and I could see he swallowed vodka like water. He asked Claudia if she was ready to go, but she insisted on staying a little longer to celebrate with the girls.

The Russian government was evacuated before and during the siege of Moscow to Kuibyszow. It was the nerve centre of the nation. With them, came all the top cultural enterprises, the Bolshoi ballet, the Leningrad Ballet, the symphony orchestra and all of the foreign embassies. Two U.S. movies, the Great Waltz, with Peter Gravet and Norma Shearer and Winter Serenade with John Payne and Sonia Henie, came to Beziamenka. That was  the extent of the entertainment there.

There were small concerts in the house of culture, featuring accordian players and singers of patriotic songs, which I was getting tired of. This is not to say I didn't like Russian music. I loved the nostalgic songs about the end of the war. They were all  romantic. But you heard them day in day out.

It was almost impossible to get tickets for the bigger events in Kuibyszow. Claudia had an idea. Let's take some Sundays off and spend them in Kuibyszow, where it was more pleasant. Besides, she had the connections through the factory to get tickets for those great events in Kuibyszow.

We began to live a cultured life in Russia. Nearly every second Sunday we spent in Kuibyszow, going to concerts and symphonies. It was hard to believe we were in harsh Russia at these events.

I didn't want to think too much about the situation Claudia and I were in. But, I wondered about Claudia's marriage. She didn't talk about it and I didn't want to ask.  In my situation, I couldn't provide her with an alternative. I knew she understood this.

From what I could gather, her husband was an alcoholic and seldom came home. It seemed  a marriage of convenience. That's all I knew, so meanwhile, we loved each other and tried to spend as much time as possible together.

It was obvious the war would end soon and I would try to return to Poland. There was no way I could take her with me. She knew and

I knew it was going to happen. But we didn't want to think about it.

She had a close friend, Tanya, whose husband was in the army. Once in awhile she gave Claudia a key to her apartment, allowing us to spend some evenings together.

In the winter of 1945 I caught a bad cold and went to see my doctor at the policlinic. After checking me and presenting me with aspirin, he gave me a permit to stay home for a few days. As usual, he wanted a pair of valinke. His wife's birthday was coming and he wanted to surprise her with another pair, if possible pure white. He promised again to sent me to the rest home. He told me about one near Kuibyszow that was luxurious and where some top people in the aviation industry went. I knew we were making a deal. I left and told him I'd do my best.

A pair of white valinke was not easy to make, especially for women. Pure white wool was hard to get and was usually reserved for bigshots. I decided to talk it over with my manager Zacjew. I told him my girlfriend is having her birthday and I would like to present her with a pair of white valinke. He agreed to help me and in a few days he let me have a pair. I treated him to a bottle of vodka.

In a few days, I got my papers to the rest home, the doctor over-joyed with the volinke and had the papers ready.

I was picked up by a special bus, on which everyone was well dressed. The ride was colorful, through the thick forest with big majestic trees covered in snow. It was a cold, but sunny day. It looked like something out of a fairy tale. The shores of the Volga were very high, its cliffs winding, creating a kind of fiord.

We came to a massive building. This was our destination. As we came closer the picture became even more unreal.

On a high cliff, overlooking the Volga stood a huge castle or a monastery. It looked like a castle I'd seen in Poland, Czechoslovakia or Germany. We entered the gates and parked in front of a huge stone building. We were shown to a room. The place was teeming with people going up and down huge, white staircases. I was assigned a bed on the first floor with six other men. In the corner, stood a tiled oven, next to it a pile of wood for heating. Now, this was a real rest home.

Because of the cold, most of the activities were inside. The food was good and plentiful. The place was clean with large steambaths. There was a place to play cards, dominoes and chess. It had an excellent library and newspapers arrived daily

They told me more females came during the summer, but I did

not care. I missed Claudia very much. The first part of my stay was quite boring, including my roommates. I didn't get involved in any conversations. All they talked about was food, drinks, sex, popular songs and books, and of course,the war and the victories of the Russian army. The successes of the allies was not a desirable topic to discuss.

I tried to be friendly, but tried mostly to talk of trivialities. On sunny days, in the late morning people would get dressed warmly and descend from the castle down to the frozen Volga. It was a kind of physical exercise, because it was more than a couple hundred steps to go down and then up. On such a day, walking up the river we encountered hundreds of German prisoners of war, walking in a single line towards the centre of the river, under the escort of a couple of older Russian soldiers. They were in terrible physical shape, hardly dragging themselves. You could only see their eyes. The rest of their faces were covered with old shawls and rags. We stopped to watch them passing by.

In our group, there were some military men and quite a few big bosses from the upper floors of our rest homes. You could distinguish them from the others by the way they were dressed in their long fur coats and expensive fur hats. We knew that on the upper floors lived the cream of the crop of the aviation industry. The only time we saw them was at this morning walk. One of the military men started to talk to one of the Russian guards leading the prisoners.

He raised his hand and the column stopped. He asked the guards where they were taking the prisoners. The guards pointed out to a little island, not far from the shore. You could see in the distance a few trees and dried, tall grass, which was burned and used for heating and cooking.They are going there to collect firewood, to bring to their camp, located not far from the fjords. This task was their daily exercise. The prisoners seemed to be happy to stop for a rest, especially because most of us including myself, offered them a cigarette. One of the leaders tried to strike up a conversation with the prisoners, but to no avail. I moved a little closer to hear the question, and I translated it to the prisoners. A circle of people formed around me and everybody wanted to ask them questions and to hear my translations.

In general, they didn't want to talk much. They were afraid. Some complaining bitterly about the way they were being treated, fed and housed. They quoted the Geneva convention about the treatment of prisoners of war. We asked them if they had followed the rules in dealing with the civilian population and Russian prisoners of war. One of the bigshots told me I should tell them that Germany is losing the war on all fronts and that the Russian army is entering Poland. I did and they told me I was lying. Hitler was going to win the war and Germany is going to rule the world, they responded.

Those prisoners were members of the SS division and were treated more harshly than other prisoners of war. We continued our walk and the prisoners walked towards the centre of the river to collect their firewood. I looked at them and could not help but feel a certain sympathy for them, even thought I knew, by now, they didn't deserve any pity.

The group of people from the upper floors, most of the engineers and designers of military planes, kept to themselves. They knew each other and walked separately. Most were middle-aged and some older, with the exception of one young, tall, thin individual, maybe a few years my senior. He must have taken some interest in me, probably because of my knowledge of German. He approached me and introduced himself, asking if he could walk with me. From the introduction, I recognized the famous name of the top Russian plane designer. This was his son who was spending some time with his father. He was also a young engineer. He was interested in where I learned German. I told him I had learned it in high school. He wanted to know more about schools in Poland, about the curriculum and sports. He was pleasant and tactful, never starting a conversation about war or politics. When we said goodbye he told me he was going to invite me to play table tennis.

He kept his word. The next day he came down and asked me to go upstairs with him. It was a different world, a world I had never seen in Russia. This was a palace with plush furniture, paintings, huge rooms, people sitting at coffee tables, smoking and drinking tea and reading newspapers. The huge library was comfortable. We entered a recreational area with several huge pool and ping pong tables. We played a few games of each and then I had lunch with him — probably the best I'd ever had. We ate caviar, chicken, sliced beef in huge amounts. I stuffed myself for all those hungry years. We drank some wine, which made me sleepy. I finished it with a good tea and cakes. After, he presented me with a package of cigarettes I'd never seen before. I was so tired I was looking forward to my room for a sleep.

When I got back to our barrack, everyone was complimentary, admiring my looks. I had gained a few kilos. The abstention from Claudia contributed a lot to it.

217

Father was happy to see me and I hoped one day he could go on this type of vacation.

With constant news of victories of the Red Army, the mood of the people had improved. Everybody waited for more involvement in the war by the allies, to quicken the pace of the war to final victory.

The spring and the warm weather also seemed to uplift the mood of the country. Everybody was anxious to return home. But, every passing day we heard more news about the atrocities committed by the Nazis. The newspapers and radio didn't single out the Jews as the victims of the atrocities. To them, they were Russian, Ukrainian, and Polish, not just Jews. At our meeting in the Polish centre, where the majority of the members were Polish Jews, we learned more about the fate of our people. The news was scattered and there was lots of hearsay. But as time passed, the reports became gloomier and gloomier.

Our meetings in the centre became more frequent and more and more people came. Everybody had a feeling that our day of return to Poland was getting closer. News of Allies' progress became more prominent and I knew Germany's days were numbered.

My affair with Claudia continued and we enjoyed every moment together. Our outings to Kuibyszow were pleasant and we became experts at getting the tickets for the best performances in the city. We knew our way around the city, and even found a place in a pre-ferred restaurant to have a meal. It only catered to the bigwigs, but Claudia managed to get the permits.

On one of our outings during the summer, we arrived in Kuibyszow quite early. The weather was bright, sunny and quite warm. We lined up in front of a store to get ice cream. Suddenly, I felt a terrible cold. I started to shiver. It was unbelievable. I couldn't describe what was overcoming me. I could not understand what was happening. Here I was on a hot day, shivering in the cold. For a moment I didn't want to say anything to Claudia. I thought it would go away, but instead it was getting worse. When I told her, she had one look at me and said I had malaria.

I quickly returned home and laid down. Father covered me with everything possible, but nothing helped. Claudia wanted to take me to the hospital in Bezemianka, but I wanted to go homefirst . Burning with a fever, we walked to the hospital, where I stayed for about two weeks.

They gave me quinine pills and I started to improve, but was still very weak. When my appetite came back, they fed me well.Claudia

218

visited me almost every day on her way from work, always bringing some goodies.

When I was released from the hospital, I received another week's vacation to recuperate. I rested and began to regain my full strength.

I had more time, so I visited the offices of the Polish organization more often. There, I met quite a few people I knew. There was always news and more rumors and all kinds of discussion about the war.

The Red Army was deep in Poland and more news became available. The non-Jewish members were much happier than the Jewish members. Most could go home to their families. To whom we would go home was becoming more and more questionable.

I was happy to go back to work to forget the thoughts about the future and what awaited us. I had little zest or interest in my work. Before I was trying and often succeeding in streamlining the operation, made more suggestions. Now, I was just biding my time and at every opportunity trying to listen to the radio or read the newspapers.

Claudia noticed the change in my mood and my nervousness. She understood me well. Her life in exile in Siberia, where she lost most of her family, made her understand my moods. We knew that any day soon we would say goodbye to each other. We tried to think only of the present but it was not easy. She too was waiting and hoping to return to her beloved Moscow and then possibly make a decision about her marital situation. Somehow I wanted the time to go faster, but it seemed to stand still.

I anticipated the final victory soon, after so many successes on all fronts. I thought the victory would come any day, but I was wrong. The Germans were retreating, but never giving up. I knew the longer it lasted, the more slim were my chances of seeing my beloved family ever again.

How long could the Jews survive under the Germans? If the Germans were losing, I was sure they would take even bigger risks with their innocent victims. I didn't share those thoughts with my father or Claudia. They were more optimistic than me. I hoped I was wrong. Maybe, subconsciously I was preparing myself for the worst.

Claudia tried to get more tickets to many excellent concerts, ballets and plays in Kuibyszow. People were becoming more relaxed. The somber mood of previous years was disappearing fast, in anticipation of better times ahead.

Everywhere we went, including Bezemianka, we encountered German, Hungarian, Romanian and Italian prisoners of war, working at all kinds of outside projects. The Russian people passing by hardly noticed them. Occasionally, some would spit on the ground and swear. I was angry with myself for not hating them as I should. Looking at those frightened young boys, I just couldn't. But on the front I'm sure they were different. Here, in their dirty uniforms, unshaven and skinny with their cheekbones protruding, they presented a pitiful picture.

No one had a clear idea about the holocaust and the atrocities they had committed in the name of their Fuhrer. I found out a little later that the prisoners of war we saw working on the roads, were members of the Wermarcht, mostly the regular army. The members of the SS, SA and the Gestapo were sent away to Siberia and the Arctic Circle to pay a stiffer price for their deeds. I'm sure most of them never made it back to Germany.

In early spring, 1945, with the tremendous thrust of the Allies and Russians on all fronts, it became clear the war;s end was imminent. I stayed in the barrack late at night, listening to the reports of progress. The newspapers were full of good news, but the news on the radio was always more up to date. There was little news about what was happening in the occupied territories,with the Russians euphoria about their many military victories.

My work performance in the shop started to slip. I could not concentrate. I was also trying to go often to the Polish post, where serious registration for eventual return was going on. People from all over came to register, especially from smaller towns, including couples who intermarried locally, and wanted to move back to Poland.

My affair with Claudia continued unabated. We came to understand it would not last forever. She understood I had to go back and she knew that she could leave any time soon. We would try to keep in touch and maybe we would solve our problems and meet again. We knew this was a remote possibility. But we also didn't know what kind of geography and what kind of world it would be after the war.

***

Finally, the great day, the day we had yearned for years arrived. The war was over. The armistice was signed. People were celebrating, dancing in the streets. Everyone left their jobs. It was greatest joy, a relief of the constant tension. People were overcome with unprecedented happiness. It was hard to believe. The end of killing and war and atrocities. We had been expecting it since the victory at Stalingrad, but it was still a long way off, but when it happened, it was hard to believe.

Claudia brought me to her laboratory. There was a great, wild party going on. Her husband came down from the office. Suddenly, huge amounts of food and drink became available. The party lasted into the wee hours. Everybody got drunk.

When returned to our barrack, the lights were on and everyone was awake eating and drinking tea. They were listening to the radio, blaring with news and music. I embraced father and we both started to cry. Soon we would find out about our family and face reality.

Everybody in the barrack was cheerful, but the mood was different than the party at the plant. To them, in most cases the fate of their families was known. They knew of the casualties, most of the them suffering through this long war. Nearly everyone lost someone dear to them. We lived with hope against hope. We needed a miracle.

Our friends in the barrack knew they would stay in the Soviet Union. They lost many relatives and were also wondered if they could return to the homes they left.

In the morning I went to work, but half the workers didn't show up. The ones that did, came with no enthusiasm for work. They had been celebrating and drinking all night. Zacjew called everyone together for a pep talk. He understood the workers' happiness, but now that the war had ended we had to work harder again to supply our population with necessities.

I understood Zacjew. He had to show a reason for not coming up with today's production. The pep talk meeting would give him a good excuse. I was excited. My mind was not at work. How soon would we be able to return and to what would we return to? I never dreamed that it would take almost a year until our return would begin.

At the meetings in the Polish office, there were all kinds of rumors, news and innuendos. We all hoped we would return, but no dates were mentioned. Father and I were glued to the radio. All of Europe was in turmoil. All the talk was of victory over the Germans. Father begged me not take anymore risks. He wanted me to stop trading at the market, stop going to Kinel for tobacco and food. We should get along with the little we get, he advised. This was no time to take chances that could complicate our return.

I promised to be extra careful. The only thing I couldn't do was end my affair with Claudia. Claudia told me her husband knew, but she wasn't sure how much. So, I tried to be more careful.

About a month after the war ended, her husband started to go often to Moscow on business. It gave us more time together. Claudia's mother liked me very much. Her relationship with Claudia's husband was not good. She was their cook, maid and nanny.

*** 

Life was becoming more pleasant and smoother. The supplies of food were becoming richer. The fear of being caught on the black market was diminished. The constant check by police and military police lessened. People became more relaxed, friendly and hopeful for a brighter future, perhaps even more freedom. They also hoped that becoming friends with the Allies, especially the U.S.A., would enhance their freedom and well-being. The Russians hoped the tremendous suffering they endured for so many years, would finally bring them better tomorrows.

Most of the Russian people by now knew what their personal losses were, but not us. We were promised a speedy return, but it never materialized. There was all kinds of confusion, lack of transportation and on the other end, an unstable government in Poland., Little by little, news of the outbreaks of brutality and the extermination camps started to trickle in by news and returning soldiers, but still the Jews specifically were never mentioned.

The postal services were returning slowly to normal. I immediately sent a letter to our address in Krakow, but I never got an answer. There was no other way to communicate. I sent a letter to relatives in the United States, but an answer was not forthcoming. Thousands of people were writing letters, but apparently the territories being occupied by the Germans for such a long time, had all their post offices destroyed.

From the news I could gather, especially from the Polish post, which was now a Polish government post, I and the others came to the conclusion that not very many Jewish people could have survived the occupation. I laid at night in my bunk in the barrack figuring how my family could have survived. Maybe they were hidden by some people, maybe in Zabierzow, a village near Krakow, where my mother was born. Maybe my sister Niusia, so strong and so good looking, maybe my cousin Herman, the Hercules of our family a Polish officer, survived. Maybe my cousin Samek, the youngest one from Cieszyn, blonde and blue-eyed who spoke German so well survived.

The nights were the worst. I could not chase away those gloomy thoughts. Even spending the evenings with Claudia, wasn't the same anymore. I would feel more depressed. She knew what was on my mind and tried to cheer me up.

I shared all the news and rumors that I heard during the day with Father, but we never shared our thoughts. He was thinking the same way I was. We didn't want to scare each other.

Work became my only solace. But the shop was not the same anymore. Some workers were returning to places where they were mobilized. New employees were hard to find. More and more we depended on prisoners of war.

Time went by slowly, maybe because I wanted it to rush by.

I went to the movies in Beziamenka more often with Claudia and my friend from the barracks. Most of the Russian movies were pure propaganda, but occasionally they showed ballets. After all these years, they were still showing again and again the two American movies, The Great Waltz, and Midnight Serenade. I knew them by heart, every scene, every word, every piece of music. I would close my eyes and daydream and fantasize. It was a form of relaxation for me.

Months were passing by, since the official end of the war, but our situation was standing still. Another winter was closing in the same fight for hygiene and warmth, though I was equipped better for the winter with good valinke and quilted jackets. With the first snow and grey skies, our spirits would go down. The long darkness would increase our depression.

On the radio, the news was full of joy and victorious spirits, stories about reunions with heroes of the Red Army, soldiers returning home, reuniting with their sweethearts, with their mothers, stories about the bright future awaiting everyone in the Soviet Union. When I read in the papers or heard on the radio about those joyous reunions, my eyes filled up with tears hoping that maybe something like this was awaiting me in the near future.

There were no signs that our departure was being organized. They started the first transportation from a place much farther east than we were, mostly from eastern Siberia and the Asian republics. We started to hear more often from people who had received letters from eastern Poland. They were related to soldiers stationed there. They would bring their letters and read them to us. It was hard to believe what we heard. We heard about whole Jewish communities wiped out. There were almost no Jews to be found, except a few survivors hiding through the years and some partisans who were fighting in the forest, being supplied and armed by the Russians. Some letters mentioned the soldiers returned to their hometowns and villages, not finding any Jews at all. The officials didn't want to deny what was in the letters, but advised us to be cautious about this information. Maybe they knew more, maybe they didn't. Maybe they just wanted to protect us from anxiety.

But since the news started to filter in and came from letters, newspapers and radio, the extent of murders and barbarism, the atrocities became clearer. The description of concentration camps, including Auschwitz, not far from my hometown of Krakow, liberated by the Red Army was unbelievable. It was impossible. But the news persisted and there were more eyewitness accounts in letters. My hopes started to dwindle.

It had been almost eight months since the armistice had been signed and we were still  in Bezemianka. People gathered at the Polish office, expressing their dismay. All the papers and registrations were ready, but not our day of departure.  I wanted to get over the uncertainty.

It was  difficult living in this limbo. My co-workers and Zacjew understood. They all knew I would be leaving for Poland soon. They were away from their homes, but at least they had families and they knew what had happened in their hometowns. They also hoped to return to their towns and cities.

The majority of people registering to return to Poland were Jewish, because they were the ones who ran from the Germans. They came from all over pre-1939 Poland. As former Polish citizens, they had the right to return.  But, Poland's borders were completely changed. All eastern parts, from the very north to south became part of the Soviet Union and amalgamated to the Ukraine, ByloRussia and Lithuania. After the war in compensation, Poland got part of the German territories, adjusting her borders on the western side. Now, Jews living in Eastern pre-war Poland could choose to stay in the Soviet Union and eventually return to their former homes. Most decided, though,to return to Poland. They were the first to receive the terrible news about what happened to their relatives and friends who were overrun by the German invasion of Russia in 1941. There's was the first despair.

People were begging for advice about what to do. These were important life decisions to make, but who could help them. We didn't have this problem. Krakow remained  in Poland and we had to return to face whatever was awaiting us. In the shop even the Hungarian prisoners found out that soon father and I would return to Poland.

One afternoon,while working in the office, someone knocked quietly on the door.  In walked a German speaking Hungarian, who seemed to be the leader of his group. He asked for permission to talk to me in private. In his heavy accented German, he told me he was from a family of Hungarian elite, who were large landowners. His family belonged to the Hungarian aristocracy. His family lived in a castle, not far from Budapest. He heard I was going back home to Poland and he wanted me to take a letter from him to his family in Hungary. He didn't know if the family now had any money to reward me. But they had many valuable paintings and I would be handsomely rewarded. The letter would be written in Hungarian, and if I wanted he would add a German translation.

I told him I didn't know when we are leaving. He could write the letter if he wanted, and I would decide before my departure. He begged me for a few pieces of stationary and a pencil, which I gave him. A few months ago I would not have hesitated and I would have easily done this favor for him. But after hearing about all the atrocities in all of eastern Europe and the Hungarian collaborators, my view off the Hungarian workers had changed. Why did they fight along with the Germans against Russia? I also heard that most Jews in Hungary perished with the help of Hungarian collaborators.

*** 

The pace of preparation for our departure in our Polish office was picking up. The officers were openly discussing days of departure. It would be some time in February 1946, almost a year after the end of the war. We were advised and told to prepare to wind up our personal commitments and to be ready on short notice. Our places of work would be notified and we would soon receive a a final date of departure.

We put our belongings together. Father and I decided to buy a valise to make the move easier. We settled on a good-sized wooden valise called *czamodan*. It looked quite impressive, but it was quite heavy, yet we were able to put most of our possessions in it. Until this very day, nobody can believe that I still had my belongings that I had taken from Krakow in September 1939, when we fled from the Germans. We accumulated a few belongings, most of it winter clothing and felt valinki. We also accumulated a few rubles and didn't know what to do with them. We weren't sure we would be able to convert it to Polish currency. I tried to accumulate some extra mahorka for our journey home. I made a special trip to Kinel and while there I said goodbye to my friend the doctor and other people that were helpful to me.

The tension grew every day. Our thoughts were already home. We weren't sorry to leave, but we were thankful we survived here. Except for the time we were in the camp in Nuziary, we weren't treated any worse than the Russians themselves. We didn't like the tyrannical dictatorship any more than the majority of Soviet citizens. But I will never forget the sacrifices, heroism and determination to defeat and destroy Nazi Germany.

The saddest part was separating from Claudia and maybe never seeing her again. But we knew this from the beginning. The history, the changes and the circumstances made our decisions for us. We had no choice.

There was not enough time to do anything about it now. If I wanted to leave Russia I had to leave now. Who knew what the future would bring.

Finally, word came that we should be prepared to leave by the end of January. We were overjoyed. In the Polish post there was lots of singing after having a few extra drinks of vodka. I didn't want to hear anymore news to kill our joy and excitement.

When the final order came, it looked like we'd be departing in February. We had to be ready at any time. We started to say good-bye to our friends in the barracks, with whom we lived in friendship and harmony for so long. We thanked them, and especially Mr. Lev, for letting us live in their barrack. Some of them couldn't understand why we were going back to Poland.

In the shop, Zacjew and all the co-workers bid us goodbye. The Hungarian officer handed me his letter. I took it with a little apprehension. I wasn't sure what I was going to do. Besides, who knows maybe we would be searched before leaving the Soviet Union or on the Polish border and having the letter could be dangerous.

I kept seeing Claudia as often as possible. We tried to go to movies and concerts for a few hours to forget. We held hands, both having the same thoughts. Maybe this movie or concert was our last together.

How complicated life was and how little control we had over our destiny. When we parted in the evenings, we stood embracing for a long time, our eyes full of tears, I was dreading the moment we would have to say the final goodbye.

We were given two days to meet at our Polish post with our belongings. From there, we would be transported to the morning train to Kuibyszow. We asked lots of questions. How long was the journey? Should we take food with us? Our leaders had few answers but lots of assurances. Everything was going to be taken care of. We were going back as proud Polish citizens. We will be treated with respect. I had my doubts, but hoped it was true.

I had to tell Claudia the news of our departure. I met her at the gate of the factory and we walked home together. We walked slowly after I told her I was leaving in two days even though it was cold and the snow was falling with brisk winds that fell like needles in our face. Before entering her apartment, we found a niche between buildings that was sheltered from the biting wind. We stood silently embracing for along time. Tomorrow we would meet for the last time.

Claudia made arrangements for us to have one last night together at her friend's apartment. We walked slowly and silently. Her friend was there and she invited us inside to a beautifully set table for two. She told us she was leaving and wished me luck.

We drank and ate in silence, commenting only on the beautiful dinner and drinks. It was so hard to talk. We could not make any promises for the future. It was almost midnight when we left and I walked her home. We embraced while tears flowed freely from our eyes. I tried to say goodbye, and she put her finger to my lips and said don't say goodbye yet. I was surprised and didn't understand what she meant. She kissed me and ran upstairs to her apartment. I stood for awhile hoping she would come back, but she didn't.

Slowly, I walked to my barrack, not feeling the cold, wind and snow. Father was awake waiting for me. He was terribly worried that I hadn't come earlier. We had to leave early in the morning. He knew where I was. When he looked at me sitting at the table,he didn't say a word. He understood. I was frozen so he gave me a cup of hot water and begged me to lay down for a few hours. We knew that we had a hard day ahead of us.

I fell asleep for awhile, but was soon awakened by Father. It was time to leave. We had a long walk ahead of us to the Polish office and we had to carry our heavy valise and a full bag of food.

Quite a few of our friends got up with us to say goodbye. Some were going to work and offered to help us with the luggage. One of them was Liowa, Mr Lev's son. He was going in our direction toward the station, heading from Bezemianka to Kuibyszow. Liowa was a tall, strong lad of about 16. He attended school in Kubyszow, where he lived most of the time in a school dormitory. When we parted with him, he told me where his dormitory was in case we were delayed in our departure from Kuibyszow. I didn't expect to see him again but we did.

We came early but there were already people ahead of us. We dropped our luggage not far from the entrance, went inside where we received our travelling papers, including a document stating our Polish citizenship.

I was sure from my previous meetings at the centre, that I knew most of the people in the area. But to my amazement, people, whole families who I had never seen, were there. One of them to my great surprise and joy was the Feldman family I met in Kinel.

Soon, the trucks started to pull in front of building and we were told to put our luggage on. Those trucks were to take us to the train from Bezimianka to Kuibyszow. We were all milling around because there was lots of time before going to the station, which was close and familiar to me. So many times Claudia and I had left from there to go to Kuibyszow.

We were supposed to take the 9 o'clock train. The trucks were filling up fast and it seemed everything was well organized. By 8:30 we were all on the platform with our luggage. I tried to put my valise as close as possible to the entrance of the train. I put it down and when I straightened up, Claudia was standing next to me. I didn't know how to react. I hugged her and gave her a kiss, but I didn't know what to say. I was a little embarrassed because Father was standing next to me.

She was dressed so beautifully with a fur hat, her golden hair covering part of her face. The fur coat and the leather trimmed valinke completed her wardrobe. I could never forget her standing there on the platform. She looked so much like Julie Cristy in the film Dr. Zivago. When I finally asked her what she was doing here, she matter of factly told me she wanted to be with me until my departure. That was why she didn't want to say goodbye to me yesterday.

The train arrived, unloaded the passengers from Kuibyszow and in a few minutes we boarded for our trip. I was so happy to have Claudia sitting next to me.

It was a short ride and soon we arrived in Kuibyszow. Following our leader, we walked slowly towards the main railway station. It was slow going because everyone had a lot of luggage. At the station, our leader went to get information about our train.

It was far away on sidetracks. We got closer to our destination, away from the main station and we noticed several cargo cars with some people milling around. That was our Western Express to Poland. At first glance, it reminded me of the train that took us to the east in 1940. I was a little scared.

We were assigned to one car with a few people already inside. They were filling one side of the cars first. They were exactly the same as the ones that brought us to Russia. But inside they had built two- tiered wooden bunks with some straw on them. In the centre was a stove, and for toilet facilities was a little booth with a hole in the middle. I was expecting a regular train to take us back to freedom and democracy. I was greatly disappointed.

We found out it would take a few days before our transfer was completed. They were waiting for people coming from all kinds of places around the region, some as far as 100 kilometres away. Father and I took a corner bunk. It was cold in the car and after putting our bundles down, we huddled around the hot stove.

Claudia was disappointed and worried about our accommodations. She knew the city better than I. We found Liowa's dormitory, but he was not there. We let ourselves in and waited for him. Liowa finally showed up. We ended up staying there for three days.

We checked on the train situation every day. Our car was filled to capacity and they kept adding more cars. It was going to be a long train. We received every day a ration of bread and walked to the station for kipiotok and sometimes we could purchase a bowl of hot cabbage soup. Most of the people, like ourselves, brought lots of food with them.

During those three days, Claudia would come in the late afternoon and bring me some goodies. I asked her not to do this because I knew she took chances taking this from the plant. She brought me two bottles of vodka and advised me to use it wisely, only to keep warm.

One evening was our last, though we didn't know it. She asked me to give her my address in Krakow where I lived before the war. I gladly gave it to her, hoping to find someone there. I printed the address in Polish on a piece of paper.

It was close to midnight and we had to make sure Claudia caught the last train to Bezemianka. We said goodbye and she said as usual I'll see you tomorrow, but it was the last time.

The next morning they told us we would be leaving in two hours. Nobody informed us when and where we would arrive in Poland. I'm sure they didn't know themselves.

The train moved slowly through the city and suburbs, but once we passed, I could determine we were going south. The doors of the cars were not closed and on any stop we could open them freely. There were no armed guards to watch us and we could leave the train on the frequent stops.

In the middle of the train was the caboose, where the director of transport and a couple of officers lived. They were responsible for feeding us and managing the train. Apparently, they were responsible for delivering us to the Polish border. Sometimes the train would stop in the middle of nowhere, for hours. In one car, there was a kind of food warehouse, from where they gave us bread, salted fish and a little sugar. Hot water was always available. Most people had brought enough food with them, so nobody went hungry.

Our biggest problem was getting some wood, or coal to run our stove. We picked up every piece of wood we could find and sometimes we stopped close to the trains carrying coal from the west, and stole as much as possible.

I was dreaming about warm summer weather in Krakow and the Vistula River, where I went swimming practically every day — the beaches and especially the big swimming pool in Blonie. I thought about walking in my shorts, short-sleeved shirts and sandals; the summer camps I attended yearly in the mountains in Zavoja, Rabka and Zakopane. I yearned for warmth. I hoped that in my years away from Krakow, it hadn't changed too much.

I tried in my daydreaming to block out the nagging question: Who was going to await me there? The progress of our transport was slow. Sometimes we spent more time standing than moving.

Lately, we had difficulty finding enough fuel to keep our stove going. The wood we found was wet and didn't burn enough to light the little coal we had.

When the train stopped at the station, we had an opportunity to get hot water to warm up a bit. But when it stopped in the middle of nowhere it was terrible. The only way to keep warm was to huddle together in our bunks.

In a few days, I realized we were beginning to go south and I remembered a city called Tambow, from our deportation from Lvov to Camp Nuiziary. If we went farther south, we would probably get to Poland the same way as we left in 1940. I knew the Polish border had changed when all of eastern Poland was seized by the Soviet Union.

The ride to the Polish border was taking a long time. But with all the difficulties we felt better. We felt free. We weren't coerced by the director of our train and the soldiers to do anything. They were, most of the time, polite and warned us not to overstay on our stops and not to get lost because it would complicate and delay our return. We were going sharply to the south now and came to the Ukraine, close to the city of Charkow. I found out by asking people at the small station.

Everybody spoke now in Ukrainian and there was no doubt that we were getting closer to our destination. The weather was getting a little warmer and there was less snow on the ground. The forests disappeared and the land was flat. Here, we could see more of the destruction caused by the war — burned out villages and towns and burned out military equipment, near the railway tracks. Some stations were completely destroyed. At some stations, we could buy a little food, but mostly the local farmers wanted to trade. Most of the Ukrainian traders had little four-piece packages of American cigarettes and chocolate bars, also American. I could not figure out where they got it from. I found out later it was a part of the Marshal plan. I bought one pack of American cigarettes and brought it with pride to my father. After a bite to eat we lit one each. When I inhaled deeply, those great smelling cigarettes, my head started to spin and father started to cough terribly. We looked at each other smiling and extinguished our Camels, putting them back in the little flat package. We decided we were too weak for these smokes and rolled our Russian mahorka in a Russian newspaper and enjoyed our smoke without difficulty. The Russians had told us we would get used to everything there. I guess they were right. Mahorka was our tobacco, now.

Going west, we noticed huge, long trains loaded with coal, going east. At one station, I found a few huge chunks of coal laying on the tracks, that had fallen from one of the cars. This coal was hard, shiny, black and heavy. I picked up those few chunks and brought them into our car. With a little hammer we broke the huge pieces into small ones, put them in our stove on the top of a little firewood. The coal started to burn immediately. The stove became red and hot. We soon found out that this was Polish coal from Silesia, being exported to Russia. From now on, we watched for those coal trains on our stops and when we found one, we helped ourselves.

*** 

When we finally came to Kiev, the capital of Ukraine, I was sure we were going to cross the southern part of Poland on the line heading for Krakow. We stayed outside the stations of Kiev for awhile. People came close to our cars, trying to sell us things.

Many Jews lived in the Ukraine and on every stop I would look to see if I could spot a familiar face. During the war many were evacuated, but I knew from the people in our barrack in Bezemianka, that many had no time or a chance to run away.

So many thoughts suddenly filled our heads. Where would we go first? Who would we meet? Who is alive? Who is not? What are we going to do? Where are we going to live? Will I go to school? What is father going to do? Over five years had passed by. So many different places, that we had lived in, fought in and worked in. So many events we witnessed in those years. I was sure that a lot had changed in Poland, especially in Krakow.

231

Father and I talked about everything. But, our fears and hopes we kept to ourselves. We understood each other well.

We left Kiev after a long stopover. The train picked up a little speed. This line was more frequented with trains going both ways. At Tarnopol, we were in the former Polish territory. In 1940, when we were going to the camp, under the watchful eyes of guards and in closed cars, we had made a stop there.

I went down to look around the station. There were no more friendly faces. People seemed gloomy and I could not see any Jews. I sat down on a bench at the station, sad and disappointed.

The gloomy reality was sinking in. I wished we could hurry up and get over the uncertainty. But our train was in no hurry. Most of the stations after Tarnopol were familiar to me from geography. And I knew soon we would come to Lvov, where I spent almost a year and from where we left on our Russian odyssey.

As we were getting closer to Lvov, at the smaller stations, very few spoke Polish. I didn't know who was Polish or who was Ukrainian. Only a few years ago, this was Poland.

It was late March. The weather was much warmer and I liked to sit outside the stations and watch people do their daily chores. On some stops, I saw small peasant markets. There were stands with some food, mostly people were trading goods. And the horse-drawn wagons were going in all directions. I looked and envied them. I knew that most of them had a hard life, but they had probably lived there for generations, with their families, and had small expectation in their lives. Maybe this impression was deceiving. A few years ago, they were Polish citizens and they didn't like it. They always wanted to have a free Ukraine. Now, they had a Ukraine under Stalin's communism, which they hated.

When we were close to Lvov, I started to think about the friends I'd left behind. I hoped to find somebody with more information.

Our train was not a priority and often there were long stops. At last, in the early evening we came to Lvov. When we opened the door, we realized we were very far from the central station. Lvov was an important railroad centre and I wasn't sure where we were parked. There were lots of coal trains around us. We helped ourselves to some. With all those coal trains we met on our way to Russia, it seemed they were taking out all the Polish coal and bringing it to their country.

We stayed about two days in the same spot, but later in the afternoon we were towed closer to the station. The platform was teeming with people. I scanned the faces, trying to find someone familiar, but with no success. I went back to the train and stood with Father and a  group of other people. It was chilly but everybody chose to stay outside to get some fresh air.

Two passersby, poorly dressed, came up close to my father and quietly asked him a few words in Yiddish. A lively conversation followed. They lived in Lvov before the war and  joined the Russian army. When they came back, they were discharged here in a few months after the war ended.  They hadn't found any family members alive so far, and they were coming often to the station, hoping to find some family or friends on the train going back to Poland. The story  they told us about the Lvov Jewry, caught by the Germans in 1941, were terrible and unbelievable. Only those who ran away to the east and outran the Germans, survived. the community of about 80,000 Jews. The rest were wiped out.  A few came back to Lvov to look for relatives and when they did not find anyone, they went back to Poland. At that very instant I decided to tear up the note given to me by the Hungarian prisoner, and not to deliver it.

They wanted to know if we had anything to sell or trade. As long as we had enough food to eat, we wanted to take our belongings with us.

But we found out from them that we were on our way to Przemysl, which lay on the border of the Soviet Union. They warned us to be careful about our belongings, because we were going to be thoroughly searched at the border.

Father and I had nothing to worry about, because we didn't have anything to speak of.

The conversations with those two Jewish men upset me terribly. I started to cry.  In those few years in the Soviet Union, I hardened myself, but when I thought about my mother,  sister and family now, I just couldn't hold back my tears.

I fell asleep late and didn't  hear the train starting to move. When I woke up, the train had picked up speed and people had begun their morning routine. I didn't get up with everyone, but moved to the corner and started to analyze the conversation with those men in Lvov. Maybe in Poland the situation was different.  It was not a war zone. Maybe the people who had survived in Lvov moved to Poland already. Maybe we would be the lucky ones. I was thinking of mother and my sister Nusia and how well our Christian neighbors liked them. Even the  priest in our neighborhood was kind to us.

We lived in a predominantly Polish neighborhood. We all spoke perfect Polish. Mother even spoke German. The one person I was sure must be alive was my powerful, super-strong cousin Herman.

I could not take the uncertainty any more. Poland meant to me, a country where I wasn't afraid of anything, a country that didn't have gulags. What kind of Poland was I going to now?

It was late afternoon. The day was bright and the sun was high in the sky when our train stopped. I opened the door and, as usual, I looked for the name of the station. It said Przemysl. I couldn't believe it. We were in Poland.

The station was teeming with people. I jumped down and lo and behold everyone was speaking Polish. I noticed some soldiers in Polish uniforms. When most of the people jumped out on the platform, I could see some hostility on the faces of the Polish people. Nobody tried or showed any welcome sign. I came closer to a group of Poles and at the entrance of the station I overheard their conversation. One of them was loudly saying to the other: "Look how many of "ours" are coming back." Momentarily, I didn't understand what they meant, but sure enough the other Poles said: "Look, only Jews."

At this moment, I understood we were not welcome. People in the car were upset. Some were called "dirty Jews", directly, while others heard remarks like: "Look how many still survived and who needs them here."

The majority of Poles left Russia with the Anders army in the early '40s and went with them to the Middle East. Few Jews were inducted into the Anders army. Mostly, they took former Polish soldiers, doctors and a few officers. We were taken illegally by the Russians in Stalingrad, on our way to Saratow, to join the Anders army. Had we not been taken off by the Russians, we would have left with the rest of them,on their way to Iran and Palestine, where many Jews ended up, including Manachim Begin, the former Prime Minister of Israel.

We were surprised to cross the border without being searched by the Russians or the Poles. Apparently, we were checked enough in Russia and the Polish authorities knew how we obtained our Polish documents.

Our train was put on a siding, not far from the station. At night, I noticed our train was watched by uniformed men, walking back and forth along the railway. I could not distinguish the uniform. We stayed overnight. I couldn't sleep. Finally, I fell asleep and had terrible dreams. I woke up in a sweat and realized I was in Poland. I lay down and fell asleep again.

Through all of this, my nerves took over me. I forgot about the place I left and even about Claudia. Now, that we had crossed the border, I started to think about her again. We were now in different countries. How free would the borders be? Could I travel to see her? Could she come to see me? She taught me about life, devotion and love. She was my only teacher, about the finer side of Russian life and Russian people. I always wondered why she loved me so much. She often told me how loving, gentle, and thoughtful I was. This meant to her more than anything. Probably, I was much different than the men she had met in her hard, unhappy life.

Early the next morning, I decided to go outside towards the station to look around. I was anxious to talk to some people, but I felt a little uncomfortable to start a conversation. I walked along the tracks, towards the locomotive, but I didn't see anyone. I assumed we were not going to leave soon.

In Poland, especially in the smaller towns, the train station was the focal point. In the evening, residents would go for a stroll there and socialize, waiting to see who was coming and going.

I walked the streets, hoping to see a Jewish face. I didn't see any. I approached a man on a horse-drawn wagon. I remarked on the weather and his well-groomed horse. He must have recognized me as one of the returning refugees because of my Russian jacket. He asked where in Russia I was coming from. He told me many transports had been coming for months and he said, with disappointment, that most of them had been Jews. I guess he thought I was one of the minority Poles returning. He told me the Polish government was communist and that people didn't like it. Times were hard, shortages were the way of life. He asked me if I had seen the trains full of coal from Silesia, going to Russia. They take everything from us. People here are freezing in the winter because they can't afford the coal and it's all going to Russia.

He was friendly and talkative and I decided to ask about the Jews. I played naive and told him I was in Przemysl in 1940 and there were lots of Jewish people there then, but I didn't see any now. The question opened a Pandora's box and he started to talk non-stop. Almost all the Jews here had been killed by the Germans, but many ran away to Russia. A few came back with the transport, stayed a few days, but when they couldn't find their families, they left. There might be a few still here, but he wasn't sure. He began to express his opinions about the Jews, calling them Christ killers and how they had all the money. They were also communists, just like the government.

Our conversation ended and my official informer had told me more than I wanted to hear.

I returned to the train just in time. We were leaving soon. A Polish officer informed us we were leaving for Krakow.

I didn't tell anyone about my conversation with the peasant.

The train ride to Krakow should only take a few hours. It was late in the evening when we left Premysl. On every stop the doors were opened. This next stop, someone called out Tarnow. I had relatives there and in nearby Zglobice. I used to come here with my mother to visit when I was a few years old, during the summer.

It seemed our last leg of the journey would never end. The morning light came and the door opened. It was cool outside and everybody wanted to look, but not me. I stayed on my bunk, trying to look at yet another small station, when someone yelled, "Krakow!"

I jumped down from my bunk and looked outside and saw the sign at the station that said Krakow. But I had never been here before. It was a simple station on the outskirts of the city. The station was actually Krakow-Plaszow, but people figured we were close enough to our destination, so they got off the train.

I went inside the station to buy myself a pop. They took the rubles, but hesitantly. We were deep in Poland and people were using the Polish zloty. I had no idea about the exchange rate or the value of the zloty. I tried to find out when we would be taken to Krakow proper, but nobody knew. It looked like it would take a long time because they uncoupled the locomotive.

Later, I found out how busy the Plaszow station had been during the war. Most of the Jewry from the ghetto were transported to concentration camps from here. They were packed inhumanely in cattle cars and sent to Aucshwitz. This station became famous in the movie Schindler's List. It was in Plaszow that Schindler saved almost 1,200 Jews, quite a few of them my dear friends from before the war. But now, the station was quiet. Not every train stopped here. The few Polish people around gave us unfriendly looks and made cruel remarks.

When I saw the locomotive was gone and we were in for a long stay, I started to worry we might arrive at the Krakow station at night and where would we go from there.

Father and I decided our first stop should be to get to our apartment, where we lived before the war and find out from the owners, the family Syrek, whatever they knew.

Deep down, I hoped they would have been able to help to my mother and sister during the war. I had even a spark of hope to find somebody waiting for us in our apartment. I never dared say this to my father, but we both agreed this should be our first step.

As the hours dragged on, there was no word about our departure. I could see some homes in the distance, but they looked unfamiliar to me.

***

At the side of the station, I noticed a couple of horse-drawn wagons with the drivers chatting nearby. The driver approached me and asked me what I wanted. Without hesitation, I blurted out I would like to go to Krakow. He was a burly man with a smile and he answered he would take me, but it was far and would cost lots of money. I gave him our address, 34 Barska, in Dembniki. He was willing to go, but for a price and the haggling started in earnest. He quoted me in Polish zlotys. I didn't have any. I told him I had rubles and he quoted me a sum I didn't have. He asked me if I had anything to sell or trade. I took out an American cigarette from one of the little packages I had from the Ukraine and offered him a smoke. When he saw the Camel cigarette, he accepted it and took out a huge wooden match to light it. How many of those cigarettes did I have, he asked. I could tell he wanted them more than anything else, certainly more than rubles. I felt we could strike a deal. I told him I had quite a few packages. I knew I had kept them for a reason.

I started to bargain with five packages. When I showed them to him, I could see he wanted them badly. But he played his game and said that was not enough. I had more in my pockets, so I went to the station and in a few minutes came back and told him I had 12. We struck a deal.

I asked him to wait while I went to get Father and gather our belongings. We said goodbye to the people we travelled with. Father was delighted with the arrangements I had made.

I told the driver he would get the cigarettes upon our arrival. I sat on a wooden plank next to the driver and Father sat in the back next the luggage. I didn't feel safe from the beginning and kept a knife under my jacket, just in case. I wasn't sure if he knew we were Jewish. I suspected he didn't. It was eerie to be on our own after having been surrounded by people for years.

Once we started on our way, with the steady trot of our horse, first on a dirt road, then on the cobblestones, a terrible excitement came over me, fear over what awaited us. I was shivering I could feel

237

my body was in a sweat. Father was in his thoughts and I didn't say a word. He only worried to make sure we were going in the right direction. The driver became very talkative, asking me hundreds of questions about Russia.

We were close to a part of the suburb called Podgorze. When we arrived at the outskirts of Podgorze, I knew which way we would go towards our address. Father was sitting quietly, deep in his thoughts, not saying much. I would have done the same if not for our driver who was bent on a constant conversation and flooded me with all kinds of questions. Suddenly, Father told the driver he wanted to go in a different direction. He wanted to pass by the Hotel Royale, our old restaurant. I explained to the driver Father's reason. He sighed a few times, but after promising him an extra package of cigarettes, he agreed.

I understood my Father's reason. He thought maybe the restaurant was still there and maybe we could find somebody. The area where the Royale was located was on the outskirts of Kazimierz, about one kilometre towards the centre of the city, the Rynek Glowny. The streets were familiar, but not the people. By now, I felt more comfortable with our driver and I decided to ask him what had happened here. Why didn't I see any Jews. Well, he gave me more information than I expected or wanted to hear. Our Jews, he said, were killed by the Germans. Only a few survived. They came back looking for their families but didn't stay too long because they didn't find anybody.

He started to tell me about the ghetto and the camp in Plaszow and the things he'd seen. The Jews were nice people, he said, and didn't deserve what the Germans did to them. He knew quite a few Jews and was very fond of them. He felt sorry for what had happened. He also said there were a few Jews in Kazimierz and Krakow, but he didn't know how many. It was the first time someone had told me there were some Jews here. He didn't know where they were, but had heard there were some. I was so immersed in his report that I didn't notice we were entering Kazimierz. I started to look around and a cold shiver and sweat took hold of me again. The streets were quiet. Who were these people? Where had everyone gone? The Kazimierz had been synonymous with Jews. Where were the Hassidim and Orthodox Jews with their long black coats and wide-brimmed hats? Where were their stores and stands teeming with customers? There were none. Where were the children playing on the sidewalks?

Only some strange faces walked the streets. Our Kazmierez was gone. I sat now quietly, keeping my head down, trying not to look around anymore.

We passed the park that was two blocks from my beloved gymnasium. Only a few years of absence, and everything around was so strange, like I had come back to some strange planet. In a short while, we got to the Royale. We entered the wide thoroughfare of Krakowska and Stradom. The streets were the same, but there was no life there. The huge dry goods stores were gone. There was no traffic near the Jewish business school.

The huge advertising posters were gone, all the stores were closed. We were coming closer. I could see on my left side the Wawel Castle. We crossed through the street and here on the right stood the Royale, better to say the former Royale. I told the driver to stop. It was exactly the spot where several droski used to have a stand to bring and pick up their fares. There was no sign of them. We got out and walked the few metres to the building. The only familiar thing was the building itself. We walked around and looked. There was no hotel, no restaurant. There was a sign of a government office. The Moulin Rouge was also gone. We didn't speak a word to each other, just turned around and practically ran to the wagon. I looked at Father, his face was full of tears and he was sobbing quietly. I hadn't seen him this way for a long time.

From here on, I told the driver how to go. We turned towards Wawel, practically circling around to the bridge, crossing the Vistula to Dembniki, my place of birth and youth.

I looked at the Wawel, where I visited yearly and walked around it daily on my way to school. It hadn't changed a bit. It was the same huge, powerful and awesome structure. It survived another invader. They came and left, but the castle stood and would probably stay forever. I didn't look on the street at the people walking by. They were strangers. The buildings were inhabited by strangers. The only familiar one was Wawel itself.

We emerged on Groble Street, from where I could see the Dembniki Bridge, which took us to our street.In a few minutes, we came to the busy Zwierzyniecka Street, with heavy traffic going in both directions. We must have looked odd to people. Our horse and wagon was out of place on the busy street. Nothing had changed here in those few years, except a few missing small stores. As we entered the bridge, I felt I was going to explode. How many times in those years had I dreamed about returning home, about this bridge and the streets. I never dreamed it would be so strange and empty of people. The bridge was the same, and the same murky waters of the Vistula underneath.

I tried to think how many times in my life I had crossed this bridge. It was so pleasant in the summer, watching people on the beaches and all sorts of kayaks and boats — the Vistula was part of my life. I spent countless hours swimming and kayaking and laying on her shores.

As we crossed the bridge, on the right side stood a stone wall covered, as always, with placards announcing the passing of people. But the road from the bridge was wider and straighter. I told the driver to go the same way I had walked in the neighborhood years before. Madalinkiego was a short, busy street, with a drugstore owned by my best friend and schoolmate's father Daniel Appel. Across the street was Ignace Bank. At the corner of Barska Street stood a huge Catholic chapel. We were only a five-minute walk from the house of my aunt and uncle Brenner and my cousins Niusie, Herman and Moniek. Moniek was in Russia; he was deported in 1940, before me.

I didn't know what to do. It is impossible to describe the thoughts that went through my head. People came home from wars, but they knew to whom and to what. Out on the corner near our apartment stood a newspaper kiosk, as always. On the left was a huge sanitation garage and across from it a barber shop, that was still operating. At the next intersection was a street leading to the public school, the church and our little synagogue. As my apartment appeared in the distance, my eyes became misty. I started to pray. It seemed to take so long as we passed Mr. Nedziaski's little grocery store, the beer house next door and finally reached the end of the block. We parked in front of Barska 34, the home I left in September 1939. How long I had waited for this moment; dreamt about it. But as we sat on the wagon, we were afraid to go in.

Father, in a pleading voice, urged me to go in on my own. I looked around and saw the stately home of Professor Savitski with its huge garden and high chain-link fence. I looked back at our building and noticed that everything looked the same, until I looked at the entrance. The beautiful garden, with its fruit trees, cherries, plums and pears, was gone. The meadow behind the house, where we played soccer and tennis, was also gone, replaced by a busy highway.

I took a deep breath, opened the door and went inside. I walked slowly up the 12-step stone staircase, trembling. At our apartment, there was a strange name on the nameplate, but the landlord across the hall, the Syreks, was still the same. I knocked on their door. It opened a small crack and then wide and there stood Mrs. Syrek. She looked much older and heavier, with white hair. I am sure she recog-

240

nized me, but she did not utter a word. Then, as though waking from a trance, she ran to me, lifted her arms and shrieked: "Jesus, Maria, this is our Samek!" As she put her arms around me, we both began to sob. Jadwiga came out of the apartment and Hela, who didn't recognize me at all. We kissed and hugged and then ran out to Father. Some people from the street stopped to look, but didn't recognize us.

We went inside the Syrek's apartment and were served milk, bread and butter. Everybody was there: Stefan, Hela and Jadwiga. When I asked about Mr. Syrek, there was silence; he had died three years previously. The son, my childhood friend Mietek, was an officer in the army, stationed in Tarnow.

They knew I was anxious to ask, so Mrs. Syrek started to talk about my family. Things were very bad for mother and Nusia. Hounded by the Germans, Mother would stay with Aunt Frania at the Brenners for days. When Jews were being moved to the ghettos, mother, her sisters Frania and Manya, my sister, and Brenners' Nusia and Manya's children left Krakow, and moved to Bochnia. Mother sold whatever she could and left. The Syreks said all the Jews in Krakow were taken sooner or later. All the families in Dembniki were gone.

We told them we didn't know what to do or where to go. We asked them if we could stay overnight. Mrs. Syrek kissed me again and said we could stay as long as we needed to.

I spoke with the oldest daughter Jadwiga. She told us about the occupation and the situation now. They endured hardships after Mr. Syrek died, the lack of income then and now. With all the excitement she forgot to tell me about my youngest cousin, Samek from Cieszyn who ran away when they took my mother and all the family and came back to Krakow to seek help. The Syreks kept him overnight and fed him, but there was no way to keep him in the small apartment, where everybody knew everyone's business. They had given him what they could and he left, never to be heard from again.

The only Jew that Mrs. Syrek knew who survived was the daughter of the tavern keeper. Her name was Ceskia. She married an owner of the garage. She converted to Catholicism and was now running the tavern. She was older than me, and knew my cousin Herman from her near-drowning in the Vistula.

I excused myself from the apartment and went to the bathroom down the hall. I lost all my composure. I started to sob uncontrollably. My spark of hope was gone. For almost six years I had dreamed of my return and I returned, but to what? I must have stayed in the bathroom too long. Father was worried and came to get me. As I entered with my eyes red, they knew why I was gone so long.

The door opened and in walked Hela with her little girl. She was the Syrek's daughter, who lived in our old apartment. Hela told me she had heard from somebody that two sons of the owner of the drugstore, Mr. Appel, returned and lived in their home. I jumped up, left my soup at the table and excused myself. I had to go see them right now.

I set a record running to their two-storey villa, on the outskirts of Dembniki. I ran up to Rolna Str #7, stopped and my head was spinning. I couldn't catch my breath. Slowly, I opened the gate, looked at the door and noticed several nameplates on the frame. There were six or seven names. Could it be that so many people lived here? On the bottom of the list, was the smallest card, hardly visible, with the name Appel. Well, they were here. I was all shook up. I went back on the street and tried to look through the window. Where could they live.?

Before the war, when I went to see them, I whistled a certain signal and Danek would come down and open the door. I looked up to the window, where Danek's room was. I tried to whistle, but I was out of practice. It wasn't loud enough. I tried and my whistle was getting louder. I entered the gate and tried the door to the villa. Suddenly, it opened. Danek ran down the stairs. He had heard the whistle. But he couldn't believe it. We hugged each other. His brother Leszek, came running, too. People opened their doors, hearing all the commotion, but we didn't pay any attention to them. Danek looked the same. But Leszek, who was several years younger, looked completely different. He had grown up. We went upstairs and passed the hallway to their room, which was the last one in the corner of the stairs. We got inside a sparsely furnished room. I sat on a chair, they sat on a bed. For a few moments, we just stayed quiet looking at each other. We didn't know where to begin.

When we finally started to talk, we did it all at once. It seemed so unreal being in this small room in their huge home. But we started with the most important topic, which laid so heavy on our chests. Their parents and other family members had all perished. They were in Plaszow, from where they were deported to Auschwitz. They had been separated and Leszek was sent to Auschwitz later. Danek had lived through several camps and was liberated in Mathausen in Austria. It took several months after the liberation for them to find each other. They had been in Krakow for a while now. When they returned to their villa, it had been occupied. When the people found out they were the owners, they decided among themselves to vacate one room in the house for them. What an irony.

They planned to move soon to Krasinskiego. It was impossible for them to live here. It was too crowded and psychologically too hard for them.

I told them in a few words about my experiences and how I had found out about them. I told them about my father waiting at the Syrek's apartment. Then, of course, the main question: What did they know about my mother and sister. They didn't know anything about them. They were taken to the Krakow ghetto, but had not seen her there. They had only heard about my cousin Brenner. Somebody told them that he came to look for his families, but did not find anybody. He left and lived somewhere in Silesia, close to Katowice. They also told me the best thing for us was to go right away to Dluga Street #42, where a Jewish committee was located. They would help us and had helped all the returnees.

I said I should go because Father would be worried. We decided to meet the next day. It was dark when I left, but I knew this road by heart. I walked slowly, my head full of thoughts. Everything was so familiar, yet so strange. I felt like a stranger here.

When I returned, Father was surrounded by the Syrek women. Mrs. Syrek had prepared a place for us to sleep. I was tired and fell asleep, dreaming of a different return. When I woke up I wasn't sure where I was. I waited impatiently for the morning to arrive.

At first light, I got dressed and went down to the street. I walked our long block to the first major intersection, leading to the public school that I had attended for four years. I looked at every house where our Jewish neighbors had lived. I turned to see our small synagogue. In the window, I saw some curtains. It was obvious some people now lived there. The door opened and a man emerged with a bundle and a lunch box on his way to work. He looked at me with suspicion.

When I returned, Mrs. Syrek was in the kitchen brewing coffee. We had breakfast and prepared to go to the Jewish committee.

I took the papers I had, my report card and I told father that we should stop at the Brenner's residence, to see what we could find out. They were the closest family we had and everyone knew them.

We passed a couple of stores, a grocery and variety store and found ourselves in front of their former store and apartment. The store did not exist anymore. Everything had been converted to apartments. I looked up to see the balcony on the second floor where we used to play and take pictures. Their store and apartment was across from the open market.

I went inside the building, looked at the nameplates and went up to the second floor. Everything was strange and there was no sign of the Brenners. Their neighbor, Mr. Bieloruski still lived there. I knocked on the door and it opened. They didn't recognize me. Mr. Bieloruski looked older and I probably had changed a lot in those six years. I had known them well. He had spent hours at the Brenner's store, talking politics with my Uncle Samuel and the customers.

I told the Bieloruskis who I was and they let me in. They insisted I sit down but I declined. I asked if they knew anything of the Brenners. They started to wail and then they told us that only Moniek was here a few weeks ago. But after not finding anyone, he left.

I left and walked towards the bridge. I stopped at a toiletry store. The son of the owners, Zbyszek, had been a close friend of Moniek's. To my surprise, he was in the store and recognized me right away. His father had died. He got married and was running the store alone. He had told me about Moniek's visit a few weeks ago. He had spent quite a long time with him. Moniek had slept overnight and told him everything. Nobody from the Brenners, except Moniek in Russia, had survived. He was sincerely sorry about what had happened and asked me if I needed anything. I told him I needed a toothbrush and some toiletries.

The only important information that I got from him was that Moniek was married, had a baby boy and lived not far from Katowice. I was very surprised, because I could not imagine Moniek married while living in Russia. I also found out Moniek's uncle, his father's brother, that I knew vaguely, survived the holocaust and worked at the Jewish committee. Moniek had visited him when he arrived.

I said goodbye to Zbyszek and promised to see him again. I wish I could put into words the feelings, the thoughts and the frustrations and helplessness. This first day was the worst.

We crossed the bridge, and descended to Zwierzynieka Street to wait on the stop for our tram. The stops and streets were all the same. The tram took us close to the Jewish committee office. Father and I walked faster and didn't talk much. The few passersby walked in the opposite direction. Most were carrying packages. they looked Jewish, but I wasn't sure and didn't want to stop to talk to anyone.

In front of the building on Dluga #42, at the entrance was the sign of the Jewish committee. In front, stood a man with a rifle, who checked people entering. When we tried to enter, he asked us a few questions and we showed him the papers from Russia. Father started to speak Yiddish and we went inside. There were many people milling around speaking Polish and Yiddish, loudly and excitedly. We ended up in a courtyard. It was packed with people standing in small groups. Often, I heard a shriek if someone had found a relative or friend. They hugged and kissed and cried. I walked around looking at everybody, trying to find a familiar face, but I didn't. I didn't know too many people from before the war. Our family was close knit and small. Almost all of Father's family was in the United States. The people I knew before the war were mostly school friends and my friends from the neighborhood.

In a few  minutes, Father recognized someone. It was one of the droski drivers from the Royale Hotel. In no time, he was surrounded by people he knew. They talked and gestured, while he tried to tell his story in a few minutes. They told Father we should register with the committee. They also gave us a few hints about what to ask for.

Most of the people here appeared to be returnees from Russia. Most had no luck finding their families. They had settled their affairs with the committee and were now getting ready to emigrate to Germany and other European countries, into DP camps and many of them wanted to eventually get to the United States and Canada.

While Father was talking to his friends, I went to find out about registering and to find out where Mr. Brenner worked. They told me he worked down the basement, in charge of a warehouse and supplies. My Uncle Brenner did not recognize me, which I didn't expect. So, I called him Uncle Brenner and re-introduced myself. He smiled and I detected a sadness on his face. He was short and chubby, just as I had remembered.  But he seemed very different.

After I answered his few questions about where I survived and when I had arrived, he told me about Moniek, confirming what Zbyszek told me.  He added that Moniek lived with his in-laws in Bytom, not far from Katowice. Also in Katowice lived my Uncle Marian, who had returned with the Polish army and some distant cousins, lived there, as well. In Cieszyn lived Uncle Steiner.  He had heard that his son Samek had survived the German occupation, but he didn't know his whereabouts now. The rest of the family had perished at the hands of the Nazis, in camps and ghettos. He squeezed my hand and his eyes were tear-filled. He told me to register and he would come to see me later and help us any way he could.

He had the address of Uncle Marian in Katowice. This was very important to me. He wanted to talk a little more, but he had work to do.

I found Father in the courtyard talking to a few more people. I told him I had talked to Uncle Brenner and shared all the sad news with Father. We embraced and silently shed tears.

We left for the registration office, where they wanted to know all about us. We were interviewed and they asked us what we needed or what they could do for us. We were given a thorough medical examination. I recognized the ear and throat specialist, the best in the city. His name was Klasa-Bruicki, who had removed my adenoids before the war. He gave us a clean bill of health, at least not anything some good food wouldn't cure.

On the committee, was a man who finished the gymnasium a couple of years ahead of me. He gave me a short list of students and professors who survived. There were only a few and most had come and gone. Beside Appel, I found another friend, Gustav Halpern, who was in the city. He gave me his address. He also told me there was a school for Jewish children, who survived the Holocaust. In charge of botany was a professor from our school, Dr. Goldwasser. She was my most beloved teacher and I was one of her favorite students. This was uplifting news.

They gave Father a small amount of money and told us not to hesitate to come back any time. Father and I went downstairs for some supplies and to see Uncle Brenner. Father spoke to him and he told father the same news he had given me, but no details. He told us in time we'd find out everything.

We received a few pairs of underwear and socks. They would also provide us with shoes and clothing if we needed it. Most importantly, he gave us Uncle Marian's address. We said goodbye to Uncle Brenner and thanked him. Loaded with our goods, we went back to Dembniki.

Never in my life had Father or myself needed charity in Poland. I will never forget how well organized, warm and helpful the Jewish community was after the war, thanks mostly to the Jewish-American organizations. It made me proud to be Jewish.

We decided to stay in Krakow for a couple more days, before going to see Uncle Marian in Katowice. I wanted to see Prof. Goldwasser and get advice about my education.

I was anxious to go back and see Danek and Leszek Appel, because we still had many things to talk about. I took out my precious sports jacket, shirt and pants from my valise and asked Jadwiga for an iron. I wanted, from now on, to dress the best I could and change my lifestyle. I had enough of being a refugee.

I went back to the Appels and whistled for them. They met me at the gate and we hugged again. It was a feeling and a confirmation that we were alive. We sat around a table and I asked them more detailed questions about the concentration camps. This was my first eyewitness report of the holocaust. What they had been through was worse than anything I had been through in Russia. I was completely shaken by what they told me. I listened to them for a long time, without interrupting.

At the end of the war, they didn't know that either of them had survived. I just could not believe or digest their stories. They had spent a lot of time in Krakow and knew the fate of some of our friends. There were very few left.

We spent endless hours that night talking. They told me they had sold their parents' pharmacy to a woman and she helped them financially and steered them in the right direction.

I left quite late and everyone at the Syreks was asleep, except Father. I told him about my evening with my friends, so he understood. I couldn't fall asleep. I couldn't understand or imagine what I had heard. Crematoriums, gas chambers, the unbelievable stories about the murder and annihilation, organized murder of our brothers and sisters, our families.

The part of the story I heard from the Appels was only a small piece of what I would learn later. I had terrible nightmares that night.

The next morning, Father and I went to the Roman baths. It looked neglected and empty. Gone was its former opulence. The steambath was still in operation and few Russian soldiers were there. I filled my tub to the brim and soaked myself up to my neck. It was heaven. It had been six years since I had this luxury. It felt as if I was washing away all my heavy burdens.

After our bath, Father went back to the Jewish committee and I went to visit Dr. Goldwasser. My legs automatically carried me to my school, the Hebrew gymnasium #445. This was my second home. I stood in front of the buildings, wondering if I should go inside. I was hesitant. My hands started to tremble. I went inside and everything was intact. Suddenly, the recess bell rang so familiar and clear. The classroom doors opened and students came running out in all directions. As they all poured out, I floated into my old classroom, directly to my desk. I sat down for a minute, got up, looked out the window to the courtyard filled with children. I wanted to run out and leave. As I was leaving, I saw a man who asked me what I was doing here. I told him I had gone to this school before the war.

I said goodbye to him and ran out as fast as I could onto the street. My eyes filled with tears. I kept running only turning around to look at the place.

The road to the school where Prof. Goldwasser taught in the former yeshiva, Hachmey Lublin, led to the heart of Kazimierz. For centuries, it was the centre of the Jewish settlement in Krakow. Seventy-five per cent of Krakow Jews lived there, mostly the Orthodox.

I passed the huge temple, the only reform synagogue in the city. I passed this Jewish landmark. It was closed. So I walked towards the market. It was an eerie feeling to walk those streets, which had once been crowded with Jews, in my time and for centuries before me. There had been hundreds of synagogues, all led by different rabbis. It was the busiest part of the city. Now, as I walked those streets, they were almost empty. No stores, no markets, no people, rushing and pushing and talking loudly and arguing. In only a few years, all this had evaporated.

I stood in front of the yeshiva. In front stood a guard. I had to explain who I was. He told me where Prof. Goldwasser was. I walked upstairs and towards the classroom. I could hear children's voices. The door of the classroom was open. There were boys and girls sitting in desks. I was thrilled there was still a Jewish school. The teacher was drawing something on the board. I recognized her immediately. She turned around and I could see her face. It was her.

When the children left for recess, I walked in the classroom. Quietly, I moved closer to her desk. I finally uttered: "Good morning, Prof. Goldwasser." She turned around, looked at me and greeted me with a kiss and a hug, calling out my name. I was so happy she recognized me. She didn't have much time, so we spoke quickly. She had survived most of the occupation with her son Tosiek, teaching and living in a convent close to Warsaw. I told her a little about my experiences and asked her advice about my education.

She advised me to enroll at the university. I showed her my 1939 report card that I had kept and she copied some data from it. She told me I needed another document that would enable me to go to school immediately. This made me feel good. She gave me the names of a few professors that had survived, but most had left Poland already. We parted in a hurry. I told her I would visit her next week.

I felt more cheery and walked the long road back to Dembniki. Every building and street reminded me of somebody or something.

Now that I had seen the school, it made me feel a little better there was still some Jewish life in Krakow.

I walked into the Syrek's apartment and quickly told Father my plans to attend Jagielonian University. Father was full of news from the Jewish Community Centre. He had met former employees and friends and they all had a story to tell. Everybody had lost their families, their belongings and their businesses.

We decided we would take a bus to Katowice the next morning, to see Uncle Marian and the remnants of our family. Privately, Father told me what he had heard. It was very disturbing. Right after the end of the war, survivors from camps and hiding places would return to their cities, towns and villages to look for their families. Usually nobody was found and the returnees faced unfriendly neighbors. They left immediately.

Two months later, after this rumor was heard, the Jewish Committee had heard about an incident in Kielce. Before the war, this city had a sizeable Jewish population. A mob there was incited by a girl who had gone missing. The centuries-old rumor that Jews killed children for blood began to circulate. They attacked the Jews in Kielce, killing 42 survivors of the holocaust. It was hard to believe.

The culprits were apprehended, tried and shot. I became apprehensive about attending school here, now. Father and I began to talk more about emigrating to the U.S.A. His parents had died there, but he still had two brothers and two sisters living there. We would get in touch with them immediately. We decided to call ourselves by Polish names, so as not to let on that we were Jewish. It was too dangerous.

We packed for our trip to Katowice and said goodbye to the Syreks. We bought a bus ticket and were on our way. I was consumed with thoughts of meeting our family. What would I tell them? What will they tell me?

We arrived in the afternoon and got directions to the address we had. I had never been in Katowice. We walked up to a three-storey apartment house, well-kept and neat. We saw the name of Mr. Bilgoraj, who was a good friend of Uncle Marian's before the war. I rang the bell and the door opened. I was in the arms of Uncle Marian. We stood there embracing and crying. I looked around to find a bunch of people I didn't recognize. Uncle Marian brought us into another room, so we could talk privately.

It had been four years from the time we had separated in 1942 in Austrachan. He looked good and rested, much better than when

249

we left him. He told us that a few months after we separated, his wife Hela had died. He buried her on a little island on the Volga, where he worked for about a year. He decided to go east to Taskent, in middle Asia. After an incredibly long journey, he arrived there and met a few of his friends from Poland. There, he joined the Polish army with them and returned to Poland in 1945, almost a year before father and I. He searched all over, trying to find any trace of our family, but unfortunately couldn't. He found only one cousin, Samek, the youngest one from Cieszyn, who had survived the German occupation and was a witness to the murder and destruction of our immediate family. He did not give any details.

There was another second cousin here, Henek Silberstein, in the apartment in another room. This was all that remained of our family. We cried together for a long time. Uncle Marian then shared some good news with us. He had married a woman, Elsa Waldner from Cieszyn, who I remembered. This was the woman Uncle Marian had been in love with many years before the war. But the two families disapproved of their courtship, so they ended their relationship. When he returned to Cieszyn, he found out Elsa was alive and they met and married. She had survived the Auschwitz concentration camp.

We decided to stay overnight. We still had many things to talk about.

In the morning, we drifted into the kitchen with all the residents of this apartment. I couldn't believe how many people lived here. Everybody went off to work and Marian told us of his plan to open a soap factory. If successful, they would find a job for Father. We told him of my plans to go back to school and how we wanted to get in touch with father's family in the United States.

Because it was so crowded at Marian's apartment, we were to stay with a relative, Izydor, who lived close by in the town of Chorzow. Father wrote his letter to the United States and Marian promised to mail it.

Izydor brought us to his apartment. He showed us a large bedroom and told us we would be comfortable here. Father and I talked about what we should do next. We didn't know what the rest of the family was planning to do. Were they going to stay in Poland? Father started to hint there was no future here. Maybe it would be best to join his brothers and sisters in the U.S.

Chorzow was a gloomy industrial city with drab buildings, all looking dirty from the coal dust and pollution of the steel mills. We stayed here for about a week, calling Uncle Marian often from a store telephone. We took a tram on the weekend to visit him at his apartment, where he had arranged a family meeting. When we arrived we found my cousin Moniek, Uncle Henek, Henek Silberstein and the rest of the friends. I was disappointed that my only cousin who survived under the Nazis wasn't there. He had already left for France, with the intention of going on to Palestine.

The rest of the family I hadn't seen since 1940, before our deportation from Lvov. It was a lively but sad meeting. Nobody had any firm plans about their futures. They were trying to make a living here in Poland, but they had no idea what the future held for them. The emigration possibilities from Poland were slim. Israel did not exist yet and the English were only letting in a trickle of people legally into Palestine. Canada was severely restricted and the U.S. quota was filled for years. The only possibility was to get to DP camps in Germany and wait for a chance to emigrate.

We returned to Chorzow late in the evening, not having come to any conclusions.

Eventually, I decided to go back to Krakow. Dr. Goldwasser was working on my papers. They would be ready in a few days. Most nights I spent with the Appels. There was no shortage of horror stories from the war.

My papers for school were finally ready and I went to pick them up. I talked with Prof. Goldwasser briefly and she wished me luck in my endeavors. I never saw her again.

I was to attend the Jagelonian University of Krakow.

The next day, I dressed in my best clothing and walked swiftly to the university. The main university was in a park-like setting in the Planty. I entered the impressive building and found the registration office. I presented my papers and told them I intended to enter medical school. It was the middle of the school year and I realized it was impossible. But, I was immediately accepted as a student in the general science department and was advised to take as many courses as possible, relating to the first year of medical school. I was to begin my classes the following week.

I returned to the Syrek's apartment and asked Mrs. Syrek if I could stay with them for free while I attended the university. She agreed. I decided to go visit Father and Uncle Marian before school began.

When I got there they were gone. Elsa told me they were at the soap factory, where Father had a job as a soap distributor and sales-

251

man. When Father got home, I told him all about school. He told me I should only consider going temporarily because he had firmly decided to go to the U.S. It was logical he wanted to join his family.

I returned to Krakow by train, excited that I was to attend classes the next day. I got up early, shaved, put on my best clothes and left early, equipped with a notebook and pen.

I was one of the first to enter the lecture room. It was a amphitheater-type room with seats in a semi-circle, descending down towards a desk with a huge blackboard behind it. I sat in the back, not far from the exits. Slowly, the room started to fill up with younger boys and girls, in groups chatting cheerfully to each other. Most were dressed casually and I felt a little overdressed. The professor entered and everybody stood up. He nodded and everybody sat down. The minute he started to lecture, people frantically began taking notes. I tried to follow but I was getting lost. I couldn't write that fast. After the intermission, one boy I met, Mietek, explained there were no textbooks because the Germans had confiscated and ransacked the university library, destroying most of the books. Scores of professors and lecturers had been arrested and sent to camps where they perished.

The Germans had been rough with the intelligentsia. They did not want or need them. According to Mein Kampf, they were supposed to be slaves needed for one purpose, to serve and build their empire. In their eyes, the Poles were swine, sub-humans. Of course, the masses of people didn't realize this and hadn't read Mein Kampf. Maybe if they would have, they would have helped the Jews a bit more.

Mietek and I became quite friendly. He showed me around the university. He introduced me to his friends and we helped each other with our homework.

I had few friends because all of my weekends were spent visiting Father in Chorzow. Time flew and I had lots of studying and catching up to do. I did better than I expected. I was hungry for knowledge. To my surprise I got A's on all of my exams and papers. In June, I was expected to finish a semester, or maybe even two, which I did.

I didn't know of any Jews at the university. One day I spotted a girl with dark hair and a doll-like face. I struck up a conversation with her. She looked Jewish. She introduced herself and told me her name was Marysia, from the city of Bielsko. I had distant relatives

252

there and asked her if she had ever heard of them. I noticed her face went white and after hesitating, she said she hadn't heard about them. From then on, she avoided me and would never sit next to me. I couldn't understand her behaviour. I was sure she was Jewish, but she didn't want to acknowledge that. She was no exception.

The school year was over and I attended with Mietek many parties and did lots of drinking.

Economically, our situation improved. Father was working and help from our family in the U.S. started to arrive. We received money and a few packages of clothing and food. The dollars were worth a lot in Polish currency. Letters to the U.S. took weeks to arrive, as did all the documentation we were waiting for. At the advice of our family, we had applied for a U.S. visa in Warsaw. We were told it would be a long wait because of the Polish quota.

I spent most of my summer vacation with Father and once in a while I would return to Krakow. I met many girls and started to date. I think I was womanizing for all those lost years. I felt very unsettled. I had no job or profession or a country. The few girls that survived the concentration camps were all in a hurry to get married. I was not.

Father was worried about my health because I was getting skinny. He proposed I should go away to a summer resort, close to Bielsko, called Szczyrk.

It was beautifully located in the Beskidy mountains. I had a nice room with a view of the mountains, covered thickly with trees and a mountain brook that flowed by my window. The food was great and rich, and I gained some weight. I had a wonderful time.

I didn't want anyone to know I was Jewish. I had been told of anti-Jewish activity in this area. My cousin had told me of a young Jewish girl who had tar poured on her head and her hair cut off. Another Jewish boy had been killed while trying to cross the border to Czechoslovakia. He had apparently been killed by a Polish underground army, who fought the Nazis during the war and now were fighting the present government.

I tried not to stray too far from the hotel. I was afraid of these stories. The press seldom mentioned these incidents. But by word of mouth it only took a few days to hear. At the resort, I ate most of my meals in the dining room and relaxed for the rest of the summer.

It was time to go back to Chorzow, to see Father. I was looking forward to my studies in Krakow, too. I spent the remainder of my summer vacation catching up on my studies. I went out with my friends to the nightclubs in the evenings and swam in the city pool during the day.

School finally started and I met my friend Mietek and another boy Edek, from the previous semester I had known and been close to Edek for several months before I found out he was actually Jewish. I hadn't been invited to his home, and knew very little of his private life. It came about rather gradually that I began to have suspicions that he might also be Jewish. I finally worked up the nerve to ask him. In those days, we had a rather careful way of finding out, to protect ourselves. We would ask one another if we knew the meaning of the word "Amchu," which in Hebrew means "my nation." Anyone knowing the word would certainly be Jewish. Should they not know the word, the questioner could simply also deny understanding of the word, saying only that he had heard it somewhere and wondered what it meant. When Edek recognized the word, we were both delighted, and immediately our relationship became much closer. I became a regular guest at his house, and we both decided to become more brave and forthright about being Jewish. I met another friend of mine, Lolek, who was now living in Warsaw. I told him I would soon be going there to get my passport and he insisted I stay with him when I get there.

Obtaining the passport was not simple. I made an application to the Department of Foreign Affairs in Warsaw and after everything was approved, the passport had to be picked up personally in Warsaw. The trips to Warsaw by train had become dangerous, because of the instances when trains were stopped by the undereground AK army. Sometimes Jews were removed from the train and in a few instances were killed.

Warsaw had been destroyed by the war. Only one or two hotels were left. The lines at the ministry were kilometres long. When I finally went to get our passports, word had got around that I was going there. Several people asked me to pick up there's too. They offered me a price to do this favour for them.

I bought a first-class ticket and sat among some high-ranking officers in uniforms, but without insignia. Of course, we talked of the war, the occupation and so on. I had a book with me and excused myself, saying I had to catch up on some reading. I didn't want to get involved in this conversation. We passed small towns and villages when one of the civilians remarked that before the war most of the small towns were Jewish, but now they weren't. Everyone began to express their opinions on this topic, saying Poland would manage just fine without Jews.

One man said some Jews were productive, but a vast majority were not. I was surprised that the high-ranking officer did not take part in this conversation.

I was listening, but kept my eyes low, pretending to read my book. I was hearing nothing new. One man piped up and came to the defense of the Polish Jews. He made a speech about how he had been in Palestine and saw what a wonderful and innovative job the Jews had done with the desert land. He said he had never seen farms like this in his life. They produced more per hectare than any of our farms in Poland. He added that without persecution, these people had built a beautiful land out of nothing.

There was dead silence in the compartment when he finished his speech. The topic was finished. If only I could have congratulated that officer.

We arrived in Warsaw. The station had been damaged by bombs, but it was functioning. The destruction of the city was unbelievable, with whole streets in rubble. There was a strong smell in the air, a mixture of smoke and dead bodies.

The city was now fighting back to rebuild. If not for the extensive sewage system of Warsaw, they probably would have not rebuilt it on its original site. It made more sense to move it.

The wide sidewalk I was on came to an abrupt end. I planned to meet my friend Lolek at the office building where he worked. I took a taxi there and entered the building guarded by soldiers. I told them I was there to see Lolek Buchaister, who was the first adjutant to the Polish Marshall. They searched my valise and I was frisked for weapons. I filled out a paper stating my business and momentarily, Lolek appeared.

He took me up to his office and later we shared a great meal together and I stayed overnight at his apartment. Much to my disappointment, he shared his opinions about his leftist, communist feelings. I didn't say a word.

The next morning I made my way to the ministry for the passports. Lolek had arranged a car with a chauffer for us. Lolek wore his impressive uniform with dozens of medals. He had joined the Polish army in Russia and all through the campaign against the Germans, displayed unusual bravery. He had been wounded several times, but not too seriously. He had worked his way up the ranks the hard way, by courage and guts.

We arrived at the ministry building. I could see people lined up for blocks. We entered the building without delay, as soldiers and officers saluted Lolek at the entrance. He demanded to be taken to the passport office and without delay, we walked right in. Lolek requested to see the man in charge. We were ushered into a large room, where we explained the reason for our visit. I presented all my papers and we were told everything would be ready in a few hours.

We left and went for a ride around the Jewish ghetto, that was filled with rubble and skeletons of buildings.

Lolek took me out for lunch at the Hotel Polonia. He seemed to enjoy his high position. He was only 23 years old.

We returned for the passports and I spent one more night in Warsaw. I was driven to the train station, with everyone's passports and I was to receive a hefty profit for a job well done.

I didn't see Lolek again until 1965, when I went to Israel.

Back in Krakow, my studies proceeded well. Every subject came easily to me, even after my long hiatus from school. I had time for everything, dating girls, going out with my friends and playing tennis. I had more money now and became popular.

One day, I received a letter from my Uncle Jerry in New York. He asked me what I would like him to send. Without hesitation, I wrote to him, telling him we were fine, but could use some American cigarettes. They were expensive and hard to get. A couple of months later, I received a notice from the Ministry of Post and Commerce telling me there was a package for me. The parcel contained 25 cartons of cigarettes. They wanted me to pay an exorbitant duty to pick up the parcel.

I consulted my friends and we decided we should fight this nonsense. With the help of the student organization and the university secretary we wrote on university stationery, several appeals to the Post and Commerce ministry. I stated I was a student without income, a heavy smoker and why should I be penalized when I was only trying to get help from my family.

Within two weeks, I was notified to pick up the parcel, without charge.

There were all kinds of cigarettes in the parcel, Pall Malls, Camels, Lucky Strikes and Kools. I kept some for myself, gave some to my friends and put some away for selling. This was a good way to make money. I became so rich, I didn't need my allowance from the Jewish committee. I could afford almost everything..

We were constantly in touch with the family in the U.S., now. We were always filling out papers and applications and mailing them to the U.S. embassy in Warsaw and hoping for our visa to come through.

256

Time was passing and our chances of emigrating to the U.S. were waning. We got a letter from the U.S. consulate. They had registered us on the regular Polish quota. It would take years before our turn would come. Our family in the U.S. was disappointed and disgusted that all the papers and efforts were in vain.

After they exhausted all efforts to get us out of Poland, they asked me if it was possible for me to go to Czechoslavakia. They would try to get me out from there, maybe on a student visa. Father would have to stay in Poland. This was discouraging news.Almost every Jew wanted to emigrate out of Europe.

We only wanted to go to the U.S., to be with our relatives. We also had one surviving aunt, my mother's sister, who lived in New York.

Soon, the 1947 school year would be ending and here we were still in limbo. The first enthusiasm of returning to Poland was long gone. We now had a new uncertainty to contend with. I had pretty well forgotten my life in Russia, except for Claudia, who I always thought of. I hadn't heard from her in nearly two years.

I passed all of my exams and went to Chorzow to contemplate my future and the possibility of going to Czechoslovakia. I also wanted to see my Uncle Henry in Cieczyn, which was on the border of Czechoslovakia. Uncle Henry had a good friend living in Prague. I wrote a letter to the U.S. telling them I would find some way to get to Czechoslavakia.

Upon my return to Krakow, a great surprise awaited me — a letter from Claudia. It was a short letter. She said it was her third, but I never received the others. Then I noticed a mistake in the address, which she made in the translation from Russian to Polish. She told me they were still living in Bezemianka and was anxiously awaiting her return to Moscow. She had told her husband about me. They still lived together with her mother and child. They would decide their future when they returned to Moscow.

The letter shook me up. I wrote her back and told her of my plans to emigrate. It was a hard letter to write. I had a feeling it would be the last one. We were drifting farther and farther apart.

An added stress came while having dinner one day with the Syreks. Hela, one of the daughters, told me about a man who had harassed and blackmailed my mother while she was still living in our apartment after the German occupation began. He had harassed her over having a radio, and made things very difficult for her. Hela told me that the man, josef Wujcik, was now living here, and worked in a print shop not far from the university.

I stalked the man for weeks, determined to have my revenge. I found his workplace, saw him, learned the routes he took to and from work. Finally, one day, Mietek and I followed him into a park. I introduced myself, reminded him of his deeds. I watched his face grow white and listened to him deny things before I began to strike him.

He was heavier, maybe even stronger than I was, but I was enraged and determined to have my revenge. I beat him until he fell to the ground, then told him to go ahead and report me, I didn't care. I never heard anything about it. Making the assault public would have been just as dangerous for him as it would have been for me. My knuckles were sore and bloody, but my mind was at ease.

The end of the school year was fast approaching. I had a few exams to write and I finished with good marks. I said goodbye to my friends and left for Chorzow again, to stay with father. It was going to be a short visit.

A letter arrived from our family in the U.S.A., stating that a student visa would be forthcoming to Prague. I should immediately make arrangements to get there.

Within a few weeks, I left Poland and arrived in Prague, moving in with Uncle Henry's friend, Alfred Hartman. It was supposed to be a short visit, but it lasted almost a year. Mr. Hartman, who still lives in Prague with his family, became one of my best friends. I am still in contact with him today.

I had been refused the student visa to the U.S.A. because I had registered for a permanent visa on the quota at the U.S. embassy in Warsaw. I was again in limbo.

My stay in Prague was a great experience. I lived for the first time in a democratic country, where I never encountered a trace of anti-semitism. Unfortunately, the freedom didn't last long. In February, 1948, the Communists overtook the democratic government and this beautiful country and held it in bondage for years. Life changed almost immediately. I had made lots of friends there, but I was dying to get out.

One of my uncles in the U.S. had cousins in Windsor, Ontario, Canada. With the help of the Muroff family, I obtained a Canadian visa with a year contract to work on their farm.

# EPILOGUE

I arrived in Canada, in July 1948, where I was met by my aunts from the U.S. and the Muroffs. I worked on the farm in LaSalle, near Windsor, with the Pajot family, the oldest farm in Essex County.

My father left Poland a few months later to Germany, from where he left for the U.S.A. in 1949. We were reunited on a visit to Washington, D.C. He stayed there with his sister, Rose. In a short time, he got married and worked at a famous restaurant as a chef. At the age of 93, he died in Washington, D.C.

I married my wife Olga in 1951 in Windsor, where we reside today. Our two daughters, Dr. Roseanna Honig and Debbie Conn, and our grandchildren Natalie and Adam, reside in Toronto.

The remnants of my family, two cousins and two uncles and the majority of my surviving friends emigrated to the state of Israel.